# I Ching of a Thousand Doors

Breaking Wave Publishing

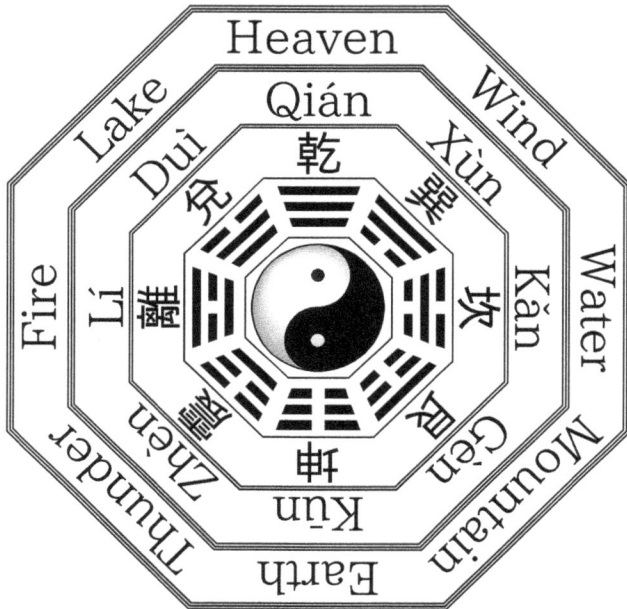

Yin-Yang and the Eight Trigrams

# I Ching of a Thousand Doors

**The *I Ching*: How to Use It, What it Meant, and What it Means.**

www.iching.wiki

---

## James R. Olsen

---

Illustrated by James R. Olsen

*Breaking Wave Publishing*

Breaking Wave Publishing
150 North Fourth Street
Post Office Box 270
Hamilton, Montana 59840
www.BreakingWavePublishing.com

*Breaking Wave Publishing*

*For more on the I Ching from the author see www.iching.wiki*

Library of Congress Control Number: 2019917928.
Olsen, James R.
Illustrated by James R. Olsen
I Ching of a Thousand Doors

Includes Bibliography and Index
ISBN: 978-1-7342332-3-0

Printed in the United States of America
Lightening Source Printing 2020

2 3 4 5 6 7 8 9 10

Cover by James R. Olsen. Cover includes a modified version of the wood block print 神奈川沖浪裏 "Great Wave
off Kanagawa" by Katsushika Hokusai, 1832. Image from Metropolitan Museum of Art, entry 45434. H. O. Havemeyer Collection, Bequest of Mrs. H. O. Havemeyer, 1929 File: Tsunami by hokusai 19th century.jpg Wikipedia.

Dedicated to

The Big Creek Coffee Café Society

   and

My mother, Barbara Jean (Street) Olsen,
Some of whose poetry appears in this book.

*Yi Pictogram*

≡≡
乾下
乾上

王弼註

乾元亨利貞。初九潛龍勿用。

九二見龍在田利見大人。

九三君子終日乾乾夕惕若厲无咎。

*I Ching Chinese Text*

From the *I Ching* — Song Dynasty. A.D. 960–1279, National Central Library

# CONTENTS

# List of Figures

## About Words and Dates

*See **Notes and Acknowledgments** section for a complete description.*

ROMANIZATION: The Chinese language is represented phonically (how it sounds) using Roman letters — that is the familiar English alphabet with accents. Two standards have been used in recent decades:

1) Pinyin (*Hànyǔ Pīnyīn*), which is now the international standard, and

2) an older one invented by Wade and Giles around the turn of the twentieth century.

This book uses Pinyin for the Romanization, sometimes showing Wade-Giles in parentheses. For example, the character 道 is translated as "The Way." In Pinyin it is rendered as "Dao." In this book it would be followed by Wade-Giles, "Tao," in parentheses — Dao (Tao).

Similarly, the book titled *Tao Te Ching* is titled *Dao De Jing* in Pinyin — and the three words are often run together. So in this book the title reads *Daodejing*. See a complete explanation in *Notes and Acknowledgments*.

OCCASIONAL USE OF CHINESE CHARACTERS. Chinese characters are included in some places to remind the reader that the *I Ching* is written in Old Chinese.[1] For more on Chinese characters, the use of honorifics, and other editorial choices see *Notes and Acknowledgments*.

DATES: This book uses B.C. (before Christ) and A.D. (*anno Domini*, year of our Lord) for dates rather than BCE and CE strictly to honor the Western cultural traditions. See *Notes and Acknowledgments* for a discussion.

POETRY AND POETIC PROSE: These are italicized. Many are from the world's religious, mystic, and philosophic traditions. Those without citations are the author's own work.

Old Building with Trigrams

# 1

# MEET THE *I CHING*

曰 春 夏 *We speak of spring and summer,*
曰 秋 冬 *We speak of autumn and winter.*
此 四 時 *These four seasons,*
運 不 窮 *Revolve without ceasing.*

So Says *The Three Character Classic*[1]

*Yin–Yang Symbol*

The *I Ching* began 3000 years ago as a divination handbook, then became a book of ethics, and is now used as a book of psychological insight. What does it do?

Every great book of wisdom can be studied, moving your mind and spirit to greater insights. The *I Ching* takes you further — you don't just read it, you interact with it. It then becomes a great sage, sitting face-to-face with you, in your time and place, first listening to you, and then speaking to you. When this happens, the *I Ching* becomes the ultimate personal-growth book, bringing you to your center, giving insight into your own mind, providing insight into the present situation and revealing how your future might unfold.

You will be rewarded if you learn to use the *I Ching*, understand its culture, embrace the insight of its metaphors — learn how it views the world. The reward for many people is a lifelong companion, often called the Sage. It becomes a wise advisor, sharing its wisdom, not as some general saying, but advising like a wise friend who knows the depths of your soul.

> *Born in China, the I Ching was already ancient when history began to be written. Like a translucent sea creature, born from folk tales, spoken with the simplicity of The Dao, it swims through time, encountering the people, ingesting and filtering their wisdom, always growing.*

> *When you glance upon this mystical creature, you see the here and now. When you peer into it, through its translucent layers, you see the wisdom of the ages.*

The *I Ching* is a book that contains sixty-four short chapters that are numbered one through sixty-four. Each chapter has a name and a six-line drawing, such as the one shown here. The drawing is called a hexagram — "hexa" being six. Each line may be solid, referred to as unbroken, or have a single dash, referred to as broken.

Hexagram Example

Since each of the six lines can hold one of two possible choices, the total possible combinations is sixty-four. The sixty-four hexagrams, with their names, are shown in Figure 1.3 on page 4. The names are English translations of one or two Chinese words. The name for Hexagram 1 is 乾, which is pronounced *qián*, and which is translated as heaven or creative.

Chapter 3 provides a step-by-step discussion of how you can consult the *I Ching* by selecting one of the 64 hexagrams. The most popular method is to use three coins. For now, assume you got number 42. If you open your *I Ching* book to Hexagram 42, you will see the name and the Judgment or Decision. What you would see in one of the *I Ching* books available, *The Original I Ching* by Margaret J. Pearson, starts as shown here:

42 益

**(Yì) Increase**

**Increase. It is benefical to have a destination. It is effective to ford the great stream**

From Pearson, The Original I Ching, 180
Figure 1.1 — Sample Judgment

The judgment is cryptic, but rich in meaning. The *I Ching of a Thousand Doors* will help you understand what it meant when it was written and what it means today. For example, to "ford the great stream" refers to crossing one of the great rivers that flow though China, such as the Yellow River, at a time when there were no bridges — a hazardous journey that could end badly, or yield great rewards. Fording the great steam can also be a hazardous spiritual or emotional journey, and it can yield great rewards.

There is more. Each of the six lines has a statement, called a Line Statement. Each line has its "place," *counting from the bottom*: first, second, third… to the top place, the sixth.

Finally, the six-line hexagram is treated as an "image." There will be a statement about the hexagram image as a whole. The "Image Statement" is a Confucian statement about what a virtuous moral person would do.

On this page is a hexagram of six lines, its name, a Judgment, six Line Statements, and an Image Statement:

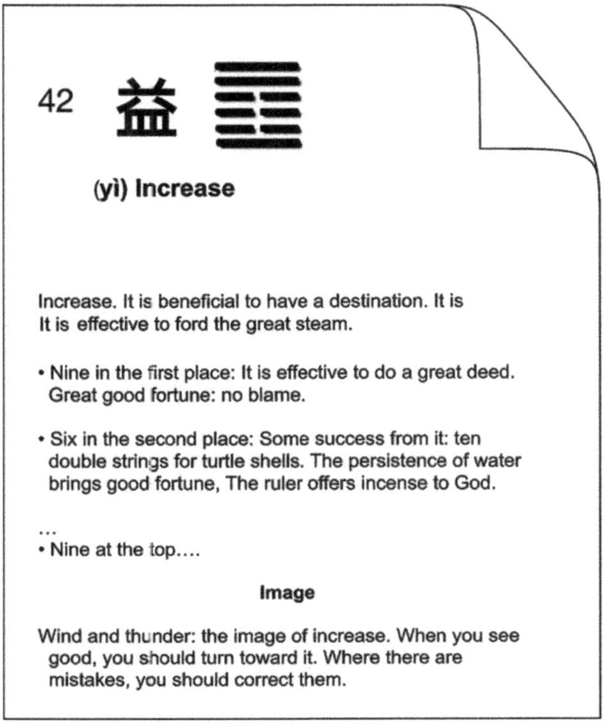

**42  益 ☴☳**

**(yì) Increase**

Increase. It is beneficial to have a destination. It is
It is effective to ford the great steam.

• Nine in the first place: It is effective to do a great deed.
  Great good fortune: no blame.

• Six in the second place: Some success from it: ten
  double strings for turtle shells. The persistence of water
  brings good fortune, The ruler offers incense to God.

…
• Nine at the top….

**Image**

Wind and thunder: the image of increase. When you see
good, you should turn toward it. Where there are
mistakes, you should correct them.

Figure 1.2 — Sample Judgment and Image

# The 64 Hexagrams of the I Ching

| 1. Heaven (Creative) | 9. Smaller Herd (Taming the | 17. Following | 25. Not False (Innocence) | 33. Retreat Retreat | 41. Decrease | 49. Molting (Revolution) | 57. Calculation (The Gentle) |
|---|---|---|---|---|---|---|---|
| 2. Earth (Receptive) | 10. Sleeping (Treading) | 18. Branch Out (Use the spoiled) | 26. Nurturing (Tame the Great) | 34. Strength (Great Power) | 42. Increase (Increase) | 50. Cauldron | 58. Joy (The Joyous) |
| 3. Sprouting (Difficult start) | 11. Peace | 19. The Forest (Approach) | 27. Jaws (Mouth Corners) | 35. Advancing (Progress) | 43. Resolute (Break-Through) | 51. Thunder (The Arousing) | 59. Dispersion (Dissolution) |
| 4. New Grass (Youthful Folly) | 12. Obstruction (Standstill) | 20. Gazing (Contemplation) | 28. Surpassing (The Great) | 36. Hurt Light (Dark Light) | 44. Royal Bride (Come to meet) | 52. Stillness (Keeping Still) | 60. Limitation (Limitation) |
| 5. Waiting (Nourishment) | 13. Friendship (Fellowship) | 21. Take a Bite (Biting Through) | 29. The Abyss (Abyssmal) | 37. Family (The Clan) | 45. Gathered (Meeting) | 53. Slight Progress (Development) | 61. Sincere (Inner Truth) |
| 6. Strife (Conflict) | 14. Great Possession | 22. Elegance (Grace) | 30. The Net (Clinging) | 38. Double Vision (Opposition) | 46. Push Upward (Pusing Upward) | 54. Homecoming (Marrying Maiden) | 62. Minor Suplus (The Small) |
| 7. Many Follow (The Army) | 15. Modesty | 23. Peeling (Splitting Apart) | 31. Reciprociaty (Influence) | 39. Impeded (Obstruction) | 47. Exhaustion (Opposition) | 55. Abundance (Fullness) | 63. After Crossing (After |
| 8. Closeness (Hold Together) | 16. Excess (Enthusiasm) | 24. Returning (Turning Point) | 32. Duration | 40. Released (Deliverance) | 48. The Well | 56. Wanderer | 64. No Across (Before Completion) |

Figure 1.3 — The 64 Hexagrams of the *I Ching*

When the *I Ching* speaks, it speaks to you, gives advice tailored to you, adapted to your time and place. And, as with a friend, you have to take the time to get to know it. The author of an *I Ching* translation will offer their own commentary suggesting how to understand the ancient text.

The most ancient words of the *I Ching* are the Judgment or Decision. As we have seen with Hexagram 42, these often have several possible meanings. It is like a friend initiating a conversation. Your friend does not repeat the experiences or culture you both share because your friend knows you understand the allusions called forth by the words they speak. Your friend not

only speaks words but displays body language and
speaks with a tone of voice that refines the meaning, giving an emotional context that goes well beyond the dictionary definition of the words being
spoken.

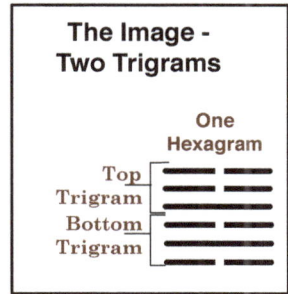

The Image -
Two Trigrams

One
Hexagram

Top
Trigram
Bottom
Trigram

*Hexagram Made Up of Two Trigrams*

The *I Ching* has its own body language and tone
of voice. To the words are added The Image. The
Image, that is the lines in the hexagram, is present-
ed for you to contemplate as you read the words. As this book will show, the
simple six lines become rich with meaning when seen as two three-line trigrams, each trigram representing a nature-image.

### ⸺∞⸺ I Ching — A Book With Several Names ⸺∞⸺

The *I Ching*, 易經, *The Book of Changes* is also translated as *The Classic of
Change,* or sometimes *The Easy Classic.*[2] "I" is pronounced "ē." The word *I*
易 means *change*; *Ching* 經 means *great book.* The word *Ching* will be found
in the title of many Chinese classics such as the *Tao Te Ching.*[3]

*I Ching* — Some of the Many Translations

The book, 易經, goes by several titles in the English-speaking world. The term "*I Ching*" has been traditionally used in English translations, dating back to the early twentieth century when the Wade-Giles Romanization was used by Western scholars. The now international standard Pinyin Romanization for the characters 易經 is "*Yì Jīng*," which is often written as *Yi Jing, Yijing,* or sometimes shortened to "The *Yi*."[4] An older name is sometimes used, 周易, written as *Zhouyi, Zhōu yì,* or the older Wade-Giles, *Chou I.* The word Zhou comes from the Zhou Dynasty (1100 B.C.–221 B.C.), which is the dynasty that created the oldest layer of text. *Zhouyi* is used to distinguish the old text from later versions that included Confucian Commentary.[5]

You will see the symbol 𝔡 for the *I Ching* on the cover of some translations and websites. This is probably the earliest form of the character for *Yi*. It is found on old bone inscriptions and is presumed to mean "cloudy changing to clear weather." The pictogram that led to the modern character of *Yi* is 彡, which may be seen on *I Ching* book covers and websites. Finally, some books will note that character for *Yi,* 易, is made up of the sun 日 over moon 月, implying *change* as the sun and moon dance across the sky every day.[6]

The change from Wade-Giles to Pinyin can lead to different English spellings for the same Chinese characters and meaning. For example, the following mean the same thing and represent the same Chinese written word: *Tao* and *Dao*; *Tao Te Ching* and *Daodejing*; *Lao-Tzu, Lao-Tze,* and *Laozi.*[7]

### ⸺ So Simple a Child Can Use It ⸺
### So Subtle the Old Struggle To Fathom It[8]

The *I Ching* is simple to use: select one of the 64 hexagrams. While selecting one of the 64 hexagrams is a random event, several traditions claim this randomness is only apparent — the selection is being guided by some underlying principle that is hidden from view. You will find no scientific proof of a non-random underlying principle for these random events. But, as this book will discuss, it is not clear that the current state of science precludes the idea either.

Carl Jung, in his forward to the first popular translation of the *I Ching*, suggested that what is going on is something he calls *synchronicity* — there is no cause and effect explanation, but there is a correlation that emerges out of the complex interactions of the universe and the human psyche's interaction with the universe.[9] There are several traditions, both ancient and modern, that also claim to explain the workings of the *I Ching*. We shall also see how the random selection of a suggestive phrase can even be seen as the *I Ching* acting in the tradition of a person-centered therapist.

There is no formula explaining how *I Ching* works. To fathom the *I Ching*, you might just have to jump in and go for the ride.

> *At this moment, the cosmos, the earth, all of the inhabitants of nature, including people with their thoughts and passions, including my thoughts and passions, are all leaning like a cosmic wave — ready to break, poised, containing the potential of the future, a future which will be released to move the universe to the next instant, minute, hour, day, week, month, year, ad-infinitum.*
>
> *The potential for the multi-fold paths of the future await my action or non-action, await the words I choose to put into the world. And, I know that words and deeds will follow my thoughts, passions, and dispassions.*
>
> *There is no mistake about it — my thoughts, words, actions, and non-action will ripple subtly through the unfolding future and shift its path, all the while holding my path in its embrace.*
>
> *If I understand the moment, I may align myself with the Way of the future.*

The effort to understand the *I Ching* is an endeavor that the *I Ching* has in common with every great ancient book. Each was borne in a particular culture and retains the birthmarks of its origins. For example, when one reads of the culture, literature, and beliefs of the people of the West through the ages, the Bible is ever present, even if you have never read it. It has had a long and powerful influence on how the cultures of the West express themselves, their art, their buildings, and their assumptions about the world. This is the same with all of the world's great religions and belief systems, including Western science. Each is a framework for how to understand the world that is often accepted without question or even awareness by the people who live within cultures who practice them.

For China, the *I Ching* is such a book. The *I Ching* retained a central place in Chinese thought until the twentieth century. By the mid-twentieth century, its central position was replaced by secular philosophies, including communist thought in the Peoples Republic of China. But, it was never forgotten, even in mainland China, where it is making a comeback. The *I Ching* has a history of scholarship on par with the Bible, and for 3000 years was read for its philosophy as well as foretelling the future. Passages were often cited to prove a point, like quoting scripture in the West.[10] For over three millennium the *I Ching* was used by the ruling class to gain insights into how to rule a society and individuals trying to figure out what to do next. It has been studied by Buddhists in the East for a millennium.[11]

Becoming familiar with the *I Ching's* cultural context will make your reading much more powerful. When we use the phrase "crying wolf," we reach all the way back to Aesop's Fables, Greek stories from around 600 B.C. Further, the passage of time changes the meaning within a culture. For example, in Shakespeare's *Hamlet, Now pile your dust upon the quick and dead.* For Shakespeare, "quick" meant "alive."

The meaning of words can also be different between cultures who speak the same language, such as the United States and England. Putting something in a boot in America is to put it in something worn on your foot. But, in England, a boot is where you store luggage in a car — the "trunk" in America.

Within the *I Ching*, the cultural references originate in ancient China — some of which are lost in the mists of time. But, when we try, our mind is stretched to not only understand the words but the wisdom behind them.

## ⸺ THE *I CHING* — A TOOL FOR DIVINATION ⸺

Divination is not exclusively concerned with future events. It is the purposeful quest to understand the hidden meaning of events in the world we sense, events in the past, present, and future.[12] Divination, in this sense, has been practiced by nearly every culture that has arisen in human history. This quest to understand hidden meanings almost always comes with a "philosophical cosmology," that is, a theory of how the universe works. Divination may or may not require magic, may or may not depend upon an intermediary diviner, may or may not assume the intercession of a divine entity, may or may not be rooted in pseudo-science — but has been interpreted from many points of view.[13]

*You predict the future every day.*[14] The *I Ching* helps you do what people do every day, predict the future in everyday life.

No one could cross the street safely if they didn't predict the future. Imagine you are standing at the curb at a stoplight. The light turns yellow. You wait because you *know* it is about to turn red. Wait a minute; how did you *know?* Unless you have done a little time travel, you have not actually experienced it. You *predicted* the light would turn red because it has always turned red.

Imagine a car is coming as you are about to cross the street. You step out to cross the street because you *know* it will not reach you before you cross the street. You *know because you predicted* it. You did not stop to compute its path using Newton's Laws of Motion when you made this prediction. But, you knew because you have observed how the world works.

When things get more complex than these everyday occurrences, your predictions become tenuous, full of doubt. This is when the *I Ching* can help. Using the *I Ching* is simply pushing this everyday ability further, giving insight into a more complex present, allowing you to predict the future that might unfold, helping you go forward with less doubt, particularly concerning the morality of your actions.

## ⟞⟶ THE *I CHING* TODAY ⟵⟝
### A PATH TO SPIRITUAL AND PSYCHOLOGICAL INSIGHT

The *I Ching* is not a religious text but has been found compelling for followers of religion by providing insight into their own religious thought. This is particularly true for the Buddhists and some Christian missionaries who came in contact with Chinese culture. The *I Ching* does not insist on a belief system, nor does it ask the reader to perform any religious rites.[15] It can go to any church and see the value in its rituals, sacraments, and teachings.

It is not a psychological treatise, but it has captivated psychologists. While the West may have been the first to coin "psychology," Chinese use of several forms of divination can be seen as "a highly developed form of psychotherapy."[16] It can help you become aware of what your subconscious already knows.

Nor is it a scientific treatise, but its underlying principles of operation are based on the *yin-yang* process, which can be a compelling insight into understanding modern science. More and more, the way the *I Ching* sees the world is how Western science is seeing the world when examining the profound relationship between energy and matter. When the *I Ching* reveals these principles, it's as if heaven and earth are speaking to humanity.

The purpose of the *I Ching of a Thousand Doors* is to encourage living a self-aware life, a spiritual life if you will. It also seeks to help in gaining an insight into our psychological, philosophical, religious, and scientific traditions, with the *I Ching* always the touchstone.

The *I Ching* can help you travel down the path you have chosen. As Mahatma Gandhi said, "Religions are different roads converging to the same point. What does it matter that we take different roads so long as we reach the same goal?"[17]

This is done with respect for *each* of the viewpoints, without pretending that they are somehow "the same" — they are not. His Holiness the Dali Lama takes Gandhi's thought further:

> To get religious understanding and harmony between belief systems, they do not need to be the same. Adherents around the world would never agree to that. Instead, each must understand and respect the other's beliefs.[18]

Nearly every spiritual and philosophical tradition, going at least back to the Greek philosophers, recognizes that the human mind understands things in different ways. When you interact with the world, three things are happening, often at the same time. You contemplate with a rational and thoughtful mind, experience with your sensual and emotional self, and sometimes get to a transcendental, spiritual insight. When you interact with the *I Ching*, you may find your mind dancing among these ways of understanding.

*Looking for fulfillment*
    *in our racing, media-driven, money-driven society*
        *is like a "two dimensional" search.*
*You don't look at the ground*
        *when you are looking for a*
*Golden Eagle.*

*Look up!*
    *The third dimension is where the eagle flies,*
        *the dimension where insight lies,*
            *where the spirit flies.*

We have an opportunity to peer into the meaning of our own beliefs. As we journey through the *I Ching* and its relationships with these beliefs, we will touch upon the original texts, the scripture, and the cultural context.

### ⤖ CHOOSE YOUR PATH ⤖

#### THE I CHING HELPS THOSE SEEKING SELF-AWARENESS AND ENLIGHTENMENT

The *I Ching,* used with meditation, has a long history among Buddhists in China and other parts of Asia. The readings inevitably move your mind toward the center, all the while providing some insight into your psyche and its interaction with the material world.

#### THE *I CHING* HELPS THE SEARCH FOR TRUE HAPPINESS.

Aristotle's thoughts on the ultimate goal of life ripples through nearly every tradition:

> *A State of Happiness, therefore, appears to be something perfect and sufficient unto itself, being the end of actions.*[19]

Every pleasure, prayer, meditation, loving thought, action is a means to this end: a state of happiness. Not pleasure that is bound to end, but an everlasting, unshakable state of happiness. There is a multitude of paths, be they living a full and virtuous life, achieving the loving union with God, living in the Dao, or through an end of suffering. Different paths, yes — paths we will examine — paths to a common goal, a real and authentic state of happiness.[20]

The *I Ching* is not a religious text, but it can be useful for gaining insight into God's will in your situation. Have you ever prayed for guidance and then opened a random page of scripture? Or, been inspired by what someone happened to say that helped your mind see the right path? So it is with the *I Ching*. The *I Ching* will suggest what the "Superior Person" should do, the person who seeks to do God's Will, follow God's commandments and live in the presence of God.

Christian priests and ministers have studied and translated the *I Ching* for a long time, including Father Matteo Ricci in the eighteenth century; Reverend Richard Wilhelm in the early twentieth century, who created the most popular translation in the West; and Monsignor Richard Rutt in recent times. From the nineteenth century through today, these Christian missionaries saw the *I Ching* as a book that was compatible with their Christian beliefs.[21]

But, most importantly, exploring the *I Ching* can bring you back to your scriptures with a fresh outlook, seeing them with the fresh openness that you had when you first read them.[22]

⊶════⊶⊶════⊷

Science does not preclude most of what we attribute to the spiritual world. The more we seem to learn about science, the more we realize what we don't know. Every time scientists think they have captured the "Mathematics of Everything," some observation of the natural world is found that cannot be explained. Indeed, that is what drives the history of "scientific discoveries."

To illustrate this for yourself:
- Take a 12-inch ruler and lay it on a piece of paper.
- At the zero-inch mark, take a pencil or pen and make a dot — that is what science knew at the time of Moses and Confucius.
- Carefully put a dot next to it, so that it touches the first dot, but moves up the ruler. This is what science knew when the United States was founded.
- Carefully put a dot next to it, so that it touches the second dot, but moves up the ruler. This is what science knew when Einstein wrote about relativity.

- Carefully put a dot next to it, so that it touches the third dot, but moves up the ruler. This is what we know now. The rest of the ruler is what we have yet to learn before we are close to understanding the Universe.[23]

Science is a good and useful way to try to understand the world, but there are other ways as well, ways that answer questions that the mathematics of science does not.

<hr/>

The *I Ching* can be part of your toolbox for pursuing whichever path you choose. The struggle to understand the *I Ching* can be frustrating because the *I Ching* suggests, hints, provides parables, gives tenuous analogies, and sometimes even prods instead giving you a convenient formula. The *I Ching* challenges you to "get it" without leaving a trail of breadcrumbs to follow.

This is common to all religions and many human endeavors. For example, Saint Augustine's writings are full of rational arguments familiar to Greek philosophers, and indeed, that is where he started his search to understand the Christian faith and the doctrine he inherited. Some may disagree with much of his logic. But, what is evident in his *Confessions* is that he found what he was looking for when a "Beatific Vision" of God flashed in his mind, beyond words, beyond rational comprehension, a vision so powerful he lost it due to the shock of it — and spent the rest of his life trying to get it back.[24] So it is that humans reach for insight into the divine through a spiritual experience.

So it was with Mary Baker Eddy who had an insight into the Might of Truth and how the "divine Principle heals the sick, casts out error, and triumphs over death."[25]

So it was when Gautama Buddha sat under the Bodhi Tree,[26] Arjuna finally saw the wisdom of his Charioteer.[27]

So it was that Muhammad, peace be upon him, was visited in a cave by the Archangel Gabriel,[28] and Prophet Joseph Smith was directed to the golden plates.[29]

So it is when the spirit that goes beyond words can be seen in the writings of Steven Hawkins and the music of the great musicians. So it was in the realm of politics when King Wén of Zhou received the Mandate of Heaven,[30] Mahatma Gandhi held tightly to the truth,[31] and the Reverend Martin Luther King had a dream.

The list is long. The *I Ching* can be a tool for getting to this kind of insight. It may suggest, but not answer, leaving your mind and spirit to complete the dialog with the Sage.

On an almost final note regarding the cultural context of the *I Ching*: You may see a patriarchal slant in many *I Ching* translations, seeing them as running counter to your culture. Some translators insist that this an accurate translation of the text, while other translators insist that the meaning of the original text was given this slant in later centuries in China such as attaching the submission of females to words such as *yin*. Historians note that womankind's status in Chinese society often suffered in historical periods after the creation of the original text. Anyone who has tried the *I Ching* and been put off by this, may wish to read the introduction to Pearson's translation, *The Original I Ching,* and give the *I Ching* another try.

As Pearson points out, the Chinese character 子, which is often translated as "man" in the phrase 君子 "superior man," is a Chinese character with no necessary gender. 君子 means the *Noble Person's Child.*[32]

Our ancestors walked through a world full of spirits. In many cultures, including China, their deceased family was believed to be still nearby, participating in family matters. The sun, the moon, each animal, and each plant, was animated by a spirit that people could sense if they wished. In our culture, we have moved the world of spirits to the movie house and the computer screen in much of our popular entertainment to recreate a spiritual world.

Does the American culture hide the spirits because science forbids their existence in our world? But, most of us still believe there is a God or some other "something" beyond our understanding. Have our ancestors become something called spirit or soul? Even more of us believe the Universe remains beyond our full comprehension.

We should humbly acknowledge that science does not explain everything.

*When we catch that fleeting glimmer*
 *In the corner of our eye,*
*It may just be the flicker*
 *Of the spirit hovering nearby.*
*It may be the spirit*
 *That underlies everything we see,*
*Or may be the spirit*
 *That gives life to our experience.*

Finally, many readers will have a mighty struggle with the fact that two apparently contradictory ideas or different meanings of a word, like Dao, can be accepted and held at the same time in the *I Ching*. When this appears to be so, it is no accident. The *I Ching* does not insist on one-or-the-other. It embraces both equally. Our culture's demand for a neatly parsed world has not been embraced by *The Book of Changes*.

~ ~ ~

*Events follow definite trends,*
*Each according to its nature.*
So Says *The Great Treatise*

Leaves Life Cycle

Western Zhou Gui Vessel

# 2

# THE ANCIENT ORACLE

*Have and have not create each other,*
*Hard and easy produce each other,*
*Long and short shape each other,*
*... First and last follow each other.*
So Says the *Dàodéjīng*[1]

Fuxi and Nüwa

The *I Ching* of ancient China is the *I Ching* of the ruling and educated elites who, because they were literate, could pass down their thoughts and experiences to us. Little is known of the peasant divination practices in ancient China. But, by the eighteenth century Europeans recorded an active trade in city streets of self-proclaimed diviners interpreting the *I Ching* for peasants and workers. For important decisions, divination was essential for making the right decision — for people around the world, for several millennia, and for many people today.

The *I Ching, The Book of Changes*, has an outlook on how the world works. The idea that everything changes, producing repeating cycles like the seasons of the year, is deeply embedded in how the ancient Chinese saw the patterns of nature in their daily lives.

## Fu Xi — The trigrams

The mythical story of the *I Ching* begins with the foundation of the eight trigrams that rose in Chinese consciousness from the mists of the founding of their culture. The original trigrams are said to have been revealed to a legendary ruler, Fúxī 伏羲 around 2800 B.C., with the hexagrams coming into being sometime later.[2] Fuxi was one of the Three Sovereigns, sometimes seen as divine. Fuxi and his sister Nüwa, 女娲 are said to have created Chinese culture and taught humans to hunt, cook, and write.[3] Other than this cultural legend, the origins of the eight trigrams are lost in the fog of the past, going back to the beginnings of complex writing and oracle bone divination around 1500 B.C.[4]

Each trigram is associated with a nature element or natural event.

Two trigrams make up a hexagram, creating a dynamic that gives meaning and movement to the hexagram reading. Thus, while the theme a hexagram is given the Judgment and the Lines, the two trigrams create a visual image of the interaction of two forces of nature.

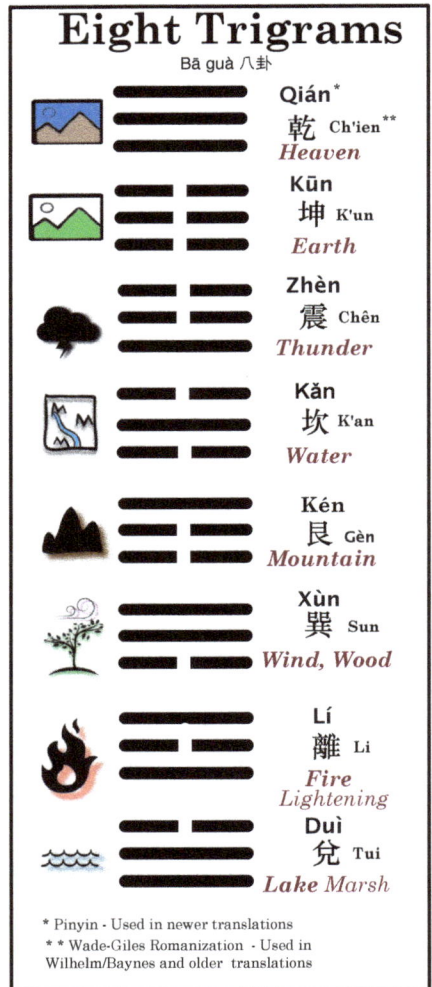

**Eight Trigrams**

Bā guà 八卦

Qián*
乾 Ch'ien**
*Heaven*

Kūn
坤 K'un
*Earth*

Zhèn
震 Chên
*Thunder*

Kǎn
坎 K'an
*Water*

Kén
艮 Gèn
*Mountain*

Xùn
巽 Sun
*Wind, Wood*

Lí
離 Li
*Fire*
*Lightening*

Duì
兌 Tui
*Lake Marsh*

* Pinyin · Used in newer translations
** Wade-Giles Romanization · Used in Wilhelm/Baynes and older translations

Eight Trigrams and Nature

The eight trigrams are not unique to the *I Ching*; far from it. They are associated with nearly all of the ancient Chinese traditions and are found in Chinese medicine, Feng Shui, and martial arts.

## ⟊ THE *ZHOUYI* — THE OLDEST LAYER OF THE *I CHING* ⟊

Trigram and hexagram images are found on ar-chaeological artifacts from the Shang Dynasty (around 1600–1046 B.C.), used for "oracle bone divination."[5] The divination was often done in association with ritual sacrifice. Turtle shells or cattle shoulder blades were carved with Chinese pictograms and characters which then were heated to create cracks. The cracks were read to get divination results. Both the question and answers were recorded.[6]

King Wén of Zhou

Some scholars suggest that hexagrams may have come first and trigrams later. Others suggest that the six lines of a hexagram are linked to the Chinese calendar of lunar cycles used in ancient China.[7] The decisions and judgments started as an oral tradition, with sages providing the interpretations of the divination results. The tradition incorporated parts of popular poems, sayings, children's songs, and stories of the time.

Around 1,050 B.C., there is the story of the man who wrote the *I Ching* Judgments. He inspired Confucius 500 years later, who, looking back, proclaimed that his dynasty reached a perfection that later generations should strive to recreate. The ruler Confucius admired was Wáng Wén, known as King Wén of Zhou.

Wáng Wén's story begins with the king of the Shang Dynasty, who had become corrupt, abusing the subjects and failing to perform the proper rituals to Heaven — *Tiān*.[8] Fearing Wén, the lord of a fiefdom, the evil king imprisoned him, during which time Wén wrote the Judgments of the *I Ching*. His fourth son, the Duke of Zhou, continued his father's work and wrote the Line Statements.

Divination Using a Turtle Shell

Wén's second son, Wu, lead his army to defeat the evil king. Wén was freed and founded the Zhou dynasty. Wén declared that inheritance was not sufficient for a king — the ruler had to have The Mandate of Heaven — a mandate that Heaven would only bestow on a just and virtuous ruler. While many historians doubt that King Wén actually wrote the Judgments, they were certainly in the form we read today around 820–800 B.C.[9] Historians agree that

Yin–Yang and Trigrams

he did claim The Mandate of Heaven, which became an important concept in Imperial China — an idea that held kings to account.

What the King Wén and his son wrote is called the *Zhouyi*, which means the Changes of Zhou. It is the core of today's *I Ching*.

The *Zhouyi* began as a tool used by the ruling class for divination. Questions were both practical and ritualistic. For example, a prophecy was recorded that:

> It would not rain if the King goes hunting; the ritual for the
> the hunt should be performed in the south chamber.[10]

*Zhouyi* divination was originally done using the manipulation of yarrow stalks to select a hexagram, sometimes being done in conjunction with cracked turtle shell divination. The cracked shell and bone methods fell into disuse sometime during the Zhou dynasty (1046 B.C. to 256 B.C.). As the written *Zhouyi* was copied and distributed, individuals began using it. By 300 B.C., the *Zhouyi* had hints of the idea of a Superior Person acting in accord with an ethical mandate, but the primary mandate for the *Zhouyi* was the regulation of behavior in accord with the wishes of Heaven, although the principles remained unstated.[11]

**The Five Classics**
- *I Ching* 易經 *Yìjīng*
- Book of Poetry or Odes 詩經, *Shījīng*
- Book of Documents (History) 尚書 *Shūjīng*
- Book of Rites 禮記 *Lǐjì*
- Spring and Autumn 春秋 *Chūnqiū*

## ⸺ THE *I CHING* BECOMES A CONFUCIAN CLASSIC ⸺

In the middle and late bronze age, the Torah, the first five books of the Hebrew Scripture and the Christian Old Testament were being written in the Middle East; the oldest Hindu Vedas were being recited in the Indian subcontinent; the *I Ching* was being written and used for divination in China. Confucians added commentaries to the *I Ching* between 500 B.C. and 200 B.C., bringing a system of morality to the *I Ching*.

When the Emperor of China gathered a group of scholars to reach consensus on an orthodox set of classics, the *I Ching* was adopted as the first of the Confucian Classics. In 136 B.C., Confucianism become the official philosophy for statecraft, and continued to be so for the next two millennia.

The *I Ching* traveled to other Asian societies along with the other Confucian Classics in the first millennium A.D., including Korea, Japan, and Southeast Asia.[12] The *I Ching* made its way to Europe and America during the last two centuries.

### ⸺ HARMONIZING THE HUNDRED SCHOOLS OF THOUGHT ⸺

The *I Ching* commentaries attributed to Confucius were written during an intellectual period that historians call the Hundred Schools of Thought, circa 500 B.C. to 221 B.C., a period which spans the Spring and Autumn and Warring States periods in Chinese political history. This burst of intellectual creativity occurred when China was in the violent turmoil, when Laozi wrote the *Daodejing*, the *Analects of Confucius* was compiled, Sunzi wrote the *Art of War*, the Legalism theory of a uniform

**A Daoist and Confucius Compare Views**

A story by Zhuangzi:

On this Confucius proceeded to give an abstract of the Classics to bring the other over to his views.

Lao Tan, however, interrupted him and said, "This is too vague; let me hear the substance of them."

Confucius said, "The substance of them is ... Benevolence and Righteousness."

"[Do] Benevolence and Righteousness to constitute the nature of man?"

"Benevolence and Righteousness are truly the nature of man. .... to love all men; and to allow no selfish thoughts." ...

"If you, Master, wish men not to be without their shepherding, think of Heaven and Earth, which certainly pursue their invariable course; think of the sun and moon, which surely maintain their brightness; ...

Why must you be vehement in putting forward your Benevolence and Righteousness? Ah! Master, you are introducing disorder into the nature of man!"

Zhuangzi, 13:7, Legge trans.

system of reward and punishment was developed, and the Yin-Yang School synthesized principles into a cosmology.[13]

The Daoists focused on human harmony with the workings of nature. Daoists use the word *Dao*, The Way, meaning something to which one would naturally and without effort conform. It is often paired with *Tiān* 天, nature/heaven, to indicate naturally and without effort, conforming to the workings of nature.

The *I Ching* exists in a cosmos whose dynamics are subject to the *Law of Change*, where all things change according to their nature, a concept represented by the yin-yang cycle and the Yin-Yang Symbol.[14]

Confucians, on the other hand, focused on human relationships. Confucius used the word *Dao,* the Way, paired with *Ren,* a good and virtuous person. Confucius portrayed the *Dao* as acting and thinking in a "virtuous and ethical" Way, which must be learned and practiced.[15]

In a spiritual sense, each of these views strive to move the workings of mankind into the proper correlative relationship with the operations of *Tian*, The Heavens.[16] The contrast is the way this is done. Daoists teach *doing nothing*; Confucians teach *doing for nothing* — doing what is moral for nothing other than morality itself.[17]

In spite of the apparent opposing viewpoints, both of these philosophies are found in the *I Ching*, the Yin-Yang Principle being ever present within the Judgment and Line Statements, while Confucian thought is spoken aloud in the Image Statement and commentaries. Thus, the *I Ching* is a synergy of these two schools, adopted as a canonical text in both, even though they differ in their view of humankind's path to coming into *being in the Dao*.

## ❧ THE TEN WINGS ❧

The Ten Wings consist of Confucian Commentaries synergized with other schools of thought that were added to the *Zhouyi*. Modern authors make the original organization of the Ten Wings invisible to the *I Ching* user. It is not necessary to try to remember what is in which wing to use the *I Ching*.

The *I Ching,* now including the Ten Wings, received Imperial sanction in

## The Arrangement of the Ten Wings

| Parts of a Reading | Example<br>Maroon Text from Legge Translation | Part or Wing Name | Orginal Text (Zhouyi) or Wing Number | Included In Sample Translations |
|---|---|---|---|---|
| Number | **17** | | Zhouyi*<br>(1100-800 BC) | Wilhelm Book 1 & 3<br>Lynn, Peterson |
| Hexagram Symbol | ☰☱ | 卦<br>Guà | Zhouyi<br>(1100-800 BC) | Wilhelm Book 1 & 3<br>Lynn, Peterson |
| Name | 隨<br>*Suí*/Following | 卦名<br>Guà míng | Zhouyi<br>(1100-800 BC) | Wilhelm Book 1 & 3<br>Lynn, Peterson |
| Judgment | ·元亨利貞·無咎·<br>Suí indicates that (under its conditions) there will be great progress and success.<br>*Time to adapt to following* | 彖<br>Tuàn<br>Or<br>卦辭<br>Guà cí | Zhouyi<br>(1100-800 BC) | Wilhelm Book 1 & 3<br>Lynn, Peterson |
| Image | ·澤中有雷·隨·君子以嚮晦入宴息·<br>.... a marsh and ...thunder (hidden) in the midst ... The superior man .... when it is getting towards dark, enters (his house) and rests. | 象傳<br>Xiang zhuan,<br>Or Great Image<br>大象<br>Great Xiang | Wing 3<br>(500-300 BC) | Wilhelm Book 1 & 3<br>Lynn, Peterson |
| The Lines | ·官有渝·貞吉·出門交有功·<br>The first NINE... going beyond (his own) gate... acheive merit | Yáo 爻<br>Line 1 of 6 | Zhouyi<br>(1100-800 BC) | Wilhelm Book 1 & 3<br>Lynn, Peterson |
| Commentary on Judgments | ·隨·剛來而下柔·動而說·隨·<br>In Suí we see the strong (trigram) come and place itself under ...<br>大亨貞無咎·而天下隨時·<br>'There will be great progress and ...<br>隨之時義大矣哉<br>Great indeed are the time... | 彖傳<br>Tuan zhuan | Wing 1<br>(Hexagrams 1-30)<br>Wing 2<br>(Hexagrams 31-64)<br>(500-300 BC) | Wilhelm Book 3<br>Lynn |
| Commentary on Lines | ...beyond (his own) gate... he will not fail... | 象下傳<br>2nd Xiang<br>Or 小象<br>Little Images | Wing 4<br>(500-300 BC) | Wilhelm Book 3<br>Lynn |
| Commetary Hexagrams 1 and 2 | *None - Only included for Hexagrams 1 and 2* | 文言傳<br>Wenyan zhuan | Wing 7<br>(500-300 BC) | Wilhelm Book 3<br>Lynn |
| Sequence | When such complacency is awakened... | 序卦傳<br>Xugua zhuan | Wing 8<br>(500-300 BC) | Wilhelm Book 3<br>Lynn |
| Miscellaneous | Sui quits the old | 雜卦傳<br>Zagua zhuan | Wing 10<br>(500-300 BC) | Wilhelm Book 3<br>Lynn |
| Explanation of Trigrams | *Commentary on the eight trigrams* | 說卦傳<br>Shuogua zhuan | Wing 9<br>(500-300 BC) | Wilhelm Book 2<br>Lynn |
| The Great Treatise | *Commentary on the I Ching as a whole* | 繫辭傳<br>Xici zhuan | Wings 5 & 6<br>(500-300 BC) | Wilhelm Book 2<br>Lynn |

\* Zhouyi is organized as Part 1: Hexagrams 1-30; Part II: 31-64 (Shown by Wilhelm & Legge)

Figure 2.1 — Name, Judgment, Image, Lines, Commentary, Sequence, Explanation of Trigrams

136 B.C. by Emperor Wu, (156–87 B.C.). During the canonization process, the core text of *I Ching* selected, the *Zhouyi*, with the Judgment and Line Statements, had been in circulation from at least 300 B.C.[18] Other versions have recently been unearthed, one with a different hexagram numbering or-

der and some differences in the text.[19] The canonized additions to the *Zhouyi* are known as the Ten Wings because there are ten volumes and were organized as shown in Figure 2.1.

Since seven of the ten volumes walk through the 64 hexagrams with their own commentary, the information is reorganized by translators to bring the relevant information from each wing into a single section, one for each of the 64 hexagrams.

The version selected by the Emperor, based upon the advice of a team of scholars, became the first of the Confucian Canon and has been transmitted with little change to what is called the "Received Text" today.[20] Many commentaries followed, developing different "schools" of interpretation of the *I Ching*, which continue to resonate to this day among the English translations of the classic.

With the addition of the Ten Wings, the classic is rounded out to be a book of political philosophy and moral development as well as a book of divination.[21] Wings 5 and 6 are parts of the same commentary, which is called *The Great Commentary* or *The Great Treatise*. It is an essay on the *I Ching* that describes its underlying meaning and operations in a synergy of cosmological, Confucian, and Daoist principles. *The Great Treatise* was complete by 300 B.C.[22] Added to this is Wing 9, a discussion of the trigrams.

The Ten Wings are rooted in Confucian philosophy but retain a synergy of Daoist philosophy. Confucianism emphasizes a hierarchical polite, orderly society, ruled by people of virtue — the ideal for the society into which he was borne. The ideal, educated Confucian embodies the European notion of a gentleman in its fullest sense, a person who embodies morality, a cultivated education, and conforms to rules of politeness.[23]

The Ten Wings do three critical things with their commentary:

1. Moved the *Zhouyi* from "doing the right action" to achieve material and social outcomes, to also "doing the right moral thing."

2. Inserted the idea of hexagram as being a field of action, the six lines of a hexagram developing the hexagram theme in space and time.

3. Reinforced the established correlative cosmology, characterizing the

changes of the 64 hexagrams and 384 changing lines as mirroring the operations of the cosmos based on laws of orderly patterns of change, such as the four seasons.[24]

The Confucian philosophy that made its way into the *I Ching* is focused almost exclusively on human relationships and the governance of society, saying very little about relations with the metaphysical or with nature.[25]

Philosophical Daoism focuses on one's relationship with the natural world, seeing it as a mirror of the workings of a spiritual world represented by Heaven and the natural world, Earth. Daoism's view of humanity focuses on "unlearning" so that one can relate to the *Dao*.[26] In spite of these apparent contradictions, the *I Ching* is part of the canon for both Confucianism and Daoism, serving as an "integrating text" for the two philosophies.

> *When I cast the I Ching, I see the yin-yang of Daoism which tells me, "See the Laws of Change. This is where you are in the changing world and how it will unfold."*
> *Then, feeling alarm rising up, I wonder, "What do I do?"*
> *I turn to see Confucius advising me, "See The Doctrine of the Mean, here is how you should respond to the coming events."*[27]

Scholars developed refined the teaching of Confucius with a body of commentary and further elaboration, the most well-known being the Confucian sage, Mencius (372–289 B.C.). The canon grew to thirteen works, with the *Five Classics* remaining at the core.

---

**The Thirteen Classics**

| | |
|---|---|
| • *I Ching* | • *Book of Poetry* or *Book of Odes* |
| • *Book of Documents* (History) | • *Book of Rites* |
| • *Rights of Zhou* | • *Ceremonies and Rites* |
| • *The Analects of Confucius* | • *Erya* (Dictionary) |
| • *Mencius* | •*Classic of Filial Piety* |
| • Three commentaries on the Spring and Summer Annals | |

---

## ∽— BUDDHISTS — LATER INTERPRETATIONS —∾

Buddhism is an imported philosophy into China. While there were isolated pockets a century earlier, a Buddhist monk Lokaksema, traveling along the silk roads around A.D. 164 from the Kushan Empire of the Steppes, and spread the Pure Land version of Mahāyāna Buddhism.[28] It spread slowly until around A.D. 400, when it became increasingly popular.

Amitabha Buddha and Bodhisattvas

The Buddhist traditions of Pure Land (*Jìngtǔzōng* 淨土宗), and Chán (*Channà* 禪) remain the primary outlooks today, often being taught together.[30] Chán is known as *Zen* in Japan and the U.S.

The Buddhist tradition of allowing synergy with other belief systems led many to be "Confucian by day," being the way society should work, and "Buddhist by night," being the way for personal development. Buddhists in China studied the *I Ching* and many adopted it as one of their classics. In turn, Buddhist ideas were adopted by Neo-Daoists and Neo-Confucianists.[31]

The Neo-Confucian Sage, Zhu Xi (A.D. 1130–1200), is credited with writing and popularizing The Four Books, which taught the core of the Confucian Classics. Zhu Xi insisted that students read these first since they were easier to comprehend. By then scholars had been studying Buddhist literature for centuries, particularly Chán Buddhist texts, so the Four Books were a synergy of Confucian, Daoism, and Buddhism. This meant new ways of interpreting the *I Ching*.[32]

**The Four Books**
• *The Great Learning* 大學
• *Doctrine of the Mean* 中庸
• *Analects of Confucius* 論語
• *Mencius* 孟子

---

### *I Ching* Travels to East Asia

East Asian countries surrounding China were influenced by Chinese culture and literature, each nation adopting much of what Chinese thought had to offer, but always adapting it and synergizing it with their native culture.

As neighboring countries imported the Confucian Classics, the *I Ching* went with them.

Japan: The *I Ching* is called *Ekikyō*. The earliest written mention is in the *Nihon Shoki* (The Chronicles), dating its arrival in circa A.D. 500. Interest in Japan made it one of the most influential Confucian texts in the fifteenth through nineteenth centuries. Scholarship included Confucians, Zen Buddhist monks, and Shinto, each accommodating it to their own belief systems.

Korea: The *I Ching* is called *Yikkying*. Arrived around A.D. 300, influencing Korean culture, being seriously studied in the sixteenth century.

The flag of South Korea includes four trigrams.

*Korean Flag*

Vietnam: The *I Ching* is known as the *Dich Kinh*, probably arriving around A.D. 100 when Chinese officials dominated Vietnam. While it penetrated Vietnam, the scholarship was not as intense as in Japan and Korea.

Tibet: The *Yi Kying* arrived around A.D. 600, but with little use, Tibetans preferring Buddhist divination methods.

---

## ⟶⟶ THE *I CHING* COMES WEST ⟵⟵

Europeans began translating the Chinese Classics to the European vernacular in the mid-nineteenth century, with James Legge providing English translations of a large body of work.[33] Legge's *I Ching* translation is out of copyright and is widely available on internet sites today.[34]

Richard Wilhelm is credited with popularizing the *I Ching* in the West, providing a German translation in the early twentieth century, followed by an English translation of the German by Baynes in the mid-twentieth century. The Wilhelm/Baynes became the "standard" for English readers, achieving Wilhelm's intent to popularize the *I Ching* in the West.[35] In the last few decades, there have been many other translations, including some which take advantage of recent archaeological finds.

Inevitably, Westerners adapted it to their cultural needs and applied it to their cultural precepts. This is the case for noted psychologist, Carl Jung, who wrote the foreword to the Wilhelm/Baynes *I Ching*.[36]

The *I Ching* has been increasingly used for a tool for self-awareness.[37]

Adopted by the counterculture by the "beat generation" in the 1950s, its popularity was given a boost in the 1960s when the American and Western European popular culture began importing and incorporating Eastern ideas of yoga, music, philosophy, and icons such as the Yin-Yang Symbol.[38]

The capstone endorsement of the *I Ching* as applicable to Western science was the best seller, *The Tao of Physics*, published in 1975.[39] Some people merge the latest physics, the *I Ching*, and Jung's concept of synchronicity along with other ideas to develop new-age spiritual practices.[40] The primary use of the *I Ching* in the West remains its continued use as a tool for self-awareness and tapping the subconscious.

> *The Sage has given me a lesson.*
> *I stare at the six lines, seeing the Image,*
> *assessing the* Judgment,
> *contemplating their insight into the present,*
> *seeking the advice of the Sage*
> *who inevitably advises responding with*
> *virtue in my heart.*

### ⚬⚬ A LIVING DOCUMENT ⚬⚬

How the *I Ching* is interpreted and used continues to change. The *I Ching* is a living document with a long and diverse history of scholarship that is seen through a lens of each scholar's own time, place, and situation, each recognizing the intellectual history of the distant past. Like many religious and philosophical traditions, *The Book of Changes* experiences a historical cycle of dynamic tension where it is elaborated upon in new ways only to have a reform movement respond to try to recapture the old. But, unlike many religious traditions, the idea of an orthodox interpretation of a reading can never be fixed because it is always interacting with the situation of the person tossing the coins or manipulating the yarrow stalks.

The imagery of the *I Ching* is similar to an Impressionist painting. Years ago, while traveling in Australia, I saw a poster announcing that Renoir's *"Luncheon of a Boating Party"*[41] was going to be displayed several hundred miles away. It was worth the trip.

*Le déjeuner des canotiers (Luncheon of a Boating Party)* — Pierre–Auguste Renoir

*As I looked upon the painting,*
*I experienced the play of the sunlight on the wine glasses,*
*the small sparkles that could never be seen in a photograph,*
*the impression of a party among friends was imprinted upon my mind,*
*not the individual expressions of the people painted,*
*but the sum of the human emotions as a whole.*
*The painting spoke not to my eyes*
*but to the part of my mind that sees the product of my eye,*
*making the experience not one of an inanimate object on the wall,*
*but a personal relationship with the painting*
*so impressions on my mind are brought to the fore.*

This experience achieved the artist's intention:

Impressionist painting characteristics include relatively small, thin, yet visible brush strokes, open composition, emphasis on accurate depiction of light in its changing qualities (often accentuating the effects of the passage of time), ordinary subject matter, inclusion of movement as a crucial element of human perception and experience, and unusual visual angles.[42]

Like a great painting, the *I Ching* evokes an impression. It speaks of the present moment, how the future is poised to unfold on many levels at once, providing both words and imagery that work together — dancing together — to communicate what is hidden.

> *The Master said, writing is not the full expression of speech;*
>     *speech is not the full expression of ideas.*

> *— So how is it possible to understand the ideas of the sages?*

> *The sages made symbols to show the fullness of their ideas;*
>     *provided diagrams*
>     *to show the full truth or falsehood of things contemplated;*

> *Appended explanations to their words,*
>     *expanding to fullness the method*
>     *of seeing what is fortuitous.*

> *— They stimulated the senses like that of drums and dances to*
>     *completely develop the spirit-like character of the Changes.*

>                                           — *I Ching*, The Great Treatise

Hexagram 42

## ANATOMY OF TODAY'S *I CHING* BOOK

The 64 hexagrams are known in Chinese as the 64 *Guá* 卦.[43] Each hexagram is made up of six lines, called *Yáo* 爻. A line may be unbroken (solid) and broken. The lines are often associated with pairs of opposites: yang 陽, yin 陰; positive, negative; light, dark.

Some *I Ching* books will use the words yin and yang to designate lines and others will not, instead using unbroken and broken, strong and yielding, or light and dark. The attachment of yang to unbroken lines and yin to broken lines occurred several centuries after the oldest layer of the text was written, during the early Han Dynasty (221–207 B.C.).[44] The translator's choice is often based on what period in Chinese history the translator chooses as the basis for interpreting the *I Ching*.

While English words vary from book to book, remember that the Chinese text being translated is always the same. The original *I Ching*[45] does not use the words yin or yang, except for a single instance of yin.[46]

Most *I Ching* translations have an introduction followed by 64 readings, one for each hexagram, organized by the hexagram number, 1 to 64.[47] Looking up a hexagram number is like looking up a word in a dictionary.

Each hexagram reading includes:

• Judgment — a brief statement, called *Tuan* 彖 or *Guàcí* 卦辭.

• Image Statement — a statement related to the imagery of the interplay of the two trigrams that make up the hexagram.

• Line Statements — a statement for each of the six lines, which are numbered 1 to 6 *counting from the bottom.*[48]

• Supplemental Commentary — additional commentary, which is sometimes, but not always, included in translations.

• Translator's commentary — the book author's interpretation, in some cases including a translation of a Chinese philosopher's comments.

The organization within one of the 64 readings can vary, but usually the order within a reading is the Name, Judgment, Image Statement, and Line Statements. The Supplemental Commentary is usually placed after the Judgment or Line Statement to which it applies.

⋆━━━⋆◦⋆━━⋆

What separates the *I Ching* from most ancient texts is that each page weaves layers of text authored over a span of three millennia. This is because the translator brings together several books of the Ten Wings to create a single chapter for each hexagram with the Judgment, Image Statement, Line Statements, Supplemental Commentary, and author commentary.

In contrast, a scripture like the Bible may span a similar time-frame, but nearly all of the books of the Bible were written by either a single author, or, at most, compiled from prior sources over, at most, a century or two.[49]

Figure 2.2 illustrates the layering of text, using two pages from the Wilhelm/Baynes translation.

> *Understand the old and contemplate it.*
> *Then add the new.*
> *With this we have an answer that will not only present itself,*
> *But will have the wisdom that comes from the many layers of*
> *thought built up over the age.*

The *I Ching* lives in three dimensions: each page containing layers of text that reach wayback in time, interacting with your mind, in your time, and your place.

~ ~ ~

> *King Wén! First to bring harmony to government.*
> *Continuing and tranquil is the Son of Heaven!*
>                     So Says the inscription on the Shi Quian Water Basin[50]

Temple of Heaven

WILHELM/BAYNES I CHING BOOK 1

55. Chin / Progress

THE IMAGE
CONFUCIAN COMMENTARY WING 3
(500 BC - 300 BC)

晉 OLDEST LAYER ZHOUYI
(1150 BC - 800 BC)

55. Chin / Progress

above LI — FIRE
below K'UN — EARTH

THE JUDGMENT

THE LINES
OLDEST LAYER ZHOUYI
(1150 BC - 800 BC)

GREEN IS TRANSLATOR'S COMMENTARY

136

157

WILHELM/BAYNES I CHING BOOK 3

36. Ming I / Darkening of the Light

OLDEST LAYER ZHOUYI
明夷 (1150 BC - 800 BC)

36. Ming I / Darkening of the Light

Nuclear trigrams CHÊN ≡≡ and K'AN

THE JUDGMENT
OLDEST LAYER ZHOUYI
(1150 BC - 800 BC)

Commentary on the Decision

The Sequence
CONFUCIAN COMMENTARY WING 6
(500 BC - 300 BC)

CONFUCIAN COMMENTARY WING 2
(500 BC - 300 BC)

Miscellaneous Notes
CONFUCIAN COMMENTARY WING 10
(500 BC - 300 BC)

565
iching1000.0006

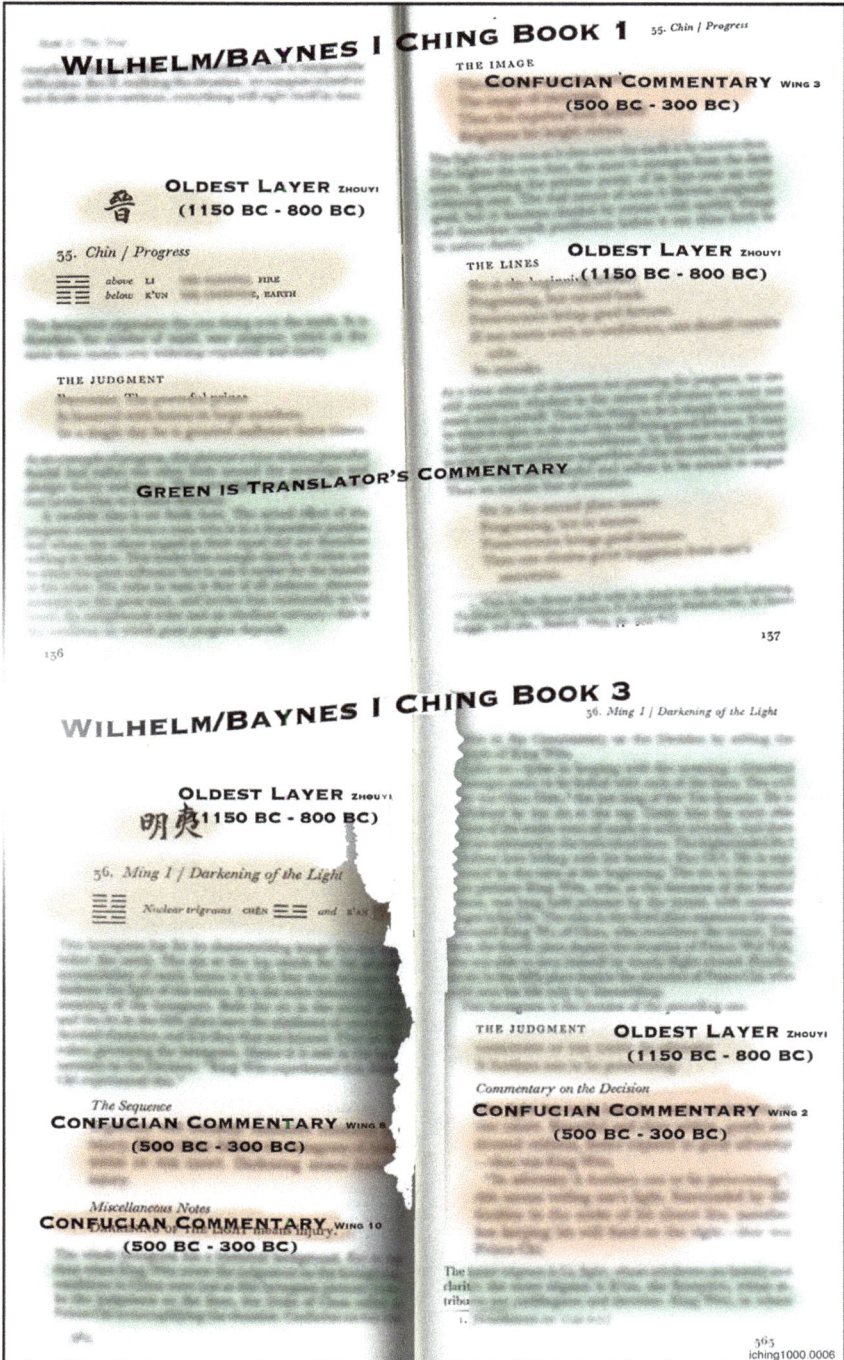

Figure 2.2 — *I Ching* Layers of Text Go Back Through Time On Each Page

Hand Painting A Hexagram

# 3

# HOW TO USE THE *I CHING*

*To heaven belongs 1;*
*to earth, 2; to heaven, 3;*
*to earth, 4; to heaven, 5;*
*to earth, 6; to heaven, 7;*
*to earth, 8; to heaven, 9;*
*to earth, 10.*

So Says *The Great Treatise*[1]

The most common way to use the *I Ching* is to select one of the 64 hexagrams by some random, or in the world of correlative thinking, apparently random process. The most common method is to use three coins. Or, you can use the traditional approach being the manipulation of forty-nine dried stalks from a yarrow plant. Many other methods exist, including beads and dice. This chapter describes and illustrates the coin and yarrow stalk methods. But, before getting to the mechanics of selecting a hexagram, we'll survey several viewpoints, recommend the creation of a ritual, and discuss the imagery of lines and trigrams.

When using the *I Ching* for divination, one may think of divination as telling the future through some sort of magic. This is not necessarily so, although it is undoubtedly seen by the ancients as well as many people today as a means of communication with the divine realm. Divination can be the act of observing the possibilities of the future through a deep understanding of the present.

The way the *I Ching* works and gives advice is centered in the Dao 道. Dao is also commonly written as the Tao in English translations, being the older Wade-Giles transcription system. Dao means The Way or The Path. When it is used in a philosophical context, it becomes a principle.

The tradition of the *I Ching* suggests that you get an understanding of how the future will unfold by aligning yourself with the Dao, The Way. Then, when you wonder how to respond to this vision of the unfolding future, the voice of Confucius points to the Way of your Superior Self.

>──── THE IMPORTANCE OF YOUR VIEWPOINT ────<

Unlike other divination traditions, the *I Ching* book itself becomes the Sage, the medium, through which insight is received. When the *I Ching* is used for divination, it can be seen in many ways. The one that works for you is likely to be based on your outlook and tradition. The viewpoints below are not exhaustive and are included only to be suggestive of one or more outlooks that might work for you:

- *Positive Affirmation — The Way of the Ancients.* The earliest recorded use of the *I Ching* was to express the desired outcome of some action being contemplated, often with a caveat *or maybe not.*[2] Spiritual traditions such as the New Thought Movement and Christian Science see affirmation as abiding in the Divine Mind, facilitated through prayer and meditation;[3] self-affirmation and positive affirmation is part of several psychotherapy methods;[4] positive affirmation is a theme in several popular books that began with Napoleon Hill's, *Think and Grow Rich.*[5]

- *Foretell How the Future Will Unfold — The Way of the Fates.* The future is poised to unfold and carry you with it. This can be seen as "fated," to be accepted, calmly acting within the fated unfolding events. This outlook spans the ages as three mythical women, called "The Fates" by the ancient Greeks and "Norns" by the Norse, weave your life-thread in the tapestry of life.[6]

- *Tap the Subconscious — The Way of the Science of Thought.* The subconscious mind thinks without words, perceiving the complex, not as a camera would, but with a framework built from experience, where experiences become expectations, and perception becomes a search for what fits and what differs from those expectations.[7] The subconscious can be brought into view by the conscious mind with the help of the *I Ching.*

*We can break the enslaving bonds of our Ego,*
*an Ego focused on its desperate desires,*

*keeping us distracted with a busy mind,*
*to obscure clarity we desperately seek.*
*But, the mind already embraces the truth,*
*quiet and waiting for us to uncover it,*
*if we can still the chatter of our Ego.*

- ***Tap the Subconscious — The Way of Therapist and the Skeptic.*** The *I Ching* can act as a person-centered therapist. Here the reading is suggestive of a general theme that leads you to fill in the particulars based on your own situation.[8] A stage performer psychic calls this approach a "Cold Reading," beginning with vague statements that apply to the vast majority of people, moving the story along based on the audience member's response. Person-centered therapy uses this same technique.

An automated "cold reading," the computer program ELIZA, that was written in the 1960s, written as a parody, fooled some people who thought there was human on the other end of the terminal, especially people not familiar with computers. It sounded like a therapist as long as one talked about themselves. But the program contained no knowledge of the meaning of the words. In addition to stock phrases, it only parsed sentences, turning the syntax around, and feeding them back. No semantic content was added to the conversation.[9] This has been compared to a Rorschach inkblot test.

This process takes advantage of the human tendency for "confirmation bias," a tendency to fit facts into your preconceived idea, a tendency that can often lead you astray. If you think the *I Ching* cast will match your situation you are likely to find an interpretation to the reading that fits. But, the tendency can be turned to your advantage when your mind matches an *I Ching* reading with preconceived subconscious knowledge.[10] Then the *I Ching* can be a tool to clearly see the thoughts that had been lurking in the shadows of your subconscious. In this way, the *I Ching* becomes a guided self-examination and awareness tool.[11] But, it's a tricky thing. Ask yourself if you really were made aware of the truth of your subconscious thought or fooling yourself into hearing what you were hoping to hear.

- ***Seek to Understand the Will of God — The Way of the Followers of Faith and Devotion.*** Many religions have as a central tenet for life's correct path the need to seek to understand and follow the Will of the Creator of all things.[12] One humbly seeks to submit to the Divine Will

in response to complex situations that all too often appear to be filled
with moral uncertainty. The *I Ching*'s help in "revealing the hidden"
may help seekers unveil the moral and righteous path.

> *Do not conform yourselves to this age*
> *But be transformed*
> *By the renewal of your mind,*
> *That you may discern the Will of God,*
> *What is good and pleasing and perfect.*
> — *The Holy Bible*, Romans 12:2, NABRE

> ~ ~ ~

> *Surely I rely on Allah, my Lord and your Lord;*
> *There is no beast but He hold it by its forelock;*
> *Verily my Lord is on the right path.*
> — *The Noble Qur'an*, Hud 11:56, (An interpretation)[13]

- *Align with the Universe — The Way of the Way*. Seek to align your
actions with the cycles of the Universe, thus becoming part of its unfolding purpose. A scientist does not dismiss faith. "Faith is the belief in something bigger than ourselves," says Alan Lightman.[14] See the
Universe as embodying the ultimate Good or seeing it as Just-As-It-
Should-Be-On-Its-Own-Terms.[15]

> *I Center my Mind.*
>     *I visualize the endless stars, the living earth.*
> *I see that the Universe has a purpose;*
> *I seek to align myself with that purpose, accepting what comes,*
>         *unattached to results.*
> *With a virtuous heart,*
>     *I choose to act;*
>     *I choose non-action.*
> *Always with virtuous intent;*
> *I approach the Sage.*

- *All Is One — The Way of the Centered Self*. When the truth is realized, we see not ourselves, but ourselves disappearing from our vision.
We see that our "selves" are nothing more than part of the organic oneness of all things. When striving toward this, the *I Ching* can become
our guide to bring our actions in line with this reality.[16]

> *He who perceives all beings as Self,*
> *for him how can there be delusion or grief,*
> *when he sees this oneness (everywhere)?*
> — *Isha-Upanishad*, Verse 7[17]

- ***It Just Works, I Know Not Why — The Way of the Practitioner.*** Most people cannot explain how their cell phone works, but it works for them. In most religious traditions there is a divine mystery that is beyond human understanding, but it works for the followers. So, if the *I Ching* works for you, it works. Simply seeing it as an experiment to try the *I Ching* out is a modern tradition. However, you should plan to approach the Sage for at least eight 八 readings before you will know if the relationship will develop.

---

*Let 8 八 and 8 八 be Joyous*
*so that*
*Double Joy 双喜 can twice be seen* 囍.[18]

### RITUAL — APPROACHING THE SAGE

People in the United States think of the culture as informal, seeming to reserve custom and ritual for church services and the playing of the national anthem. However, custom and ritual is part of our existence, often automatic, a claim that is easily demonstrated:

When you meet someone, or even if they are merely sitting at a table, you may reach out your open right hand, vertically, thumb side up toward the sky. The response is automatic and largely unconscious, the greeting ritual of a handshake. But, in America and Europe, each person knows: about how long to grasp hands, what pressure to apply, and several other nuances of body language.

When it is written down like this, it can sound like it's from one of the Confucian Classics, *The Book of Rites*. When we read about ancient customs and rituals, it is good to remember that they were as automatic and accepted as a handshake is to us. The *I Ching* includes short scenes and references to the rituals of the time, the most notable one being the Judgment for Hexagram 20, "The ablution has been made [invoking a deity]. But not yet the offering [to the deity]. Full of trust they look up to him [the person who has the ritual duty to make the offering]."[19]
— a scene of a pause at the moment of inner transformation.

Most *I Ching* guides and translations have little or no comment on ritual beyond some need to calm your mind and formulate questions.[20] There are some exceptions including *The Other Way*, by Carol Anthony,

> **The Fool**
>
> Several people I know and I have learned to approach the Sage with a serious attitude and not to ask the same question again because we didn't like the answer. When we didn't, we got Hexagram 4, The Fool — the Judgment asks we are bothering the Sage if are not seeking a serious answer.

who devotes a chapter to ritual rooted in meditation.[21] However, the Chinese classics of history make it clear that ritual and the *I Ching* went hand-in-hand in ancient China.

When sitting down to use the *I Ching*, having your own ritual can be helpful in getting into the right mindset for forming a relationship with the spirit of the book — the Sage; you will be joining many long-time users.

There are claims as to the right way to use the *I Ching,* including which compass direction to face. But, the best advice is to invent your own. Many experienced Western users have a custom that approaches ritual, including the physical setting, their favorite well-worn book, and coins that they may keep in a particular pouch. Some keep the book along with coins or yarrow stalks in a particular place or box.

So, you will be in good company if you invent your own ritual, in your own tradition or something you create that makes it more fun and exciting.

> **Ritual, Custom, and Tradition Everywhere**
>
> If an isolated group of people do not have a set of customs or rituals that help define their society, they tend to invent one, a set of rituals and customs that fits their situation and landscape.
>
> The novel, *Lord of the Flies*, illustrates this in a "social experiment" with boys stranded on an island. While dealing with many social issues, the rapidity with which ritual practices and objects are invented leaves the reader awestruck.
>
> The author spent time on three remote arctic sites, in which people who were there did tours for work of a year or more. Populations ranged from 34 to around 4,000.
>
> What he noted was that each site had an oral history, some mythology — a good story that fit the situation true or not — one or two must–read books, and a set of customs that differed from "civilization" that were both invented on the spot and passed on orally over time. The smaller the population, the more the customs would seem "abnormal" to outsiders.
>
> You can find this every–where: minority solidarity, and within sports teams, industries and even companies to greater or lesser degrees.

## A Thousand-Year-Old Ritual Example

Zhu Xi 朱熹, his honorific being Zhu Wen Kung, the Venerable Gentleman of Culture, (A.D. 1130 to 1200), was selected by *Life Magazine* as one of the most important people of the millennium in 2000.[22] He was a well-known Neo-Confucian scholar. His scholarship included a reinvention or rediscovery of the yarrow stalk method used today.

Venerable Master Zhu Xi believed that the *I Ching* should be approached with a solemn ritual. His approach to the *I Ching* involved a secluded room with a board for divination. He began with ceremonial washing. Then he would enter from the East 東, the direction of the sun 日 rising over the trees 木 of the forest and burn incense to provide a respectful greeting. The yarrow stalks, located at the north of the board, were held with both hands and passed through the smoke of burning incense when he asked for news that only the Divine Intelligence could provide with clarity.

Early Chinese philosophers saw ritual as a psychological process that gave profound meaning to the events of their lives.[23]

## A Checklist for Creating Your Own Ritual

A satisfying ritual does not need to include all of these elements, but they are provided as a guide of discovery for what may work for you:

- The materials: which book or books, the paper or journal you will draw on, the writing instrument, the coins or yarrow stalks.
- Storing materials: they may be in a certain spot or kept in a box. Coins may be in a cloth pouch or be kept on a string through holes in the middle.
- Iconic materials: any objects that are meaningful to be incorporated.
- Space: how is it arranged. This may include the direction to face, north being a traditional position of the student or inquirer when interacting with the teacher or sage, in this case, the *I Ching* text.[24]
- The gestures and words: ritual gestures, mantras, or prayers.
- Stages of meditation or mindfulness.
- Formulating the question, which is discussed below.
- The act of divination: Rolling the coins, manipulating yarrow stalks, or some other method.
- Any closing rituals.
- Of course, your ritual will evolve over time, as do all rituals.

### ⊷ A Journal ⊷

A journal of your questions and the *I Ching*'s responses is *very* useful. Indeed, sages who developed the *I Ching* use their own historical records of divination questions, responses, and results. It is apparent that the scholars took advantage of this, adjusting their interpretation based on experience.[25]

The *I Ching* interacts with you. Your outlook, personality, and way of thinking about questions will be unique to you. Thus, the *I Ching* readings and your interpretations will both be individualistic and evolve over time as you and the Sage interact. A journal will be invaluable when you receive a particular hexagram and can go back to see how it unfolded for you before.

The journal should include the date, the question, and maybe even a short stream of consciousness of what was on your mind, and the hexagram you received. You may write the number and the hexagram drawing or include the Judgment, Image Statement, and Line Statements. You may also want to record the outcome of a situation as it later unfolded.

### ⊷ Asking a Question ⊷

Here are two ways to asking a question:

- **The Old — What if I do...** This method actually should start with "clearing your mind." This can be rooted in your own tradition including meditation or prayer.[26] Then a question is formulated, but the form is important.

  The *I Ching* may indicate whether or not the situation is auspicious but, more importantly, provide hints as to how the situation will unfold. Phrasing a question like, "What will happen if I..." rather than "Should I do..." is more conducive to interacting with the Sage.[27]

  Beware! On occasion the *I Ching* will not answer the question; it will answer the unasked question that was on your mind.[28]

- **The New — Ask not.** A "general" consultation that seeks a response to whatever is appropriate. You may also jot down what is on your mind. This approach is a mediation using the *I Ching* as a guide, humbly approaching the Sage with an open mind.

*Envisioning a Universe that holds all things.*
*I pray, I meditate, I clear my mind, waiting...*
*My hands move the stalks, or grasp the coins.*
*The ritual unfolds...*
*One of 64 hexagrams is for me this day,*
*with lines broken and unbroken,*
*changing or unchanging.*

## ⸺ THE LINES (爻 *YÁO*) ⸺

The *I Ching*'s 64 hexagrams are each made up of unbroken (or solid, positive, yang 陽) lines and broken (or divided, negative, yin 陰) lines. Figure 3.1 shows the association of pairs of forces or attributes that act in a yin-yang relationship.[29] Each line can be "unchanging" or "changing" and broken or unbroken — four types of lines:

*Unbroken, Changing-Unbroken, Broken, Changing-Broken.*

In practice, as we shall see later in this chapter, casting (also called rolling) a hexagram will yield a sum of 6, 7, 8, or 9 for a single line of a hexagram. The lines, changing or unchanging, and the pairs of attributes commonly associated with the lines are shown in Figure 3.1. The "O" and "X" in the figure are simply memory aids to remember that the line is changing. Some people will simply put a check mark next to a changing line.

These numbers, 6, 7, 8, and 9, may seem like modern artifacts, but actually go back to at least 200 B.C. The oldest existing texts literally use the Chinese characters for six and nine. So, for instance, when a translation such as Wilhelm says, "Six in the first place," this is a translation of the Chinese character for the number "six" and the Chinese character for "first."[30]

Sixty percent of the Line Statements are poetic in Chinese, either rhyming or having the four-character meter of the Book of Poetry. A Line Statement can have some or all of three types of components:[31]

- Topic — A condition or object that introduces the remainder of the Line. For example: *He has fish; He walks with difficulty; Has no fish.* This can also be an "omen" of coming events.[32]
- Injunction — An action which is to be taken or avoided if the forecast is to occur or be avoided: *Beneficial to...*
- Forecast/Verification — A prognostication about how the future is poised to unfold: *Auspicious, inauspicious, danger, no blame.*[33]

# The Lines

## The Lines

**Unbroken**                                    **Broken**

━━━━━━━                          ━━━  ━━━

Yang                                              Yin

## The Changing Lines

Unbroken Line                          Broken Line
Changing         Unchanging          Unchanging          Changing
9———⊙———7————          8—━━━  ━━━—6——✕——

Odd Numbers                              Even Numbers

## The Attributes

**Unbroken**                                    **Broken**

━━━━━━━                          ━━━  ━━━

Firm ————————————— Yeilding
Positive ———————————— Negative
Bright/Light ——————————— Dark
Strong ———————————— Weak
*Earlier* Active ———————————— Passive *Earlier*
*Later*                                          *Later*
Yang                                Yin
Male ————————————— Female

iching1000.017

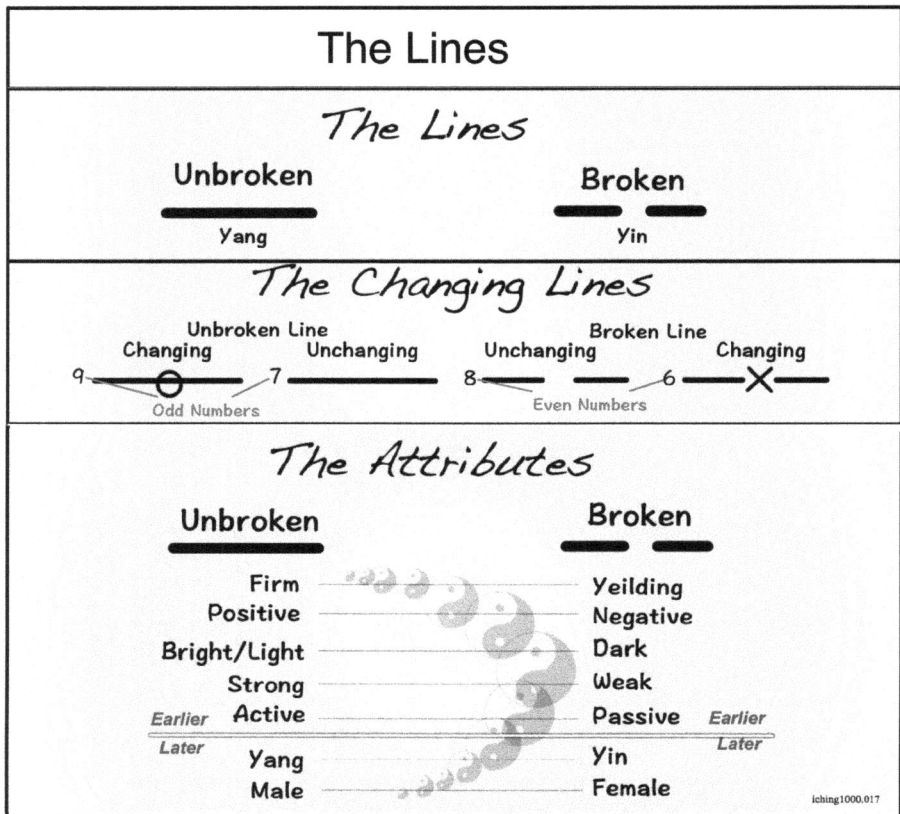

Figure 3.1 — The Lines and Their Attributes

## ⟶ THE HEXAGRAM AND ITS TRIGRAMS (卦 *GUÀ*) ⟵

A hexagram reading includes an Image Statement, in addition to the Judgment. The Judgment and Image Statement can be seen as having different viewpoints. As previously mentioned, the Judgment was written well before the Image Statements. The Judgment is a statement of your situation, providing hints as to how your fortune will unfold and contingencies that you should consider; the Image Statement states how a moral person should behave in the situation at hand.

The Image Statement interprets the nature imagery of the top and bottom trigrams that make up the hexagram. The images are either *Above* and *Below* or *Outside* and *Inside*.

Figure 3.2 illustrates the idea of six empty spaces for a hexagram, waiting for the broken and unbroken lines to be manifest. The selection of a hexagram manifests lines and the trigrams.

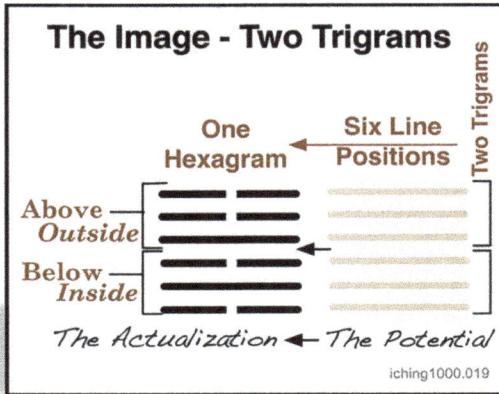

Figure 3.2 —The Image

The advice for the *superior person* arises from the interaction of the two natural forces. The hexagram is Deliverance, with *Zhèn,* Thunder, on top and *Kǎn,* Water, on the bottom.

> *Thunder and rain are manifest*
> *Bringing a state (the image)*
> *of Deliverance (from drought for example).*
> *The superior person, in accord with this,*
> *Forgives mistakes,*
> *And deals gently with crimes.*[34]

#### ⟶ THREE COINS — THE NEW ⟵

The coin method came into use in about A.D. 600 to 650[35] and continues through today because of its ease of use.[36] The "three coin" method being described here is the most common.

While many people like to use Feng Shui coins, any pocket change can be used. Each cast of three coins yields one line:

- Heads has a value of 3; Tails is 2.
- Cast the three coins and add the values up. You will get 6, 7, 8, or 9.
- You draw the bottom line first (the bottom line is the "first" line) — see Figure 3.3.

  > 6 — a changing broken line. Draw a dashed line. Put an "X" in the middle or a check mark beside it to remember that it is a changing yin line.
  > 7 — an unbroken line. Draw a solid line.
  > 8 — a broken line. Draw a dashed line.
  > 9 — a changing unbroken line. Draw a solid line. Put an "O" in the middle or a check mark beside it to remember that it is a changing yang line.

- Repeat six times until you get six lines. Figures 3.4 shows an example.
- Take the top trigram and bottom trigram and look up the hexagram number in the table which is provided in your translation. You ignore the changing line marks when looking up a hexagram. They come into use when you actually read the text.
- The *I Ching* is like a dictionary in that you look up the hexagram number in the *I Ching* book or Figure 3.5, finding the top trigram in the row at the top of the table and the bottom trigram on the left.
- Read the Judgment, Image, and Commentary that accompany them. When you get to the Lines, only the changing lines are for you. This is your reading. If you have changing lines, they are often more to the point than the Judgment and may modify its message.

If you got one or more changing lines, draw a new hexagram, redrawing the unchanging lines the same, and drawing the opposite line for each changing line — change a broken line to an unbroken line and an unbroken line to a broken line. Figure 3.6 shows an example. Look up the new hexagram — with no changing lines since they have already changed. *This is not a new reading.* It can be thought of as how things will end up.

# Coin Method

## Roll three coins to get one line: Six rolls for a Hexagram.

**Heads = 3 · Tails = 2**
**Add them up to get your line:**

**Line Positions/Changing Line Terminology**

Nine (or Six ) ...
Line 6 · at the Top · Sixth Line
Line 5 · in the Fifth Place · Fifth Line
Line 4 · in the Fourth Place · Fourth Line
Line 3 · in the Third Place · Third Line
Line 2 · in the Second Place · Second Line
Line 1 · at the Beginning · First Line

Heads = 3   Heads = 3   Heads = 3   =   9

Solid line with an O in the middle

**Unbroken Changing Line**
Nine in the Beginning

Heads = 3   Heads = 3   Tails = 2   =   8

A dash line

**Broken Line (Unchanging)**

Heads = 3   Tails = 2   Tails = 2   =   7

A solid line

**Unbroken Line (Unchanging)**

Heads = 2   Tails = 2   Tails = 2   =   6

A dash line with an X in the middle

**Broken Changing Line**

Figure 3.3 — Three Coin Method — Coin Values and Their Lines

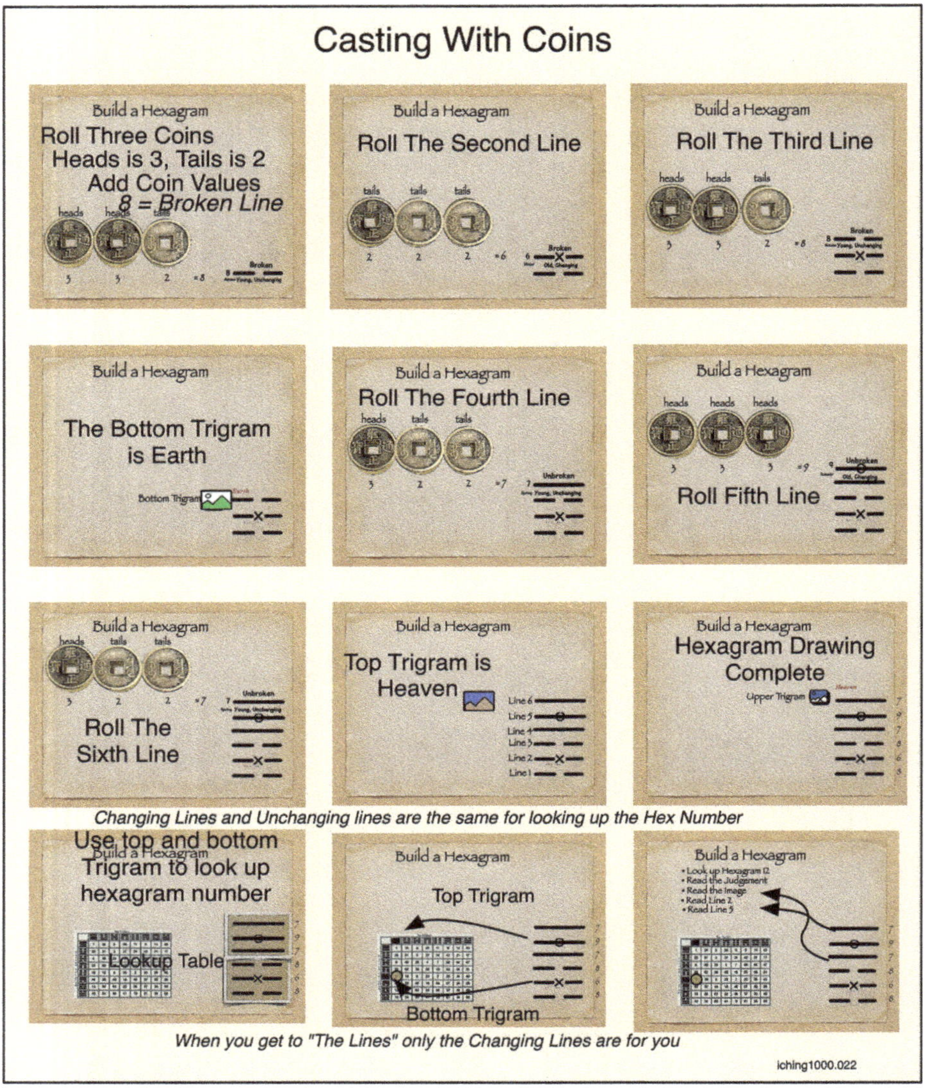


Figure 3.4 — Coin Method Illustrated

Figure 3.5 — How to Look Up a Hexagram

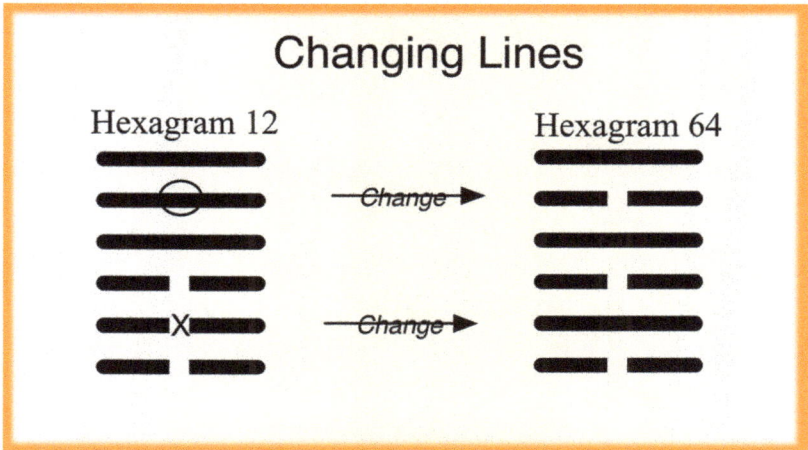

Figure 3.6 — Creating a Changed Hexagram

## ⟶∞⟶ **50** YARROW STALKS — THE OLD ⟶∞⟶

While the coin method selects a hexagram by six random events, the Yarrow Stalk Method uses dried stalks from the yarrow plant,[37] six to twelve inches long, to create eighteen random events. This is done by repeatedly separating a bundle of stalks into two, three times for each line. The use of yarrow stalks is recorded in the earliest references of the text, prior to Confucius. But, the original method of manipulation was lost.

The method used today was recreated by Zhu Xi 朱熹 in A.D. 1186, using the verse from The Great Treatise that is presented at the beginning of this chapter.[38] The use of 6 through 9 numbers to represent lines is the same as for the Coin Method, but the numbers are selected by manipulating yarrow stalks instead of tossing coins.

It takes about 20 minutes to perform the manipulation. With practice, the time shortens to about 10 to 12 minutes. An advantage of yarrow stalks is that it slows down the process so that you can attain a calm state as you contemplate your question, meditate, or pray, thus extending the ritual.

Start with 50 stalks, set one aside, and do manipulations with the remaining 49 stalks. You will end up with three bundles of stalks on the table as shown in Figure 3.7. Each bundle is like one coin; if it has 4 or 5 stalks its value is 3 (like heads); if it is 8 or 9 its value is 2 (tails).

The method illustrated in Figures 3.8a and 3.8b is:
• Begin with 50 stalks.
• Lay one aside. It will not be used for manipulation. You may use it to lay the bundles on as shown in Figure 3.8a.
• You are left with 49 stalks.
• Hold them in your left hand with your thumb.
• With your right hand, grasp about half of the bundle and lay it down on the table — it is your RIGHT pile. This is the first random event.
• Take one stalk from the right pile and hold it with your little finger in your left hand. You still have the remaining bundle held by your thumb.
• With your right hand, remove four stalks at a time and put them in a LEFT pile. Do this until you have 1, 2, 3, or 4 stalks left being held by your thumb.

# Yarrow Stalk Method

## Roll three coins to get one line: Six rolls for a Hexagram.

**Fewer Stalks = 3 • More Stalks = 2**
**Add them up to get your line:**

**Line Positions/Changing Line Terminology**

*Nine (or Six ) …*
———————— Line 6 • *at the Top* • Sixth Line
———————— Line 5 • *in the Fifth Place* • Fifth Line
———————— Line 4 • *in the Fourth Place* • Fourth Line
———————— Line 3 • *in the Third Place* • Third Line
———————— Line 2 • *in the Second Place* • Second Line
———————— Line 1 • *at the Beginning* • First Line

*Solid line with an O in the middle*

5-S$_{talks}$ = 3  4-S$_{talks}$ = 3  4-S$_{talks}$ = 3  =  9

**Unbroken Changing Line**
*Nine in the Beginning*

*A dash line*

5-S$_{talks}$ = 3  4-S$_{talks}$ = 3  8-S$_{talks}$ = 2  =  8

**Broken Line (Unchanging)**

*A soild line*

5-S$_{talks}$ = 3  8-S$_{talks}$ = 2  8-S$_{talks}$ = 2  =  7

**Unbroken Line (Unchanging)**

*A dash line with an X in the middle*

9-S$_{talks}$ = 2  8-S$_{talks}$ = 2  8-S$_{talks}$ = 2  =  6

**Broken Changing Line**

iching1000.012

Figure 3.7 — Three Yarrow Stalks Bundles per Line

- Move these to your middle fingers.
- Pick up the RIGHT pile and hold it with the thumb of your left hand.
- With your right hand remove four stalks at a time and put them in a LEFT pile. Do this until you have 1, 2, 3, or 4 stalks left being held by your thumb.
- The total number of stalks, one being held by your small finger, the stalks held with your middle fingers, and the remaining stalks should

total either 5 or 9. If they do not, you counted wrong and should repeat the process.

- **You have one set of stalks laid aside on the table with either 5 or 9 stalks. With the remaining stalks. Start Again.** (Figure 3.8b).
- Gather the stalks in your left hand and put them aside.
- Gather the remaining stalks and hold them with your left thumb.
- Repeat the process: With your right hand separate about half and put them into a RIGHT pile. This is the second random event.
- Pick up one from the RIGHT pile and hold it with your left small finger. Repeat the process of removing four at a time into a LEFT pile until there are 4 or fewer left. Hold these with your middle fingers.
- Pick up the RIGHT pile and hold it with the thumb of your left hand.
- With your right hand remove four stalks at a time and put them in a LEFT pile. Do this until you have 4 or fewer stalks left being held by your thumb.
- The total number of stalks, one held by your small finger, the stalks held with your middle fingers; the remaining stalks should total either 4 or 8.
- Gather the stalks in your left hand and put them aside to make a second bundle on the table.
- **You have two sets of stalks laid aside on the table, the first with either 5 or 9 stalks, the second with either 4 or 8 stalks. With the remaining stalks. Start Again.**
- Gather the remaining stalks and hold them with your left thumb.
- Repeat the process: With your right hand separate about half and put them into a RIGHT pile. This is the third random event.
- Pick up one from the RIGHT pile and hold it with your left small finger. Repeat the process of removing four at a time into a LEFT pile until there are 4 or fewer left. Hold these with your middle fingers.
- Pick up the RIGHT pile and hold it with the thumb of your left hand.
- With your right hand remove four stalks at a time and put them in a LEFT pile. Do this until you have 4 or fewer stalks left being held by your thumb.
- The total number of stalks, one held by your small finger, the stalks held with your middle fingers, and the remaining stalks should total either 4 or 8.
- **You should have three bundles on the table. This is one line, the bottom line.**
- You have three sets of stalks laid aside on the table.

Each set represents 2 or 3.

Five or four stalks = 3;

Nine or eight stalks = 2.

**Add them up.**

Draw the bottom line of the hexagram:

6 = broken line with an X in the dash;

7 = an unbroken line;

8 = a broken line;

9 = an unbroken line with an O in the center.

- Pick up all 49 stalks and repeat this whole process for a total of six lines:

  *Bottom Line — Line 2 — Line 3 — Line 4 — Line 5 — Top Line*
- **Look up the hexagram number using the top and bottom trigrams**. Consult the *I Ching*, reading the Judgment and Image Statement and their associated Commentary. Then read only the changing lines — only the changing lines are for you.
- Once you have the hexagram, look it up to get the hexagram in the Hexagram Lookup Table in your *I Ching* book.
- If you received any changing lines, draw the changed hexagram (Figure 3.6) and look it up as well. This is not a new reading. It informs the original reading and can be thought of as how things will develop when the situation at this moment in your reading changes.[39]

---

### Zhu Xi's Method of Reading a Hexagram

While the yarrow Stalk method used today is from Zhu Xi's *Introduction to the Study of the Classic of Changes,* the method of reading the results most commonly used in the West differs from Zhu Xi's, which is:

- If no lines change — use the Judgment of the hexagram cast. Interpret the top trigram as the question or present situation and the bottom trigram as the prediction.
- If one line changes — use that line as the prediction.
- If two lines change — use both lines, but the uppermost line is the ruler.
- If three lines change — the hexagram cast is the present situation and the hexagram as a result of changing the three lines is the prediction.
- When four lines change — the two unchanging lines are read, the bottom being the ruler.
- When  lines — The Unchanging line is used.
- When six lines change — The hexagram resulting from changing all lines is used, except that for the first two hexagrams, Qian and Kun, use both hexagrams.

— *Zhu Xi, Introduction to the Study of the Classic of Changes, Chapter IV.*

# Yarrow Stalk Method

Put one stick on table. Hold other 49 in LEFT hand with thumb.

With the RIGHT hand split the bundle in half.

Place two bundles on the table.

Left Bundle     Right Bundle

Pick up a single stick from the RIGHT pile.

Hold it with your pinky in your LEFT hand.

Pick up LEFT pile and hold it with your LEFT thumb.

< Holding the Left bundle

< Still holding the one stick

Take **4 Sticks** out of the bundle and lay them down to start a LEFT pile.

Take another **4 Sticks** and lay them in the LEFT pile.

Continue: take out **4 at a time** - Until there are **4 or fewer** left.

< 4 Removed

< One left

Move the sticks left from you thumb to your middle fingers.

Pick up the RIGHT pile and hold it with your LEFT thumb.

Count off 4 at a time until there are 4 or fewer sticks left.

< Left picked up

< Three left

Move the sticks between fingers.

Gather the sticks in your left hand. Lay across the stick on the table.

You will get 5 or 9 sticks

Pick up remaining sticks in your LEFT hand and Start Again.

iching1000.010

Figure 3.8a — How to Manipulate Yarrow Stalks — First Bundle

# Yarrow Stalk Method

With your LEFT hand take half to make a LEFT bundle.

Take **4 sticks** at a time to make LEFT bundle until **4 or fewer left**.

< Three left

Remove **4 Sticks** at a time.

Pick up remaining sticks and repeat again.

Pick up RIGHT pile and remove 4 at a time.

Pick up one stick from the RIGHT bundle and hold with your pinky.

Hold remaining sticks between middle fingers.

< Moved to Middle Fingers

Keep removing 4 at time until you have 4 or fewer.

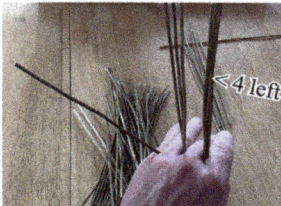
< 4 left

Hold 1 stick from RIGHT pile pinky. Pick up LEFT pile.

Remove 4 at a time until there are 4 or fewer left.

Two Left >

Pick up the LEFT bundle.

< Still holding the one stick
< Holding the Left bundle

Pick up RIGHT pile and hold it with your LEFT thumb.

Gather up sticks in you left hand and place them on the table.

You will have either 4 or 8 left

Count off 4 at a time until there are 4 or fewer sticks left.

< One left

Lay down third bundle on table. These three bundles are your line.

You will have either 4 or 8 left

Figure 3.8b — How to Manipulate Yarrow Stalks — 2nd and 3rd Bundles

## The Math

There are 64 hexagrams, 6 lines that may change in the hexagram, totaling 384 lines that may change. There  4,096 possible casts of a hexagram along with 0 to 6 changing lines in a cast.

Coins and stalk manipulation are random events. The probabilities for getting a broken versus unbroken line is 50/50 in both cases. However, the probabilities of getting a Changing Broken Line is 1/16 in the case of stalk manipulation and 3/16 in the case of coins:

| Coins | Stalks | Coins | Stalks | Coins | Stalks |
|---|---|---|---|---|---|
| 6 —— X —— | | 2/16 | 1/16 | 8 —— —— | 6/16 7/16 |
| 7 ———————— | | 6/16 | 5/16 | 9 ———O—— | 2/16 3/16 |

Zhu Xi's recreation of the stalk manipulation method worked out the process by "splitting the bundle in half" — or almost. However, the process works even if the bundle is split very unevenly since the process is mathematically one of remainders, like in the manual division process. The process works if there is a least one stalk in the left hand and two in the right: but to keep from repeating a predictable practice the left hand should have about 8 or more.

When counting off by fours, this becomes a "modulo" (or "mod") arithmetic, specifically, "modulo 4." When a number exceeds 4 minus 1 it "wraps around" to start at 0 — Euclid, *Elements,* Book 7.

When using yarrow stalks the operation becomes one of modular arithmetic:

For example, the remainder when dividing 49 by 4, the remainder is 1, which is written as: $49 \equiv 1$ (modulo 4).

"Mod" is used as a shorthand. Similar to regular arithmetic:

$X$ (mod 4) – $Y$ (mod 4) $\equiv$ $(X–Y)$ (mod 4): Minus sign meaning removing stalks.

The first operation results in 5 or 9 stalks being removed. 5 and 9 are both $\equiv 1$ (Mod 4), the same a 49 (Mod 4): 5 being 1 more than 4 and 9 being 1 more than 2 x 4.

The modular arithmetic for remaining stalks after the first operation is to subtract the remainder for 4 or 8 from the remainder of 49:

1 (mod 4) — 1 (mod 4) $\equiv$ 0.

… 4 and 8 are both 0 (mod 4).

For the next two bundles the math will be: 0 (mod 4) — 0 (mod 4) $\equiv$ 0.

It has been noted that if one starts with 48 the operations are always $\equiv$ 0 (mod 4).

~ ~ ~

*The numbers of Great Expansion make 50, 49 are used.*
*Dividing into two heaps. Representing Heaven and Earth*
*The prognostication begins. One is then taken and placed,*
*And this now represents the Three Powers:*
*Heaven, Earth, and Man.*
*Manipulated by counting by 4's,*
*This represents the four seasons.*

So Says *The Great Treatise*[40]

Yarrow Stalk Manipulation in Progress

Wall plaque in Erdaobaihezhen, Jilin, China, depicting Laozi

# 4

# THE LAW OF CHANGE

*Heaven above, Earth Below,*
*Thus, Heaven is the Creative, Qián;*
*Earth is the Receptive, Kūn.*
*Things above and below relate to each other,*
*The Laws of Movement and Rest lead to*
*Distinctions of Strong and Weak*
*Each acting according to its nature.*
*In this way*
*Fortunate and unfortunate circumstances aris*
*In the Heavens forms take shape;*
*On the Earth shapes take form.*
*And corresponding Changes and Transformations take place.*

So Says *The Great Treatise*[1]

Yin–Yang Symbol

The Principle of Yin-Yang developed as people living close to the land observed the patterns of the natural world around them. As the sky's color begins to change, the light of the stars is dimmed by the light of the rising sun. Soon, the sun lights up the sky. The people came to expect this. This pattern had been observed from time immemorial; they knew when the sun sank below the horizon that they could expect to welcome it back the next morning. The seasons changed, only to repeat themselves; the animals and the people were born, grew up, grew old; crops were sown, tended, and reaped in accord with the four seasons.

When people formed a mental model for how things changed, they were engaged in what an anthropologist calls "The science of the concrete."[2] The Western heritage left by ancient Greek philosophers was equally valid, but with a different outlook.

*Ancient Philosophers of the Land of the West*
    *Observed the things of nature, and thought,*
    *"There must be a smallest thing,"*
    *And they called it Atom. It was the Atom of Things.*

    *"A complicated thing is made up of simpler things,*
    *So that is how we shall describe the world we see."*

*But before the smallest thing, before the thought called Atom,*

*Ancient Sages in the Land of the East*
    *Saw nature and wondered,*
    *At the Way things changed.*
    *The sun rises and falls — changing,*
        *but remains the same thing;*
    *The moon shines in the night — changing,*
        *but stays the same.*
    *"There must be a pattern," The Changing of Things.*

    *"Everything changes according to its nature,*
    *So that is how we shall describe the world we see."*

*These Philosophers and Sages created their Schools of Thought,*
    *and their progeny continued thinking these Thoughts through the ages.*

*In the Land of the East,*
    *The Thinkers of Change glimpsed the mysterious Agents of Nature.*
        *They saw the changing patterns creating harmony — dancing.*
    *They created images to see what they saw,*
        *Lines, broken and unbroken, dark and light,*
            *penetrating and receptive.*
    *They saw Synchronicity.*

    *They called this The Law of Change.*

*In the Land of the West,*
    *The Creators of Atoms created symbols and rules;*
    *They called it Mathematics.*

    *They used these symbols and rules to describe those simpler things*
        *that made up the complicated thing.*

*But Atoms were not enough.*

    *The Thinkers of Atoms saw that their Atoms moved,*
        *fell, bounced, and slid;*
    *They called this Energy.*

*Ah, but then they felt urgency to master this Energy,*
  *doing much work to describe it,*
  *describe it precisely with the symbols they made,*
  *intricately arranging them to see what they said.*

*They were rewarded:*
  *It gave them the power to manipulate the Atoms of Things.*
  *It made them the Makers of Machines;*
  *And they made Machines of Wonder.*

*But Nature whispered of mysteries to the Makers of Machines.*
  *This mystery disturbed them;*
  *They felt an urgency to master it.*

  *So they did much work,*
    *inventing new symbols and arrangements.*

*Again they were rewarded.*
  *It gave them the power to glimpse the mysteries of Nature,*
    *mysteries which no longer needed to be whispered.*

  *When they looked upon this,*

*They saw The Law of Change.*

Figure 4.1 — Meaning of Yin and Yang Characters

## ⊷ THE NATURE OF YIN-YANG ⊶

Yin and yang began as words describing what people saw as they went about their lives in ancient China: *Yīn* 陰 is the shady side of a hill and *Yáng* 陽 the sunny side. Yin and yang characters each begin the Chinese written character for hill-mound ß as shown in Figure 4.1.[3] Yin the hill-mound is joined with the character for cloudy, while yang, the hill, joins the character for sunny, suggesting that Yin is dark and receptive and Yang is light and creative.[4]

When a sage or scholar is going beyond the world we sense, striving to understand the principles that underlie the natural world, they will often use an existing word and change its meaning, a meaning that goes from the concrete to the idea that is hidden behind the concrete. It is this process that led to pairing yin and yang to create the Yin-Yang Principle. The original meaning of the words hints at the deeper meaning — the idea that a hill can have a shady and sunny character. Indeed, not only is each defined by the other, but they change into each other.

> *Yang, the Creative, the Strong and Firm,*
> *the Streaming Light,*
>
> *Initiation — flowing forth*
> *in a search for completion,*
> *knowing that only Receptive can complete it.*
>
> *Yin, the Receptive, the Elastic and Yielding,*
> *the Encompassing Darkness,*
>
> *Completion — waiting patiently*
> *for the arrival of initiation,*
> *knowing that only the Creative can initiate it.*

Imagine waking up in the morning just before sunrise. You stand on your porch and look at a wooded hill. The forest seems to be asleep, its impenetrable shadows combining to make the trees appear as one. The eastern sky turns from a deep dark purple to yellow-orange, getting brighter as the disk of the sun rises over the horizon. The sunlight moves across the landscape and arrives at the hill. The hill seems to awaken; the leaves of the trees reflect back their green light; the shadows fade, seeming to push a wave of waking birds taking flight as the sun sweeps over the hillside. This brings to mind change. As the natural cycle repeats once again, each thing reacts according to its nature, in synchrony with the rise of the sun and with each other. But the hill itself is still the same hill, each tree is still the same tree, yet, they have changed.

*When night dissipates,*

*Dawn brightens the Eastern Sky,*

*Chasing Dreams Away*
— Barbara Olsen

Thus, the observed and the sensed becomes an underlying idea, becoming a principle of the changing patterns of the earth and nature and the yin-yang aspects of nature. When the sun rises, it is only a matter of time before the sun, shining the *creative* energy of life, meets the *receptive* as it dips below the water's edge of the vast sea. This illustrates the Yin-Yang Principle.[5]

*The Creative actuates the beginning of things*

*The Receptive achieves their completion.*
— The Great Treatise, fifth verse.[6]

### Science and Knowledge

The correlative cosmology of the ancients was a "unified theory" of how the universe works. While a modern reader might look back and think of it as incredibly inferior to today's science, it is good to remember that the innate intelligence of the ancients was the same as now. There were Einsteins.

The reason for humanity's progress from generation to generation is language. It is complex language that allows the creation of an inverted pyramid of accumulated knowledge. And, since scientific knowledge rests always on perception, the build–up of technology which extends perception through gadgets such as telescopes, microscopes, radars, and x–rays accelerates the pace.

The march of innovation is not smooth, but more like cylinders of study that interact and intertwine.

Thus, even though modern science has a more refined model of how nature works, there is still no unified theory. Indeed, there are still many mysteries to be resolved.

Meanwhile, the Chinese cosmology of old still provides the foundation for useful medicine and acupuncture.

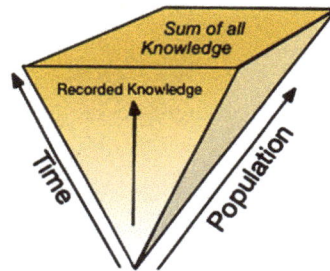

*Language and Knowledge Pryamid*

Zhuangzi and a Frog

## ⟡ THE HUMANITY OF YIN-YANG ⟡

The principle applies to the society of humans, humans in the natural world who are embedded in the operations of the Yin-Yang Principle. *The Great Treatise* of the *I Ching* begins:

> *Heaven is high, earth is low.*
> *Thus hexagram 1, the Creative,*
> *and hexagram 2, the Receptive, were formed.*
> *Things low and high relate to each other.*
> *Movement and rest follow definite patterns.*

> *Hence the distinction of strong and weak lines in The Changes.*

> *Events in The Changes sequence according to their tendencies,*
> *and things are divided according to their classes.*
> *Hence fortuitous and unfortuitous moments are manifest.*

Human activities and responses to events can be seen in the framework of yin-yang in diverse activities as psychological mechanisms, human social interactions, medicine, sports, politics, warfare, and doing business. In this realm, however, human consciousness and will play an important part. Does one understand the situation in the framework of the Yin-Yang Principle? Does one act in accordance with the framework of yin-yang or does one resist its flow? Does one fight to control nature, or live within it, adapting to its cycles, what Zhuangzi would call "easy" and Arne Næss would call Deep Ecology.[7]

This is a significant theme in the *I Ching,* as well as the *Daodejing* and *Zhuangzi* — the founding texts of Daoism. Zhuangzi tells us that even the passions in their yin-yang relationship arise from where we know not:

> *Joy and anger, sadness and pleasure,*
> *anticipation and regret, fickleness and fixedness,*
> *vehemence and indolence, eagerness and tardiness;*
> *like music from an empty tube,*
> *or mushrooms from the warm moisture,*
> *day and night succeed to one another*
> *and come before us,*
> *and we do not know whence they sprout.*
> *Leave it be! Leave it be!*
> *Can we expect to find out suddenly*
> *how they are produced?*
> *— Zhuangzi.*[8]

The Yin-Yang Principle applies to the very definition of ideas, ideas that have no meaning except in comparison with their opposite.

*We know good.*
*But if something is good — then something is made bad*

> *Existence and non-existence define each other*
> *Difficulty and ease produce the idea of each other*
> *Long and short fashion each other*
> *High and low define each other by their contrast*

*Musical notes and tones become harmonious with each other*

*Before and after present the idea on one after the other.*
> *— based on Daodejing, Verse 2.*[9]

~ ~ ~

> *To everything there is a season,*
> > *and a time to every purpose under the heaven:*
> *A time to be born,*
> > *and a time to die;*
> *A time to plant,*
> > *and a time to pluck up that which is planted;*
> *A time to kill,*
> > *and a time to heal;*
> *A time to break down,*

> *and a time to build up;*
> *A time to weep,*
> *and a time to laugh;*
> *A time to mourn,*
> *and a time to dance;*
> *A time to cast away stones,*
> *and a time to gather stones together;*
> *A time to embrace,*
> *and a time to refrain from embracing;*
> *A time to get,*
> *and a time to lose;*
> *A time to keep,*
> *and a time to cast away;*
> *A time to rend,*
> *and a time to sow;*
> *A time to keep silence,*
> *and a time to speak;*
> *A time to love,*
> *and a time to hate;*
> *A time of war,*
> *and a time of peace.*
> — *The Holy Bible*, Ecclesiastes 3:1–9 KJV

In human affairs, we see yin-yang in:

Every handshake

— hand out to initiate: hand grasped to receive.

Every ball thrown

— the thrown ball actuates: the caught ball completes.

Every dance step

— one starts to move: the other anticipates.

Every negotiation

— one offers: the other responds.

Laozi

When our interactions get more complex, the cycles within cycles may be hard to understand, the pattern hidden. Here the *I Ching* can help, the words for the Judgments, Image Statements, Line Statement, and Commentary, together with contemplating the imagey, helps uncover the crux of the matter that lies hidden under the complexity. Of course, to get to the hidden, your own mind participates. Indeed, Chinese commentators have noted that the *I Ching* mirrors peoples' minds and that a superficial reader will see shallow readings and the thoughtful reader will get deep readings.[10]

The Yin-Yang Principle, and the Dao from which it arises, have strong correlations with Buddhist thought. This was recognized by Daoists, Confucians, and Buddhists when Buddhism arrived in China.

> *The Daodejing verse cited above continues:*
> *Thus, the Sages act without effort (Wú Wéi 無爲)*
> *and give instruction without speaking.*
> *All things rise up and always show themselves*
> *Going about their business with no expectation of reward*
> *The work is done with no claiming of accomplishment*
> *The work is completed but no one claims it*
> *We are never without them.*
> — based on *Daodejing*, Verse 2

The concept of *Wú Wéi*, effortlessly acting naturally, is the seam in the tapestry where the Daoists and Buddhists meet. When translated as "doing nothing," it is properly interpreted as "doing nothing that is not natural," or, "doing nothing other than effortlessly acting in accordance with the *Dao*."[11] There is power in this:

> *If he had intelligence enough*
> *to be entirely unsophisticated,*
> *and by doing nothing*
> *to seek to return to the normal simplicity,*
> *embodying natural instincts,*
> *and keeping his spirit resting in his arms,*
> *so enjoying himself in the common ways,*
> *you might then indeed be afraid of him!*
> — *Zhuangzi*, Book 12[12]

By the time of the Hundred Schools of Thought, yin-yang as a principle is thoroughly incorporated in a correlative cosmology and presented as a key underlying principle of how the *I Ching* works in *The Great Treatise*. Commentaries are added for the original *Zhouyi* hexagram Judgments, and Line Statements. The concept of yin-yang, by then, attaches "yin" to broken lines and "yang" to unbroken lines.[13] In the *I Ching* readings you will find that the power of yin is most prominent.

──── THE SPIRIT OF YIN-YANG ────

The concept of yin and yang has a strong cosmological implication, that of the correlation of heaven, human, and nature. Yin-yang operates in all three domains with the events of the three domains affecting each other.[14] This is known as *The Three Powers*: Heaven, Human, and Earth. In a trigram the Heaven is the top line, Humans the middle, and Earth at the bottom. When two trigrams

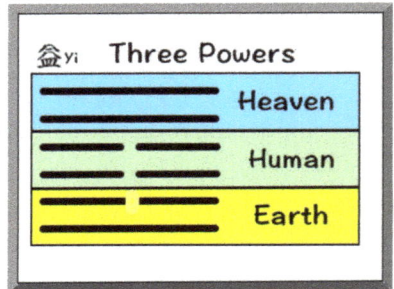

The Three Powers

combine to form a hexagram, the two top lines are Heaven, two middle Humanity, and two at the bottom Earth.[15]

The idea of correlative cosmology is that the Three Powers are each in a dynamic yin yang cycle but relate to each other in harmony. As the natural cycles of Earth act in harmony with the Heavens of the sun, moon, and stars as well as the spiritual world of the Heavens. Humans live in the middle, having their own willpower, but act in harmony with the powers of Heaven and Earth.

The idea of the Five Agents, 五行 *Wǔ Xíng*, arose out of the yin yang cycle. Elemental forces of nature, which are correlated with the forces of movement of the stars and the forces in the human body are the "Five Phases" of mutual generation: Wood, Fire, Earth, Metal, and Water. The system of five phases describes interactions and relationships between phenomena. Around 200 B.C. the Five Phases became incorporated into Chinese medicine, martial arts, Feng shui, Chinese astrology, and music.[16]

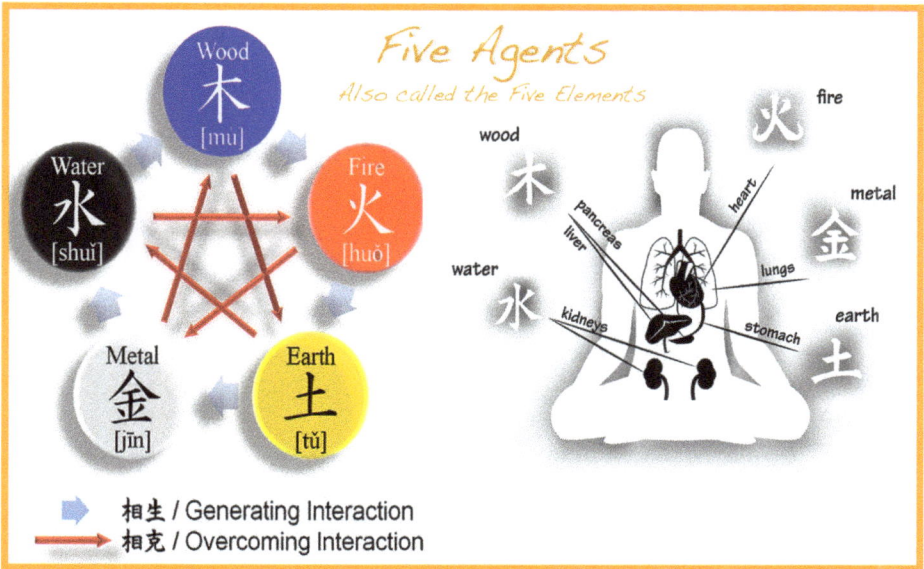

Five Agents or Five Elements

In Medieval Italy, the Yin-Yang Principle is present as well:

> *Praise be to Thee, my Lord, with all Thy creatures,*
> *Especially to my worshipful brother sun,*
>> *Which lights up the day,*
>> *and through him dost Thou brightness give;*
> *Praised be my Lord, for sister moon and for the stars,*
>> *In heaven Thou hast formed them*
>> *clear and precious and fair.*
> *Praised be my Lord for brother wind*
>> *And for the air and clouds*
>> *and fair and every kind of weather,*
> *Praised be my Lord for sister water,*
>> *Which is greatly helpful and humble*
>> *and precious and pure.*
> *Praised be my Lord for brother fire,*
>> *By the which Thou lightest up the dark.*
> *Praised be my Lord for our sister, mother earth,*
>> *Which sustains and keeps us*
>> *And brings forth*
> *Diverse fruits with grass and flowers bright.*
>> — *Canticle of the Creatures*, Francis of Assisi[17]

In India, the principle was applied to human relationships:

> *Let us live happily then,*
> *not hating those who hate us!*
> *among men who hate you*
> *let us dwell free from hatred!*
> *Let us live happily then,*
> *free from ailments among the ailing!*
> *among men who are ailing*
> *let us dwell free from ailments!*
> *Let us live happily then,*
> *free from greed among the greedy!*
> *among men who are greedy*
> *let us dwell free from greed!*
> *Let us live happily then,*
> *though we call nothing our own!*
> *We shall be like the bright gods,*
> *feeding on happiness!*
>                   — The *Dhammapada*, 15. Happiness[18]

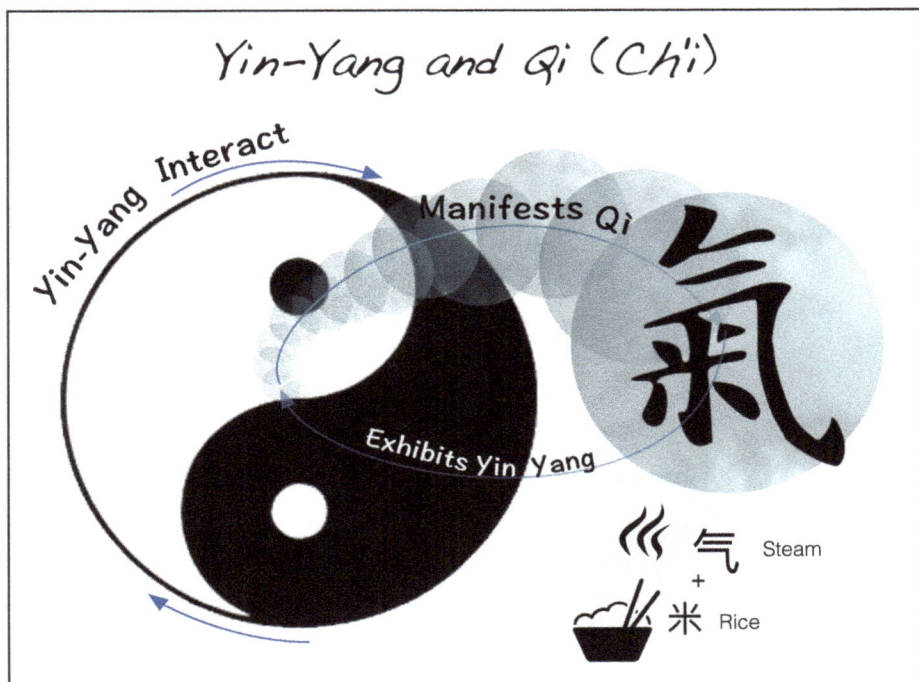

Figure 4.2 — Qi (Ch'i) and Yin–Yang

Across the oceans the principle resonates:

> *He burnt an Offering.*
> *Asking that it be seen.*
> *A sacred offering in praise.*
> *Asking that his nation be held in kindness.*
> *His strength the rays of sun.*
> *His cloak the path of the moon.*
> — Description of part of the Heyoaka Ceremony, *Black Elk Speaks*[19]

## ⸻ THE QI (CH'I) OF YIN-YANG ⸻

While yin and yang symbols appeared on oracle bones prior to the tenth century B.C., the idea of the *breath* which connects them, exhibits them, produces them, *Qì (Ch'i)* 氣, came a bit later. The idea that *Qi* flows through the *I Ching* is frequently noted in later commentaries and studies of the *I Ching*. Figure 4.2 illustrates two of the aspects of *Qi*.

*Qi* has no accurate Western word that captures its meaning.[20] Both matter and energy are aspects of *Qi*, as in Einstein's equation e = mc². Matter, even when it is at rest, has the potential for expending energy, a principle of both *Qi* and of science.[21] But, *Qi* extends to encompass "vitality" in living beings, as well as the spirit that animates a person. It is a cosmic force, a manifestation of yin-yang.[22]

Around 400 B.C., we see an expression of the vital essence in a person:

> *Wherever ships and carriages reach;*
> *wherever the strength of man penetrates;*
> *wherever the heavens overshadow*
> *and the earth sustains;*
> *wherever the sun and moon shine;*
> *wherever frosts and dews fall:*
> *all who have blood and breath [Qi 氣]*
> *unfeignedly honour and love him.*
> *Hence it is said,*
> *"He is the equal of Heaven."*
> — *Doctrine of the Mean*, Chapter 34, Verse 4.[23]

*The intention of Qi —*
*You cannot control it,*

*Except with the Inner Power of Virtue* [德 De].[24]
*You cannot beckon it,*
*Only welcome it.*
*To keep it,*

*You must respect it.*
*When you develop it,*
*You are filled with power and wisdom.*
                    — Inspired by the *Nei Ye*[25]

*De*, The Power of Virtue, can create *Qi* within oneself: *De* is "the force of moral character." By the twelfth century A.D., Zhuxi is writing about *Qi* as a universal aspect.

*When one is born knowing it is of pure Qi;*
*their moral principles are clearly in view.*[26]

While *Qi* encompasses several ideas, when using the *I Ching* it becomes the animating spirit. When properly manifest in thoughts and actions, *Qi* can bring forth your efforts as a unity of spirit, energy, and body. This can become mystical as can be seen in original Dao texts and other traditions.[27]

*That by the concentration of his Qi, he could save men from*
*disease and pestilence, and secure every year a plentiful*
*harvest. These words appeared to me wild and incoherent*
*and I did not believe them. "So it is," said Lien Shu.*
            — Zhuangzi, *Enjoyment in Untroubled Ease*[28]

This idea of manifesting *Qi* in yourself is an important and practiced concept in Qigong and martial arts. There is no reason it cannot be manifest in our everyday efforts if we adopt the same mindset. When we sense yin and yang within the operation of The Book of Changes, we see the Law of Change. When we try to peer further into the depths, what is there is not seen, not to be described in words, not to be heard, but still to be known — the Dao.

## THE NATURE OF THE DAO 道[29]

Dáo (Tao) 道 is usually translated as *The Way*.[30] It is inherently a concept that words cannot describe except in terms of what it is not, what it does and does

not do, or by analogy. It has no name or shape. It is primal essence.[31] The best
introduction is the first verse of Laozi's *Dàodéjīng* 道德經:

> *The Dao that can be trodden*
>> *is not the unchanging Dao.*
> *The name that can be named*
>> *is not the enduring and unchanging name.*
> *Having no name,*
>> *it is the originator of Heaven and Earth,*
> *Having a name,*
>> *it is the Mother of all things.*
>
> *Always without desire we must be found,*
> *If it is the deep mystery (of the Dao) we would sound.*[32]
>
> *But if desire always within us be,*
> *Its outer fringe is all that we shall see.*
>> — Laozi, *Daodejing*, Verse 1[33]

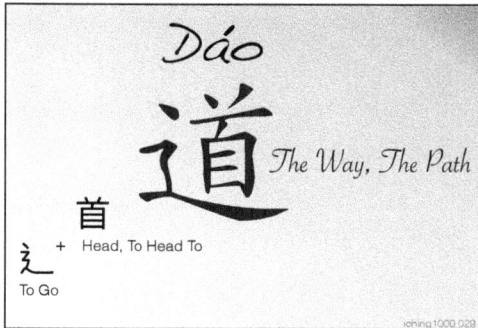

Figure 4.3 — The Dao Character

The Dao "lies underneath" yin-yang, which arises from it. The word,
Dao 道 is made up of characters for "to go" or "travel" and "head" as illustrated in Figure 4.3, implying a "correct" path. "Being in the Dao is like a
fish being in water" is an apt analogy to the invisible natural element that
holds us all.[34] Even though the fish are embedded in the water, they do not
"see" the water: The analogy is that fish can go through life without sensing
the water in which they live, so humans can live in the Dao without being
aware of it. But, even though the water is not something of which the fish is
aware, it "gives life,"[35] all the while being beyond space and time — at least
as perceived by the fish.

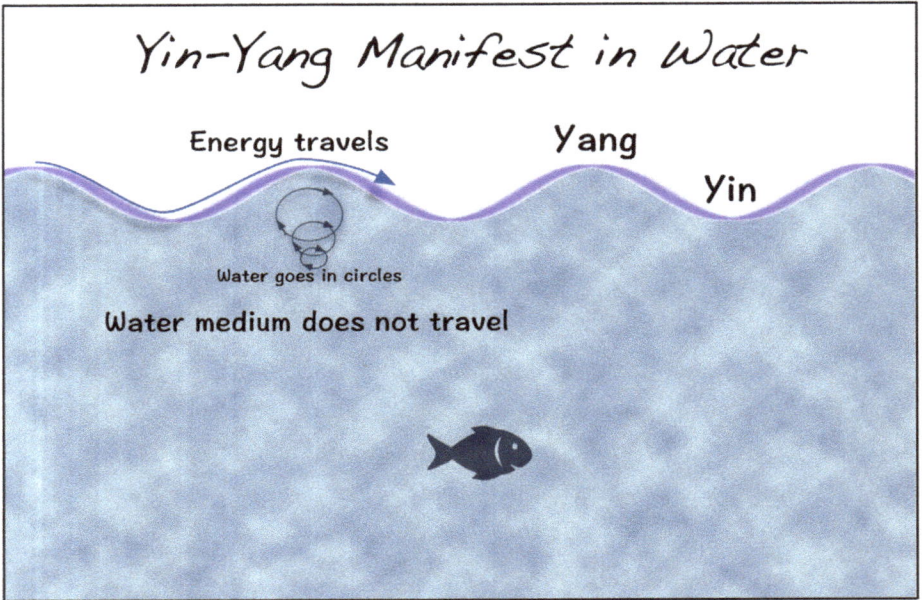

Figure 4.4 — In the Dao — A Fish in Water

Yin and yang are aspects of energy as waves move through the water medium — as illustrated in Figure 4.4. Of course, it is good to remember that this is a rough, even clumsy, analogy for understanding the Dao, which, in the end, must be seen with the mind's eye and not with pictures or words.

In the world of physics, the closest analogy is called a *Field* in physics, which is used to describe everything from electromagnetism to quantum mechanics. The *Field* fills space-time, each point having a value for a physical quantity, such as gravity or electric charge. The *Field* is the conceptual/mathematical medium through which perturbations of changing quantities flow. If it were visible it would be like the surface of a lake, with perturbations rippling across the surface. And there is entanglement in our world — two subatomic particles interact and, if separated halfway across the universe but remain isolated — what happens to one affects the other, instantaneously.[36]

As we think about the nature of the Dao, interacting with the Sage, or in everyday life, the essential question is our human relationship with the Dao.

## ⤙⤙◦⤙⤙ THE HUMANITY OF THE DAO ⤙⤙◦⤙⤙

As expressed in the *Daodejing* and *Zhuangzi*, the correct Way is to be "in the Dao," living in accord with the natural manifestations of the Dao, living in nature by living intuitively, even unconsciously. Indeed, there is a call to "unlearn" things like right and wrong and to unlearn the things that the ego uses to hold the mind in its grasp.

> *If we could renounce our sageness and discard our wisdom,*
> *it would be better for the people a hundred-fold.*
>
> *If we could renounce our benevolence and discard our*
> *righteousness,*
> *the people would again become filial and kindly.*
>
> *If we could renounce our artful contrivances*
> *and discard our (scheming for) gain*
> *there would be no thieves nor robbers.*
> — *Daodejing*, Verse 19[37]

To be in the Dao is to be in harmony with the cycles of yin and yang, in harmony with the Law of Change. Thus, the *I Ching* uses the Daoist view-point in *The Great Treatise*, which can be interpreted in psychological terms:

> *If one puts their chattering ego aside,*
> *the simple and easy can be understood.*
> *With the intuitive simple and easy,*
> *the laws of the world are sensed.*
> *When this happen,*
> *one achieves perfection.*[38]

In addition to seeing the Dao in the *I Ching* itself, an ancient Daoist med-itation practice was available to someone contemplating the *I Ching*. A book of poems titled, *Nei Ye (Nei Yeh)* was written in the same time-frame as the *Daodejing*. The *Nie Ye* is the 49th chapter of a larger text, *Guanzi*, which con-sists of chapters from several schools of thought.

*Nei Ye* is translated as *Inner Training*. The *Nei Ye* provides meditative po-ems getting insight into the Dao, through the moral force of *De*,[39] and would be a useful tool for preparation of a session with the *I Ching*.

Surf the Yin Yang

*Sitting on the surfboard, at the break line,*

*The exact place where the hard and unyielding bottom that lies beneath interrupts the circular motion of the yielding water.*

*Looking toward the horizon, you see the peaks of the swells in their yang aspects come toward you.*

*As one approaches, you can feel the water underneath subtly shifting, drawing toward the oncoming peak.*

*The swelling sea below raises the peak, and you begin to slide down the slope.*

*The power of the peak tries to rush forward, but, overreaching, it starts to break, the yin swells up from below causing it to release its energy.*

*Without effort, you glide down the face of the growing mountain of water.*

*You stand, turn, accelerating without effort, feeling the energy of the wave beneath your feet that carries you along in the moving curl as the wave breaks.*

*Without effort, you have let the Qi of yin-yang carry you forth.*

*But, as you peek back, you see how your surfboard's wake has changed the texture of the breaking wave — you and the wave embrace each other, each affecting the other.*

*The wave exhausts itself, and you are standing in the water.*

*Another wave begins to break over you. You do not fight it. You dive into the bottom of the curling wave, where you know the yin, the yielding water being pulled to the back of the wave, will carry you under the breaking yang peak.*

*You are in the water under the wave, being moved without effort back and up as the wave washes by.*

*You are in the Dao.*

## —∞— THE SPIRIT OF THE DAO —∞—

The Dao is impartial of human affairs, not cognizant of cruelty or kindness, instead, treating people as if they were "straw dogs" (*Daodejing*, Verse 5), in other words, without any feeling of benevolence or harm. The Dao is the invisible universal field in which all exists.

If there is a comparison, then *Logos* (λόγος) is a rough analogy. This was envisioned by the Greek Stoics as the logic of the universe, and Philo of Alexandria (a Jewish philosopher 25 B.C.–A.D. 50), and Plotinus (a neo-platonic Greek philosopher A.D. 204–270) as the "divine logic of the Universe."[40] The Christian tradition moved the idea of *Logos* in the flesh of Jesus Christ, the very incarnation of God, while for others it is a consequence of the Will of God. The Nag Hammadi Scriptures expressed this in a more intimate way:

> *God came forth, the Son, Mind of the All.*
> *This means that even his Thought,*
> *Takes its existence from the root of the All,*
> *Since he had him in Mind.*[41]

Dao Small Seal Script

Another rough analogy is the Brahman, not to be confused with the Brahmin caste or Brahma the Creator God in the Hindu tradition. While sometimes thought of as the Supreme God, in its metaphysical sense, Brahman is the impersonal infinite cause of the universe, having no form — changeless, but the cause of all changes.[42]

When these comparisons hint at being associated with God, it is important to remember that the Dao lies outside of the idea of God actively participating in human affairs. In fact, the *Dao* creates the "myriad of things" in nature, with all of its variety out of nothing — conceived by many in the West as a Cosmic Consciousness.[43]

> *Flashes of insight*
>     *come only to those who plug into the universe*
>     *and become harmonious with its rhythms*
>         *by communication with it.*
>                         — Walter Russell[44]

_Doing Nothing_

Doing Nothing

Wu 無 — Non-being, was expounded by Wang Bi as the unified, undifferentiated, reality that underlies the material world, the hidden mechanism that is the search of all diviners.

The correspondence between _Wu_ and You is:

| _Wu_ | You |
|------|-----|
| What is above form | What is within form |
| Dao (the Way) | _Qi_ (concrete objects) |
| Dao (the Way) | _Yin-Yang_ (manifest process) |
| Noumenal | Phenomenal |
| Hidden | Manifest |
| Totality | Particularity |
| The one | The Many[45] |

The application of yin-yang and the one and the many was applied in the West as well, a cosmic consciousness that expresses itself yin-yang and principles along the lines of _Wu_ and the many.

_Wu wei_ 無爲 — non-action, and _Wei wu wei_ — acting without action is an important idea not only for the Daoist but also Asian Buddhists and Confucians. Although they each have a different path, the end goal each is to be on the proper path, "without effort."

Daoism grew up with the _I Ching_. The oldest layer, the _Zhouyi_, was an old book when Laozi was alive. _Wu_ 無 is found in the _Zhouayi_, as the word for "never," a "negative imperative," often meaning "take no action." But, as Daoist concepts got interweaved with Confucian concepts in _The Great Treatise_, the hint of the metaphysical idea of the unchangeable essence lay quietly in the Judgment for Hexagram 48, The Well, which includes two of _wu_: "The will be no [_wu_] loss, no [_wu_] gain."[46]

*When the sun disappeared,*
      *then came the moonlight;*
*When the moon disappeared,*
      *then only mind remained;*
*When mind disappeared,*
      *then naught anywhere was left;*
*Then whither*
      *did earth, ether, and sky go off absorbed;*
*Only the all-being,*
      *all-light remained.*

— Lalla Ded[47]

Cross on Wall in Antigua Guatemala

Many mystics, particularly in the Christian tradition, strive for a version of *Wu* for a relationship with God that is not dispassionate, but passionate.

*On a dark night, ...*
*This light guided me*
*More surely than the light of noonday*
*To the place where he (well I knew who!) was awaiting me—*
*A place where none appeared.*
*Oh, night that guided me,*
*Oh, night more lovely than the dawn,*
*Oh, night that joined Beloved with lover,*
*Lover transformed in the Beloved!*
*Upon my flowery breast,*

*Kept wholly for himself alone,*
*There he stayed sleeping, and I caressed him,*
*And the fanning of the cedars made a breeze.*
*The breeze blew from the turret*
*As I parted his locks;*
*With his gentle hand he wounded my neck*
*And caused all my senses to be suspended.*
*I remained, lost in oblivion;*
*My face I reclined on the Beloved.*
*All ceased and I abandoned myself,*
*Leaving my cares forgotten among the lilies.*
— Saint John of the Cross, *Dark Night of the Soul*[48]

Saint John, alone in the dark, it is she, the soul, who is suffering — in the dark — alone — no hope of release. "God rises up out of the darkness, profound blessing."[49] The soul is helpless as God finishes her purification so she can be One with her beloved — God.

Immortal Land Yuan Jiang–Penglai Island by Yuan Jiang (袁江) A.D. 1708

## A MYSTICAL JOURNEY WITH THE ART OF THE DAO

The synergy of Confucian, Doaist, Buddhist, and Chinese cosmology continued — using both words and images. Laozi and Zhuangzi founded what is called Philosophical Daoism. A mystical, religious tradition was built on their ideas. This is a world full of spirits, magic, alchemy, astrology, and immortality. What is called Religious Daoism rose around A.D. 25, filling the gaps left by the disappearance of shamans of ancient times.[50]

The tradition includes a search for the magic elixir that will extend life and give immortality following the teachings of the Celestial Masters. By around A.D. 1000, there had developed the idea of internal elixirs which is available within the body through the dual cultivation of body and mind, while maintaining the Confucian virtues. This coincided with a mysticism movement in search of out-of-body experiences.[51]

Within this world of spirits and correlations, there exists a Oneness, the Dao. This is the summary expressed by many Daoist masters. The path to it is to engage with the spiritual world, living a simple life, and practicing disciplines such as Taiji (Tai Chi).[52]

Zhou Dunyi's *Supreme Ultimate Diagram* illustrates a singular polarity expressing itself in cycles of Yin and Yang, interactions of the five primary forces of nature, male and female, creative and receptive — that blossoms into the multitude of things of this world.[53] This is also an expression of the ultimate morality and goodness of that Ultimate Principle.

The wGnostics interpreted "The Father"

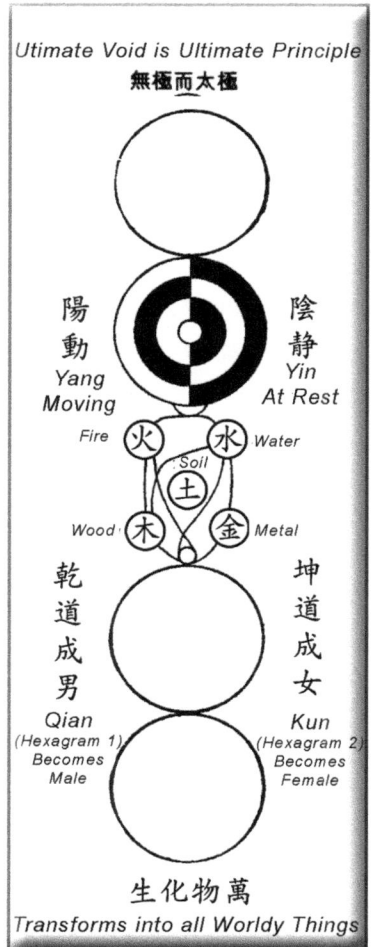

Utimate Void is Ultimate Principle
無極而太極

陽 動 Yang Moving

陰 静 Yin At Rest

Fire 火   水 Water

土 Soil

Wood 木   金 Metal

乾 道 成 男 Qian (Hexagram 1) Becomes Male

坤 道 成 女 Kun (Hexagram 2) Becomes Female

生化物萬
Transforms into all Worldy Things

Zhou Dunyi Ultimate Principle Diagram

in this same way, "The Father is singular while being many. For he is first and he is unique, though without being solitary."[54]

Carl Jung reached toward it with his collective subconscious. Others espouse an Ultimate Consciousness, the Divine Mind. The American-born New Thought Movement conceives of God as a Universal Mind which is available to humanity, an idea that was articulated by Mary Baker Eddy, founder of Christian Science as well as Earnest Holmes, founder of Centers for Spiritual Living, and Universalists who embrace a synergy of Christian and eastern reli-

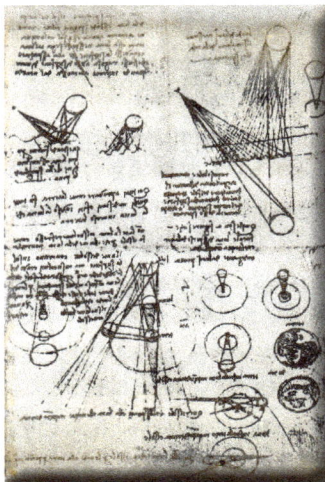

Study of the Moon by da Vinci [55]

gious thought.[56] The point of these traditions is to get us, the Many, back to the One. As Walter Russell said, *there is "...but One Mind, One force... When man knows this ... he will have no limitations"*[57] — the entangled universe, the grand and only consciousness — quantum entanglement daring to hint at a mechanism. How do humans know this? It seems to go beyond words.

The Wave by Walter Russell

Solar by Walter Russell

*The original painting of The Wave has disappeared. Any information leading to its safe is greatly appreciated. Call 1–800–882–5683. Anonymous tips use this form – https://philosophy.org/contact.html.*

People like Leonardo da Vinci and Walter Russell's quest to understand the universe was expressed through thought, words, *and art.*

Walter Russell expressed the idea in his book, *The Universal One* in the 1920s. Like Zhou Dunyi, his theories of cosmology are intimately connected with his art. One can see the Yin-Yang cycle in much of Russell's work, waves within octaves, and in his art.

People are applying the idea of art to the hexagrams of the *I Ching.* There are some websites and some books which strive for a visual emotional resonance with a hexagram.

*I Ching* books which present a Daoist outlook will have some or all of these ideas. They almost always have an introduction or a number of chapters that present the reader with the idea of connecting to the spiritual realm, viewing the hexagram relationships and cycles as an important aspect of using the *Book of Changes*, and recommending associated Daoist practices in addition to consulting the *I Ching.*

~ ~ ~

*Things grow best when left to themselves,*
*Left, and to nature's vigor rare.*
*How young and tender is the child,*
*With his twin tufts of falling hair!*
*But when you him ere long behold,*
*That child shall cap of manhood wear.*
So Says *The Book of Odes*[58]

**Web of Life Mandala**
Silk Screen and Batik on Cotton by Mary Byers

*Grow best left to themselves*

Boy in Hat, Ready to Fly

Hancheng Confucian Temple, Shaanxi, China

# 5

# CONFUCIUS ADVISES

*The superior person achieves composure*
*Before trying to move others;*
*Achieves an easy and restful mind*
*Before speaking;*
*Contemplates the principles of his dealings*
*Before seeking something from others.*
So Says *The Great Treatise*[1]

Confucius

Confucius, 孔夫子 Kǒng Fūzǐ (K'ung Fu-tzu), literally the "Grand Master Kong" — also known by the simple title, Kǒngzǐ, Son of Kong.[2] He lived from 551 to 479 B.C., a century earlier than Socrates.

Confucius had a profound influence on Chinese culture and life. He traveled to seek a prince who would heed his advice and found none. While he traveled, he taught, finding many students, attacking many followers. It was his students and followers who would become the advisors of princes.[3] His teachings were carried on by his disciples through the Confucius School of Thought, or Confucianism.[4] The philosophy and moral code developed by Confucius then spread through the Korean Peninsula, to the islands of Japan, and then into Southeast Asia, where it was incorporated into the local cultures.

For much of the history of China and well into the nineteenth century, governments were administered on behalf of the emperor by Confucian scholars, *Rú*. Because of this, Confucianism was known as the School of Scholars *Rújiā* 儒家. People from this school created the *I Ching* version that received imperial sanction in 136 B.C. It became, with little change,

Ru Seal

what scholars call the "received text."[5] Other archaeological finds have discovered hints of other versions as well as a complete version in 1973, known as the *Mawangdui* version, named for the place it was found. It has a different hexagram order and some of the Chinese text is different than the received text. Edward Shaughnessy translated it into English in his *I Ching, The Classic of Changes*.

At its core, the teachings of Confucius are about human relationships. It is a humanitarian philosophy that began from the hierarchical society into which Confucius was born, emerging as a sophisticated philosophical system designed to transform a people into an ethical and virtuous society.

An important point made by the Confucian School is that its philosophy must be taught, must be learned by individuals, who learn both its proper customs and its inner moral code — something to be practiced daily. The grand vision of Confucianism is that a virtuous society will arise when it is populated and ruled by these educated and moral individuals.[6]

Confucius recognized a relationship and dependence upon Heaven as it was understood in his time, honoring the rituals that go with it. In later centuries (A.D. 800) Confucius was deified as the god of culture, with temples of worship — a cult he may have found inappropriate if he was alive.

Confucius was religious but did not develop a religious philosophy; he accepted the religion of his time and place. His philosophy was focused on a human society living in harmony, with an implicit assumption that human society would then be in correspondence with the will of Heaven.

Before Confucius, the *Changes* was used sometimes as a moral guide. As early as 603 B.C., when a youth talks about his political ambitions to a prince, the prince remarks later that the outcome of his aspirations without virtue can be found in the top line of *Feng* — he builds a large house, soaring in his pride, he will be alone and there will be evil. The young man died at the hands of his subjects within a year. Confucius and his students codified these ideas.[7]

Confucius developed these ideas in a unique way for the age, with reasoning that did not need to appeal to the divine nor the concept of an immortal soul as in Western and Indian thought during this period. He appealed to the ideal past, to the beginning of the Zhou Dynasty, founded by King Wen, who is said to have written the Judgment Statements of the *I Ching*. This was the ideal ruler that Confucius sought to describe, what the classical Greek philosophers would call the Sage-King.

## RECIPROCITY — THE UNIVERSAL GOLDEN RULE

Confucianism developed in China in the period philosopher Karl Jasper calls the Axial Age (800 B.C. to 200 B.C.), a time when much of the foundation for today's religious beliefs were laid in various societies throughout Eurasia.[8] It is during this critical developmental period that many common moral themes emerged, including the Golden Rule, "Do unto others as you would have done unto you." This was also when societies began to see people as moral agents who were accountable for their acts and deeds based on a moral code, going beyond loyalty to a tribe or king.

The Golden Rule is virtually a universal ethic throughout the world. Possibly the earliest document containing the idea is a wonderful Egyptian poem, *The Eloquent Peasant,* which is a poetic appeal by a peasant to a ruler for the return of his confiscated trade goods:

*Act upon the man as you would wish him to act toward you.*[9]

In the Eastern Mediterranean region the Golden Rule was articulated as both a religious and Classical Greek ethic:

- Greek philosophy: *If we never do ourselves what we blame in others.*[10]

- Zoroaster, the founder of a religion that was firmly established in Persia by 500 B.C., made a similar statement: *...that nature is good when it shall not do unto another whatever is not suitable for its own self.*[11]

- Hebrew Bible and Christian Old Testament: *...thou shalt love thy neighbor as thyself...* — *The Holy Bible,* Leviticus, 19:18 KJV

- Christian New Testament takes it further to *love your enemies: And as you wish that others would do to you, do so to them.* — *Luke 6:28 ESV*

- In the Qur'an the Golden Rule is reflected in an emphasis to giving to the poor: *And let not those of virtue among you and wealth swear not to give aid to their relatives and the needy and the emigrants for the cause of Allah, and let them pardon and overlook. Would you not like that Allah should forgive you?* — *Noble Qur'an,* The Light, Surah 24:22

The idea of the golden rule is present in the religions that arose in India:

- Buddhism: *One who, while himself seeking happiness, oppresses with violence other beings who also desire happiness, will not attain happiness hereafter.* — *Dhammapada,* 10 Violence, Verse 131

---

In China, Confucius was teaching the Golden Rule:

己 所 不 欲 , 勿 施 於 人
*Jǐ suǒ bù yù , wù shī yú rén.*
*What you wish not for yourself, do not do to other people.*
— Confucius, *Analects*[12]

This doctrine gives a word to live by:

> "Is there one word which may serve as a rule of practice for all one's life?"
>
> The Master said,
> "Is not RECIPROCITY (恕 Hue) such a word? What you do not want done to yourself, do not do to others."
> — Confucius, *Analects*[13]

When Confucius was asked what "constitutes perfect virtue," the response was, "Courtesy, generosity of soul, sincerity, diligence, and kindness [Reciprocity]."[14] For Confucius, the Golden Rule does not stand alone, but is an integral part of the superior person so often discussed in the *I Ching,* a person who embodies another universal idea — moderation.

## ⸺ THE DOCTRINE OF THE MEAN — UNIVERSAL MODERATION ⸺

This universal idea of reciprocity is expanded in another key Confucian document two generations later in the *Doctrine of the Mean, Zhōng yōng*, which goes on to develop the idea of moderation. It is attributed to the grandson of Confucius, Zisi. The *Doctrine of the Mean* is both the name of the book and a principle of moderation.

> *Earnest in practicing the ordinary virtues, and careful in speaking about them, if, in his practice, he has anything defective, the superior man dares not but exert himself; and if, in his words, he has any excess, he dares not allow himself such license.*
> — *Doctrine of the Mean*[15]

This is much the same idea as The Rule of the Golden Mean in Western philosophy, which is a philosophy of moderation and self-control.

> *Excess and deficiency are characteristic of vice*
> *Hitting the mean is characteristic of virtue.*
> — Aristotle, *Nicomachean Ethics*[16]

An example given by Aristotle includes gluttony and self-starvation, both of which he considers vices. The Golden Mean lies in moderate eating. Examples abound in nearly all aspect of life and human feelings. Aristotle, like the *Doctrine of the Mean*, associates the Golden Mean with virtue.

In the Abrahamic (Judaism, Christianity, and Islam) religious traditions these ideas are motivated by a relationship with a living, present God.

> *But the fruit of the Spirit [the gift of Grace from God]*
> *is love, joy, peace, longsuffering, gentleness, goodness,*
> *faith, meekness, temperance [moderation]...*
> — *The Holy Bible*, Galatians 5:22 KJV

The Buddhist Middle Way is a similar idea:

> *Avoid extremes.*
> *Follow the middle way.*
> — *Dhammacakkappavattana Sutra*[17]

The Doctrine of the Mean is almost ever present in the Image Statements. An example from Hexagram 10, Treading:

*The sky above, and below it the waters of the marsh forms* TREADING. *The superior person, in accordance with this, distinguishes between high and low, and gives contentment to the aims of the people.*

Within the humane person lies Reciprocity and the Doctrine of the Mean, a person Confucius would call *Ren.*

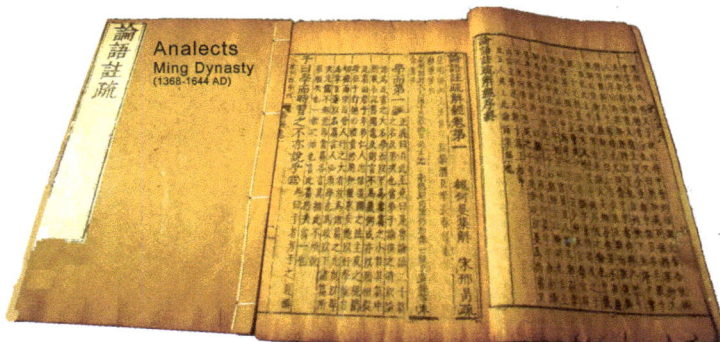

Analects of Confucius Ming Dynasty

### ⟶ HOW THE COMMONER BECOMES THE SUPERIOR PERSON ⟵

In the *Analects*, Confucius raises an ancient term, *Ren,* which earlier merely meant people, to the highest principle, that of humaneness, human-heartedness.[19]

"The people," 人, and the proper interaction between them, "two" 二, creates the character *Rén (Jen)* 仁.

*Ren* became a central concept in Confucian thought — perfect humaneness.[20] *Ren* is something to be cultivated over a lifetime. The *Doctrine of the Mean* includes *Ren* as one of the three virtues to practice daily, Learning/Knowledge, *Ren*, and Energy/Courage.[21]

The word Dao is used by both by Laozi in the *Daodejing* and Confucius, each using the word as meaning "correct principle of action." For Laozi, the correct principle is to let your intentional will fall away and be in the Dao. For Confucius, it is to intentionally follow the Way of the Good-hearted Person.[22] The *I Ching* incorporates the idea of the Dao as a principle of nature and the moral view from Confucius as well, delivering both viewpoints in each reading.

Confucius taught that a person is not truly noble unless they have *Ren*, a subtle critique of noblemen who were self-serving. He elevated another word: Nobleman, *Jūnzǐ (Chün-tzu)* 君子 merely meant noble birth, literally a Lord's 君 child 子. Confucius transformed the meaning of the word *Junzi*. *Junzi* became the "superior person" of the *I Ching*, someone who goes beyond *Ren* to also embody a love of learning and the authentic customs of society. It became something anyone can achieve through education and cultivation, a person who is motivated by moral action and virtue.[23]

> *Love of wisdom without the love of learning*
> *leads to no understanding of principles.*
>
> *Love of being sincere without the love of learning*
> *leads a disregard of consequences.*
>
> *Love of straightforwardness without the love of learning*
> *leads to rudeness.*
>
> *Love of courage without the love of learning*
> *leads to recklessness.*
> — Confucius[24]

The concept of a superior person is developed further by Mencius (372–289 B.C.), one of Confucius's most famous disciples, in a book titled with his name. He gives numerous examples of how a superior person should behave in different situations.

> *The superior man makes his advances in what he is*
> *learning with deep earnestness and by the proper course,*
> *wishing to get hold of it as in himself.*
>
> *Having got hold of it in himself, he abides in it calmly*
> *and firmly.*
>
> *Abiding in it calmly and firmly, he reposes a deep reliance on it.*
>
> *Reposing a deep reliance on it, he seizes it on the left*
> *and right, meeting everywhere with it as a fountain from*
> *which things flow.*
>
> *It is on this account that the superior man wishes to get*
> *hold of what he is learning as in himself.*
> — Mencius[25]

For Confucius, it is this educated, humane person who travels the Dao.

## ━━ THE DAO AND THE CHOICE — EAST VERSUS WEST ━━

Two starting points for discussing human morality are:

> East: Follow the right path (the *Dao*).
> West: Make the right choice.

There is a subtle, but important, difference between these two. The starting point is "choice" in Greek philosophy as well as Jewish, Christian, and Islamic theology. An individual makes a choice to act, to do good or evil, subject to their divine beliefs or their society's agreed upon moral principles. The source of those moral principles and the motivation can be secular or religious, secular choices being made based upon a set of ethical principles, religious choices made in accordance with their belief in the will of God.

But, if humans have a moral accountability for a choice made they must have free will.[26] Turning this around, if a person has no free will then there was actually no choice between good and evil and, thus, no moral accountability. Choice is so embedded in Western culture that it might seem to be the only way to think about moral action.[27]

> *One is not generous if he finds it painful to give;*
> *they would choose wealth over noble action.*
> — Aristotle, *Nicomachean Ethics*[28]

Choice is where Western thought begins, but often ends up on a "straight and narrow path."

> *Thou wilt show me the path of life: In thy presence is*
> *fullness of joy.* — The Holy Bible, Psalm 16:8 ASV

> *I put my trust in Allah, My Lord and your Lord! There is*
> *not a moving creature, but He hath grasp of its fore-lock.*
> *Verily, it is my Lord that is on a straight Path.*
> — *The Noble Qur'an*, Hud, 11:56[29]

> *And I also beheld a strait and narrow path, which came*
> *along by the rod of iron.*
> — *The Book of Mormon*, 8:20

Confucius approaches good and evil from the other direction. Instead of beginning with "choice," Confucius starts with the "narrow path," the *Dao*, the Way. The imagery for straying from the Way is to walk a "crooked path."

The Confucian moral life is not defined by choices made, but instead by a continuous commitment to walk the *Dao,* the Way, the Path — which, when he uses the word, he uses it as a conscious commitment. In the *Analects of Confucius* the choice between good and evil is left as something implicit.[30] Good is traveling the Way. Evil is inevitable when a person or society strays off the Way.

> *Mencius replied, "The way of truth is like a great road.*
> *It is not difficult to know it."* — Mencius[31]

The idea of an individual's free will is assumed, but free will's choice is a life time continuous commitment to travel the Way through love of learning, cultivating human-heartedness and empathy (*Ren*) and striving to be part of a harmonious society in every social interaction (*Li*). This continuous practice can be seen as making the correct choice in response to events a subconscious disposition. That is, without effort.[32]

## THE DANCE OF HARMONY

The superior person integrates *Ren* with *Lǐ* 禮, the rules of propriety in accordance with one's station in society. Herbert Fingarette and other scholars see this integration of *Ren* and *Li* as *Dé* (*Te*) 德 (virtue). According to Fingarette, achieving this is nothing less than a sacred act.[33] This is how Confucius gets to the heart of the purpose of humankind — roughly summed up as a harmonious society authentically living in harmony with Heaven and Earth.

Confucius gets to the central need for society — harmony. *Ren,* the authentic and human-hearted, dances with *Li,* the customs and rituals that brings harmony to society. In the *Analects, Ren* is not described as some ascetic state of being. It is something that is in motion, that acts with society. You do not become Confucian by sitting alone in a chair and contemplating. You have to interact with your fellow humans.

*Ren* motivates the human will to act in accordance with *Lǐ,* 禮, the accepted customs and rituals of a society that are oriented toward harmony. *Ren* comes out of the humane heart to meet society, to rule a kingdom. *Ren* does this in accordance with *Li,* the external manifestation of human-heartedness and harmony.

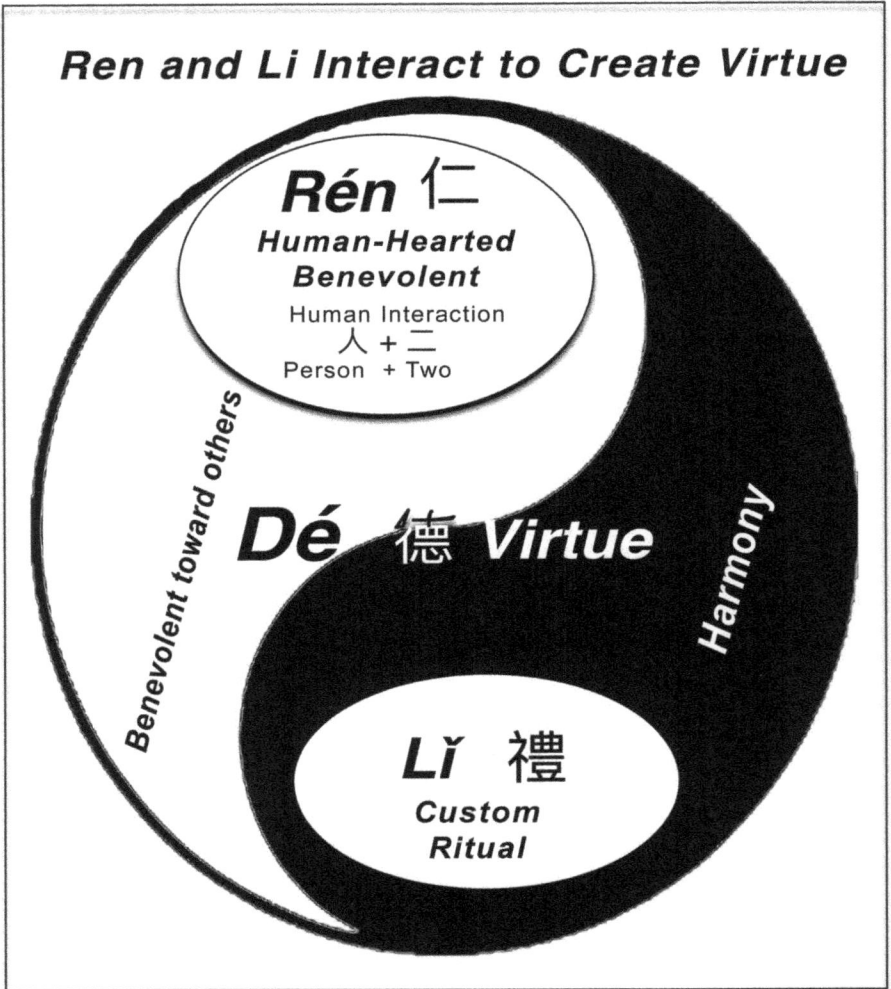

Ren, De, and Li

~ ~ ~

*Yes, here I am*
    *With a welcome heart to greet you.*
*In my mind*
    *I see a smile upon your lips*
*And then*
    *I hear your voice speak gently*
*Of friendships*
                    — Barbara Olsen

*Li* is an important concept in Chinese history, a history sometimes full of violent warfare, with *Li* being the way to replace violence with harmony throughout society, from the ruler to the family. But, for *Li* to be authentic, it must be practiced by people who have *Ren*. Otherwise, it is fake, just going through the motions, a departure from the Way. Thus, for most of Chinese history from Confucius to the early twentieth century, *Li,* the customs, were taught to every child, and *Li,* the full embodiment of Confucian practice, was taught to scholars throughout the land.

While Confucian Sage acts that are conscious, taught, and practiced, the *Daodejing* includes the Golden Rule, suggesting the Way itself is virtuous and that one can skip all of the learning and simply seek the *Dao* directly.

> *He who acts in accordance with Dao,*
> *becomes one with Dao.*
> *He who treads the path of Virtue*
> *becomes one with Virtue.*
> *He who pursues a course of Vice*
> *becomes one with Vice.*
> *The man who is one with Dao,*
> *Dao is also glad to receive.*
> *The man who is one with Virtue,*
> *Virtue is also glad to receive.*
> *The man who is one with Vice,*
> *Vice is also glad to receive.*
> — *Daodejing*, Verse 23, (Legge Trans.)

It was here that Confucius distinguished himself from Laozi on how to stay on the true path, the Way, the Dao: It is to engage in continuous, conscious practice of virtuous behavior.

> *If a superior man abandon virtue, how can he fulfill*
> *the requirements of that name? The superior man does*
> *not, even for the space of a single meal, act contrary to*
> *virtue. In moments of haste, he cleaves to it. In seasons*
> *of danger, he cleaves to it.*
> — Analects, Benevolent Unity, Verse 5

Confucianism sees the development of the individual as the superior person, not for the primary purpose of the individual reaching their ultimate potential, but as a mechanism in which a society reaches its ultimate potential, because each person is a superior person.

> *The superior person acts*
> *with kindness and grace,*
> *So another person may act*
> *with kindness and grace.*
> *It is this mutual act that*
> *fills society with grace.*
> *Holding us within its embrace,*
> *makes it a sacred act.*
> *The superior person is*
> *the consummate person.*
> *Who through kindness and grace*
> *becomes Sacred.*[34]

## ⚫━━ HOW TO RULE A KINGDOM ━━⚫

The sayings attributed to Confucius, *The Analects,* is as much a political treatise as a book of philosophy, similar to Plato's *Republic.* In both cases, the authors were faced with societies that were becoming more complex that began competing for control of resources. The competition between the small states of their time was getting more and more violent. Struggling to restore harmony, Greek and Chinese philosophers both created political treatises on how best to rule that were also books of ethics.[35] For benevolence, *Ren,* and proper customs, *Li,* to be authentic, a Confucian had to be righteous and just, *Yì* 義. This, of course, is another universal principle.

### *Li* and Mao Zedong

Mao Zedong saw *Li* and other Confucian ideas as holding back China from seeing the need for things that deserve "absolute" negation – a central idea in the Marxist/Soviet theory of Dialectic Materialism — such as exploitation of workers.

— Mao, *Mao Zedong on Dialectical Materialism: Writings on Philosophy,* 105, 158, 165

Like nearly every tradition where inner virtue and a set of rules is an important part of the tradition, the rules can get separated from the human–heartedness and become a rigid means of control. This is how many saw *Li* in China as the twentieth century opened. Things such as this misuse of the Confucian principles, plus pressures from the West, set the stage for a civil war in China with the eventual creation of the Peoples Republic of China.

The Cultural Revolution was the final act to bury *Li.* But, the essence of *Li* won't be denied.

*Guānxì* 关系 in modern China retains the Confucian idea of the trusted relationship that was embedded in *Li.*

— Zhang, *"Embracing Guanxi."*

What Confucians did, however, is recognize that justice had to "get to the truth." To get to the truth one had to call things by their proper name, that is in an American idiom, with "no spin."[36] This is called the Rectification of Names, an essential principle for understanding the truth so that the honest response is understood:

> *Names have no intrinsic value, it is only society's agreement on its meaning and attachment to reality. It is a matter of custom. Names that are clear and simple and designate a real thing are said to be good. The enlightened ruler regulates names, so as to rule well.*[37]

Xunzi is also a Legalist, one of the Hundred Schools of Thought. Legalism is a system of rewards and punishments prescribed to be applied uniformly to each person based on the role in society. For most of China's history up until the early twentieth century, governance combined Confucianism with Legalism.

This combination of Legalism and Confucianism was adopted by the Koreans and Japanese. For the practical ruler, the Confucian idea of the virtuous ruler leading by example is an idea that is, in practice, enforced by Legalism, leaving the argument over people starting out good or bad to the sages.

## ————< THE CONFUCIAN COMMENTARY IN THE *I CHING* >————

These Confucian ideas are found in the Ten Wings. The Image Statements are particularly Confucian. The Image Statements often add advice for self-cultivation — which is usually practical. An example:

> 58. 兌 *Joyous.*
> *THE Judgment: Joyous intimates that there will be progress and attainment. It will be advantageous to be firm and correct.*

Xunzi (310-235 BC)

Xunzi

A straightforward reading is a prediction with a caveat where it is best to be firm and correct in ones actions and words. One could see emphasis on *Li.*

*THE IMAGE. Two symbols representing the waters of a marsh, one over the other, form Joyous. The superior person, in accordance with this, encourages the conversation of friends and the stimulus of their common practice.*[38]

With this later Confucian addition of The Image (and the Confucian Commentary of the Ten Wings), the *I Ching* now has further advice that brings in *Ren* more explicitly into the equation. Scholars would develop Confucian thought further. When Buddhism arrived in China, it had a profound effect on Confucian thought. Buddhism's influence would, in turn, affect how the *I Ching* and how its commentaries are interpreted.

# Confucian Principles

**Five Relationships**
- Soveriegn and Minister
- Father and Son
- Husband and Wife
- Elder and Younger
- Friends

**HEXAGRAM
Relationship between Lines**

**Five Contant Virtures**
Rén 仁, benevolence, humaneness, human-heartedness
Yì 義, justice, rightuosness
Lǐ 禮, proper custom, ritual, courtesy, propriety
Zhì 智, knowledge, wisdom
Xìn 信, integrity, trustworthy, fidelity

**Some Other Important Vitures**
- Shù 恕, kindness and forgiveness.
- Xiào 孝, filial piety.
- Zhōng 忠, loyalty.

Confucian Principles and Relationships

### ⋙⋘ THE NEO-CONFUCIAN AND THE *I CHING* ⋙⋘

Buddhism arrived in China and by A.D. 420 *Chán* (Zen) Buddhism had arisen. The question for Confucian scholars was how much Buddhist thought to incorporate. The answer is Neo-Confucianism, *Sòng-Míng lǐxué*. Neo-Confucianism would become the dominate tradition from after its introduction around A.D. 800 to the early twentieth century.[40]

Neo-Confucianism built upon the golden age of culture of the Han Dynasty (206 B.C. to A.D. 220), when the *I Ching* was elaborated upon by scholars along the lines of Jing Fang, Images and Numbers School. As the Han Dynasty came to a close, Wang Bi elaborated the Meanings and Principles School.

Two main schools arose during the Neo-Confucian period, creating a tension and lively scholarship, the "Rationalistic Wing," (Chang-Zhu School) and the "Idealistic Wing" (Lu-Wang School). The rationalists have an outlook in common with classical Greek philosophy and the idealists have a Buddhist and Daoist outlook,[41] giving the *I Ching* its own dynamic tension between images and meaning, practical divination and esoteric insight. Translators of the *I Ching* may bring one of these outlooks as the "right way" to interpret the *Book of Changes*.

What these "wings" of thought have in common is the goal of permanent happiness can be summed up as the superior person who is always calm and at ease, unlike the inferior person who is constantly apprehensive.[42]

---

**Womankind and Confucianism**

In the Neo–Confucian era, up to the beginning of the 20th Century, foot–binding was imposed upon daughters primarily by upper class households, making them more "feminine" and dependent. The justification misappropriated Confucian and Buddhist principles. In particular the Confucian principle of not violating the body was lost in the process.

As protest movements spread in China in the early 20th century, including a woman's movement, the past abuses were associated with Confucianism.

Confucianism joined the ranks of all of the world's major religious and ethical philosophies in being appropriated by the powerful for their own purposes in ways the founders never intended.[39]

### ⟶⚬⟶ THE JOURNEY WITH CONFUCIUS IN A MODERN WORLD ⟶⚬⟶

Confucius began with an ethical system which has the same themes as religions and ethical beliefs around the world — the ethical advice, particularly in the Image Statements, will be familiar. Since Confucius built on the practical advice of the *Zhouyi*, any translation that includes Image Statements will give advice similar to an advice columnist or many self-help books, albeit with the language of Confucius and the mechanisms of Daoism.

Many translations are enhanced by adding "author commentary" to the translation of the *I Ching* text — by that I mean commentary by the translator or their advisor — or in some cases a translation of a Chinese Sage's com-

*The Roof Decoration of Sanxing. At Magong Beiji Temple, Taiwan*

Sanxing Deities — Prosperity (Fu), Status (Lu), and Longevity (Shou) Photo by 雲角

mentary, such as Lynn's inclusion of a translation of Wang Bi's commentary in his book, *The Classic of Changes*.

Wilhelm, in his translation, *The I Ching*, collaborated with Lao Nai-hsaün, one of the leading Confucian scholars of his day. Thus, Wilhelm got the best Neo-Confucian commentary as it existed in the early twentieth century. At that point in history, China had been subject to colonial pressure and wars, which could not help but affect the outlook of the populace, but the intellectual heritage of Confucius was alive and well. But, the major culture change that resulted from the Japanese invasion, the Chinese Civil War, and the Cultural Revolution would suggest that Wilhelm, through an accident of history, got the benefit of the pinnacle of Neo-Confucian thought.

With this, a Neo-Confucian brings the Buddhist-influenced awareness of one's interior life. This brings the *I Ching* into the realm of a psychological tool.

> *The New Confucius*
> *Layer upon layer*
> *From the material to the inner realms*
> *Brings us to the embrace*
> *Of the sixty-four hexagrams*
> *The embedded trigrams*
> *The resonance lines*
> *Of the book of wisdom and divination*
> *The Book of Changes.*

So, we reach for the full inner experience, with Buddhist-like meditation added to the ritual of the Zhou Dynasty era. Books such as Carol Anthony's series and several other authors bring us right to it — full circle from the spiritual practices of the sacrificial rites of the Zhou to the spiritual practices of meditation and prayer.

Remember, any of these levels — the practical, the ethical, the psychological, the spiritual, the metaphysical — is useful for the *I Ching* devotee. Pick out your favorite translation, and use it the way you choose — your choice is the most important criteria of all.

~~~

*The virtue of the chief of Shen,*
*Is mild, and regulated, and upright.*
*He will keep all these countries in order,*
*And be famed throughout the kingdom.*

So Says the *The Book of Odes*[43]

*Lǐ* and the Universal Social Ritual
— shared food —

*The superior person never departs from
humaneness even for the space of a meal.
— Confucius*[44]

Shared Food Creates Good Will and Good Order

Butterfly Dance

# 6

# MAKING YOUR MIND DANCE

*The eight trigrams having been completed*
*in their proper order,*
*there were in each the (three) emblematic lines.*
*They were then multiplied*
*by a process of addition*
*till the (six) component lines appeared.*
*The strong line and the weak push themselves*
*each into the place of the other,*
*and hence the changes (of the diagrams) take place.*
So Says *The Great Treatise*[1]

This chapter discusses more advanced concepts of imagery.[2] If you are new to the *I Ching* it may be easier to grasp after you have gotten some practice using the *I Ching*. It is like learning to dance, learning the choreography of hexagram so that our mind can dance to a tune suggested by the correlation, conflict, and cooperation that is exhibited by the lines and trigrams within the hexagram.

The previous chapters discussed the relationship of unbroken and broken lines with the yin-yang cycle, how this is represented by changing lines, how three lines form trigrams that represent natural agents, how two trigrams form the hexagram, and how the imagery of the interacting trigrams give insight into the Judgment. In this chapter a hexagram becomes a field of action in time and space, with line relationships that overlap and interact in the same hexagram, including yin-yang, physical height, and the assignment of a human role in a hierarchical society. Of course, these can be read as metaphors for both external events and internal psychological interactions.

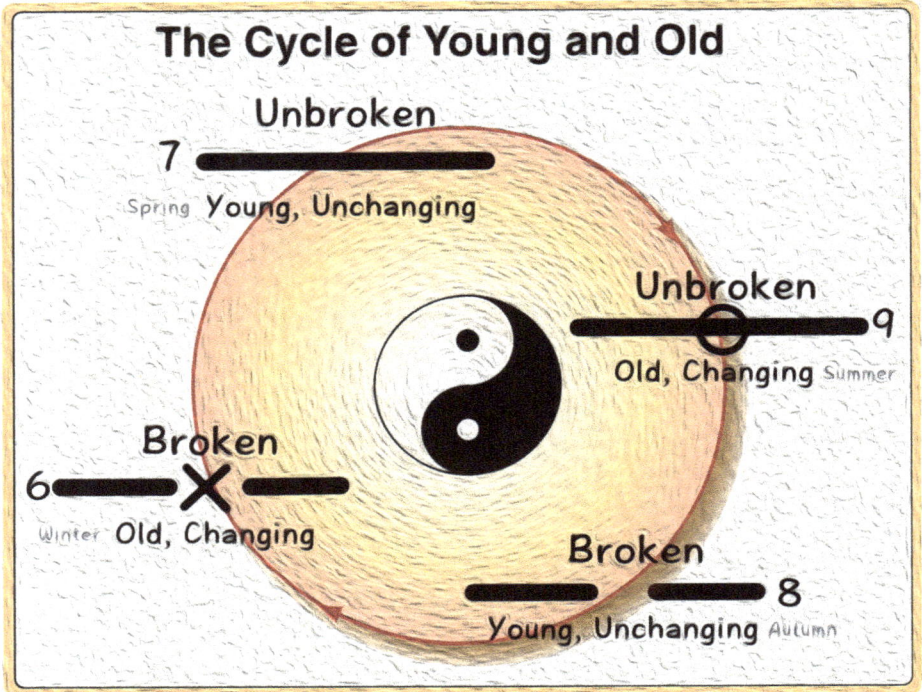

Figure 6.1 — Lines Cycle Like Seasons

## ⟶ EVOLUTION FROM THE SINGLE POLARITY TO TRIGRAMS ⟵

The *I Ching Great Treatise* contains an explanation of how two symbols, the unbroken and broken lines gave rise to the trigrams and hexagrams. Some *I Ching* author commentaries will reference this explanation and the terms it uses. The process starts with the Supreme Ultimate, the single polarity, from which all things come forth.[3] Yin and yang come forth as broken and unbroken lines. The broken and unbroken lines can be old, ready to change, prepared for reincarnation to match the four seasons (Figure 6.1).

Figure 6.2 shows how they double themselves, being two unbroken or two broken lines. When they are young — they are called Little Yin and Little Yang, unchanging, growing old. When they are old — they are called Great Yin and Great Yang, ready to reincarnate, to change. There are two lines as well, the top line is where they are going, and the bottom line is where they came from. These give rise to the trigrams which combine to give the hexagrams.[4]

# The Development of Lines

## The Lines

**Unbroken**

━━━━━━

Yang

**Broken**

━━  ━━

Yin

---

### Zhouyi - King Wen (c. 1000 BC)

9 九 Changing      6 六 Changing

---

### Dazjuan - The Great Treatise (c. 300 BC)

易有太極 With Changes, the Supreme Ultimate (Taiji/Tai Chi)
*Yì yǒu Tài jí*

是生兩儀 Produced two elementary forms (Lines, Broken and Unbroken)
*Shì shēng liǎng yí*

兩儀生四象 The two forms produced four symbols (Changing and Unchanging)
*Yí liǎng shēng sì xiàng*

| Old | Young | Young | Old |
|-----|-------|-------|-----|
| Great Yang | Little Yang | Little Yin | Great Yin |

四象生八卦 The four symbols gave life to the eight trigrams
*Sì xiàng shēng bā guà*

| Heaven | Earth | Thunder | Water | Mountain | Wind/Wood | Fire | Lake |
|--------|-------|---------|-------|----------|-----------|------|------|

• *The Trigrams, two by two, give rise to the 64 Hexagrams* •

---

## The Changing Lines

| Changing | Unchanging | Unchanging | Changing |
|----------|------------|------------|----------|
| 9 ─○─ | 7 ─── | 8 ── ── | 6 ─X─ |

Unbroken Line ..........................Yang     Broken Line ............................. Yin

Translated Chinese a paraphrase based on Legge, *I Ching (Yi King)*

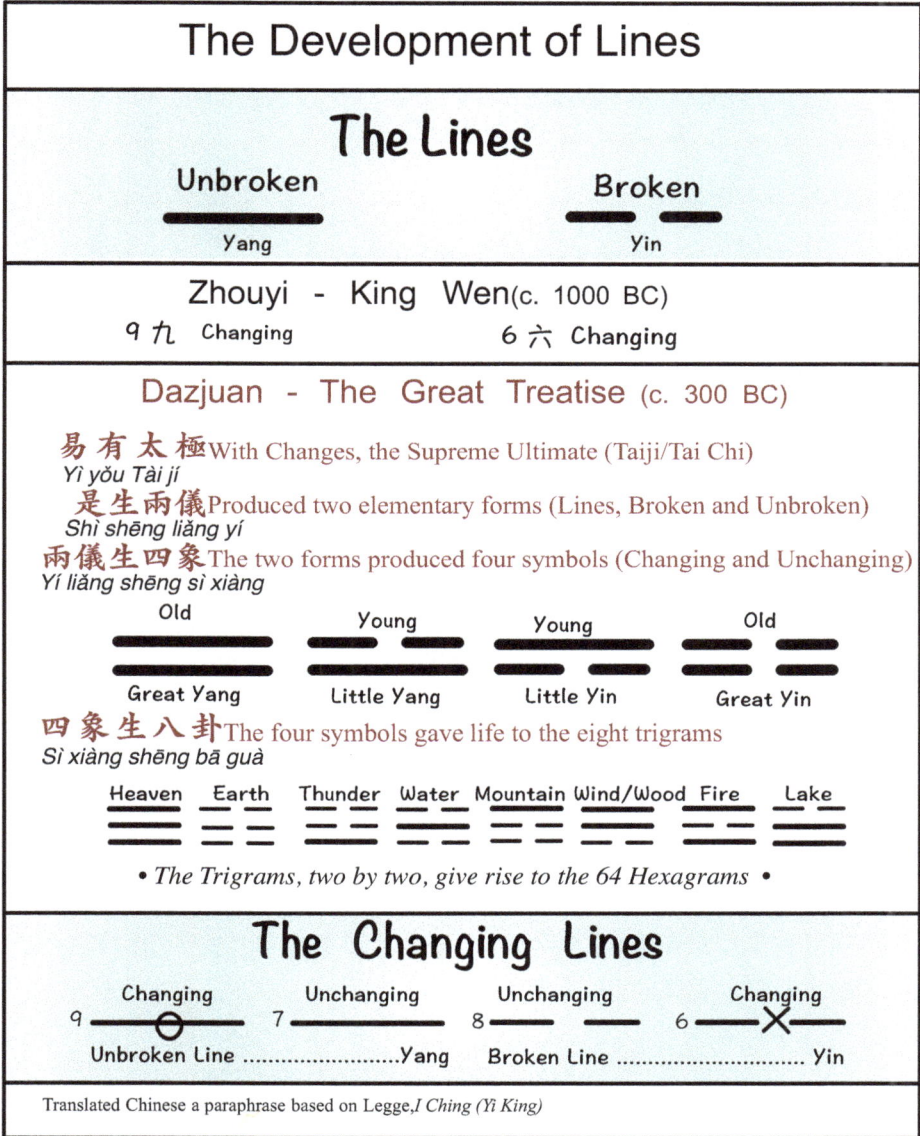

Figure 6.2 — Evolution of Lines

*I gaze upon six lines, not yet in focus, seeing first the places hidden beneath them. The places have relationships, one to the other.*

*Now the lines emerge, broken and unbroken, coming into focus. They are in their places, and the spaces define them.*

*The places have depth, some higher, some lower.*

*Now lines see their place, their place in the stack of lines, their relation to each other. And, to this they respond: Some want to move; some hold fast.*

*Six lines, shimmering, interacting, informing each other, giving meaning to the whole, creating the hexagram that they arranged themselves to make.*

### ⸺ MOVING, RESONATE LINES WITHIN A HEXAGRAM ⸺

There are several kinds of imagery used in each hexagram commentary; some or all may be present in the same hexagram commentary:

- Moving Lines: Unbroken and broken lines trying to "move" in the hexagram, interacting with lines nearby.
- Yin-Yang Positions: Yang lines are in their ideal position if they are on odd-numbered lines and yin on even-numbered lines.
- Rulers of a Hexagram: Each hexagram has lines associated with a "constituting ruler," which relates to the meaning of the hexagram and a "governing ruler," which is always a superior person.
- Line Position Relations: Each of the six lines that make up a hexagram has a position, 1 to 6 counting from the bottom, with the position being assigned a role in society, and the interaction between lines in positions having meaning.
- Development of Idea: The lines represent the development of the idea of the hexagram as Line Statements progress from 1 to 6.
- Line Position Height: The lines' position may represent the physical height, 1 lowest and 6 highest.

Odd positions prefer to be occupied by unbroken, light, yang lines; even positions prefer broken, dark, yin lines, which is illustrated in Figure 6.3. This idea of lines being "where they belong" comes into play in the commentaries. For example, a yin line in Line 5, the position of the ruler, will often indicate a ruler who is weak. This is not necessarily a negative.

For example, for Hexagram 40, *Deliverance,* the six (yin changing line) in the fifth place, the Wilhelm translation reads:

*If only the superior person can deliver themselves to virtue*
*It brings good fortune.*

*Proving to inferior people that they are in earnest.*[5]

Legge translates using the idea of a yin action:

> *The superior person (the ruler [being in the ruler's position at the fifth line]),*
>
> *Executing his function of removing (whatever is injurious to the idea of the hexagram),*
>
> *In which case there will be good fortune*
>
> *And confidence in him/her will be shown by even the small people.*[6]

Hexagram 63, *After Completion,* is the only hexagram with all of the yin and yang lines in their proper places. But, the yin-yang process is in place, as noted in the Wilhelm commentary: Finally, everything is in order when good fortune will prevail, but then disorder will soon follow.[7] Then follows its opposite, Hexagram 64, *Before Completion,* with the yin and yang lines all out of their proper places — order transitions to disorder, as the cycle through the 64 hexagrams gets ready to begin again.[8]

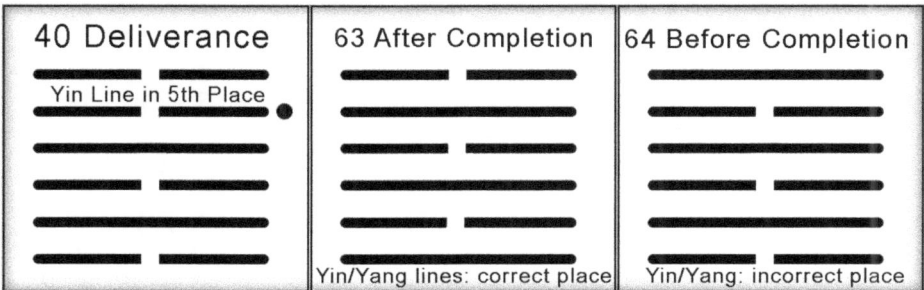

Hexagram Examples of Line Positions

## RULERS OF A HEXAGRAM

The supplemental commentaries, which may be included and which are included in Wilhelm, *The I Ching,* Book III, discuss the rulers that govern the operation of the hexagram. There are two, the constituting ruler and the governing ruler.

The constituting ruler governs the meaning of the hexagram and can be seen as the appointed or formal ruler. The line position for the constituting ruler depends on the makeup of the hexagram and how the lines interact.

The governing ruler is always a superior person. It is usually, but not always assigned to Line 5. The governing ruler and the constituting ruler may be one and the same line — this is a positive sign. When they are in different positions, it implies a non-alignment for the superior person's motives with the motives of some other powerful, but not necessarily positive force.

These come into play with the line position relationships — the interaction of the Confucian Five Relationships:
- Parent and Child — Affection — Filial Piety
- Ruler and Minister/Subject — Justice — Loyalty
- Husband and Wife — Harmony — Differentiation
- Elder and Younger Siblings —Affection — Precedence
- Friend and Friend — Trust — Honesty

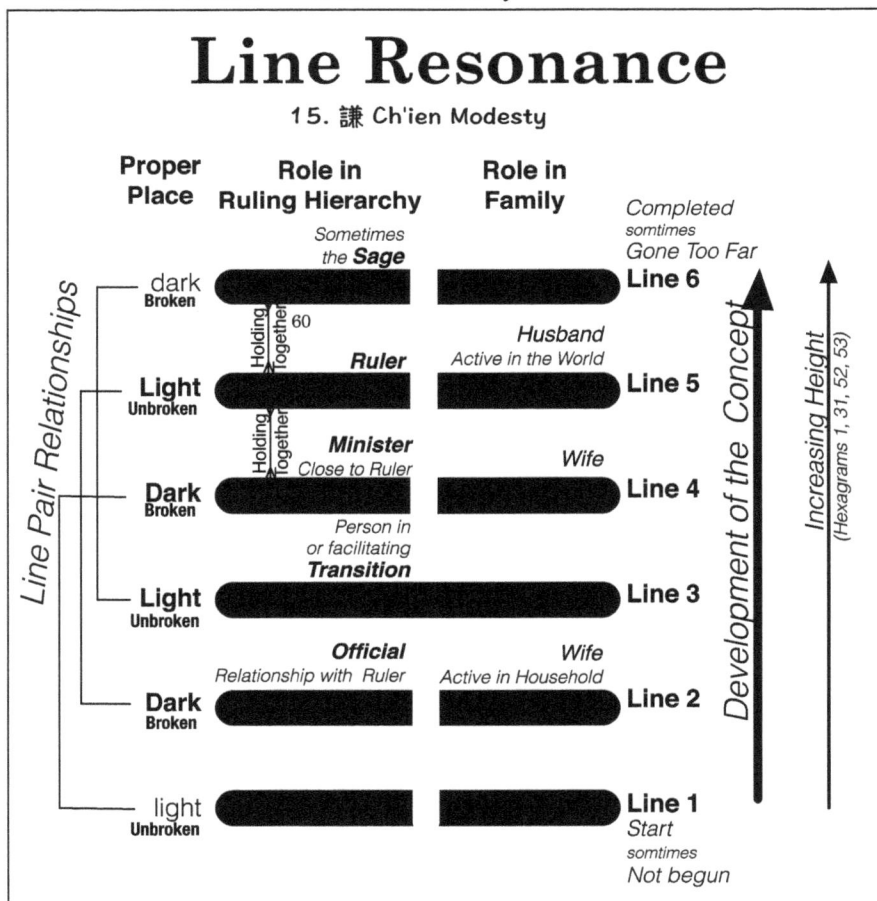

Figure 6.3 — Line Resonance

## ⟶⟶ LINE POSITION RELATIONS ⟶⟶

The resonance among the six line *positions* in a hexagram represents the Confucian relationships. Figure 6.3 shows these relationships that are assigned to the line positions. The ruler, that is the emperor or prince, is almost always assigned to the most auspicious position, Line 5. The minister is close to the ruler at Line 4. The official, in the center of the lower trigram at Line 2 seeks a relationship with the ruler, but this relationship may be disrupted by the lines between the official and the ruler, Lines 3 and 4.

Most of the time, a line's importance is its relationship with the fifth line. A somewhat sophisticated narrative from *The Great Treatise* shows the nuances of the line positions that come into play often in the commentaries:

> *The second and fourth lines are of the same quality (even numbered lines),*
>
> *but their positions with respect to the fifth line are different,*
>
> *Thus, the second is the object of much commendation,*
>
> *But, the fourth the subject of many apprehensions, from its nearness to the ruling fifth line.*
>
> *But for a line in a place of weakness it is not good to be far (from the occupant of the place of strength line 5), and what its subject should desire in such a case is (merely) to be without blame.*
>
> *The advantage (here) is in (the second line) being in the central place [in the bottom trigram].*
>
> *The third and fifth lines are of the same quality, (as being in odd places), The (occupant of) the third meets with many misfortunes,*
>
> *While the occupant of the fifth achieves much merit: This arises from one being in the noble position and the other in the mean.*
>
> *Are they occupied by the symbol of weakness? There will be peril. By that of strength? There will be victory.*[9]

Are they occupied by the symbol of weakness? There will be peril. By that of strength? There will be victory. This, together with Figure 6.3, gives a summary of what to expect in the commentaries:

- Line 5, the ruler, is generally the governing ruler. Getting this changing line is usually a prediction of good fortune.
- Line 4, the minister is generally in a position to influence the ruler in Line 5. Whether the minister has good or bad fortune depends on the ability to influence the ruler to realize the theme of the hexagram.
- For example, in Hexagram 12, *Standstill,* we see Line 4 having good fortune *if* the minister is called to restore order — which is the theme of the hexagram. However, in Hexagram 50, *The Sacred Cauldron,* the minister is not up to the task and has misfortune — spilling the sacrificial meal.
- Line 3 is usually, but not always, a line of misfortune, sometimes great sometimes small, being in a place of transition. It is often trying to make the same effort as Line 2, but with less hesitation.
- Line 2 almost always resonates with the ruler at Line 5. Its success in interacting with the ruler depends on the lines in between. A firm, yang Line 2 and a yielding Line 5 can lead to Line 2 becoming the ruler of the hexagram. Hexagram 4, *Youthful Folly,* a changing Line 2 reads, for example, *showing patience with the fools and admitting the goodness of women will be fortunate. The son is able to take the burden of the family.*
- Line 1 is outside hexagram story, so that it has nearly always just begun or not yet begun the development of the hexagram theme.
- Line 6, is the sage or someone going too far. Sometimes, as in Hexagram 50, *The Cauldron,* it is the pinnacle of success,w or Hexagram 36, *Darkening of the Light,* the search for light has gone too far, climbing to heaven only to fall back to earth.

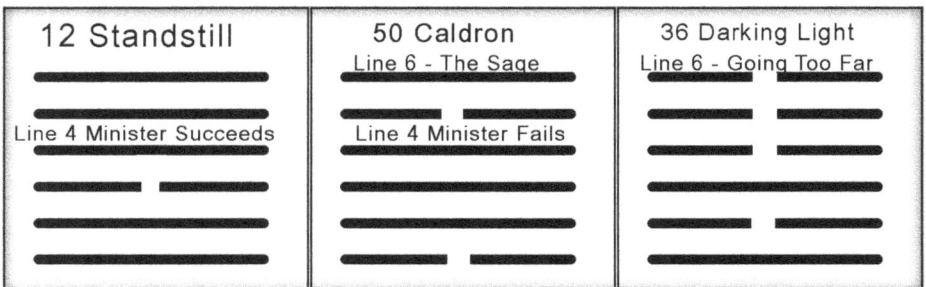

| 12 Standstill | 50 Caldron | 36 Darking Light |
|---|---|---|
| | Line 6 - The Sage | Line 6 - Going Too Far |
| Line 4 Minister Succeeds | Line 4 Minister Fails | |

Examples of Human Roles Related to Lines

Relationships in the Confucian world were seen as one of the most important ways to ensure ethics at all levels of society. In A.D. 79, *The Comprehensive Discussions in the White Tiger Hall* records this discussion in the imperial court:

> *Why must a king consult ministers?*
> *To get all the advice possible.*
> *If that is not enough to make a decision*
> *Then meditate*
> *If that doesn't work*
> *Then use the I Ching.*
> *Why must the sage who already has foresight*
> *Consult the I Ching.*
> *To make sure he doesn't act for his own benefit.*[11]

The lines sometimes represent physical height, 1 at or below ground and 6 in the sky. Hexagram 1, Heaven, the Creative, has lines that describe a dragon on the ground (or underground) at Line 1, to be arrogant enough to rise to the sky to lose touch with humanity at Line 6. Hexagram 52, *Keeping Still*, the lines discuss part of the body, starting at the toes in Line 1 and the jaws in Line 5.

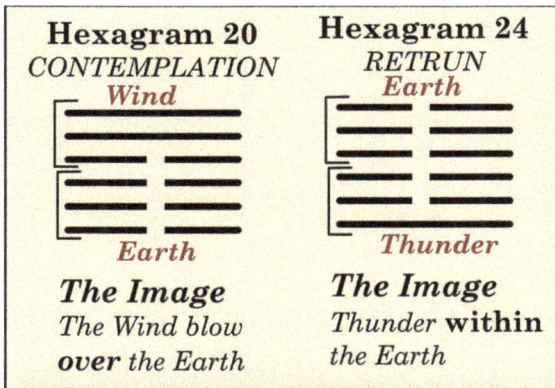

Top and Bottom Trigram Relationships Hexagram 20 and Hexagram 24

### ⚬⚬ LINE POSITION DEVELOPMENT OF IDEA ⚬⚬

The progress from Line 1 to Line 6 is to develop the idea or theme of the hexagram. This development is always present and is intertwined with the line position meaning discussed above. The Lines 2 through 5 are "within" the meaning, Line 5 being the perfected meaning. Lines 2 through 5 develop the theme of the hexagram. As previously mentioned, Line 1 is prior to, or just-about-to, the development of the hexagram's theme; Line 6 can be too far. Or, Line 6 can be the Sage standing above and beyond.

For example, Hexagram 53, *Development,* the lines tell of a wild goose flying to a mountain and then flying up the mountainside. By Line 5 the wild goose reaches the summit. Then at Line 6 the wild goose goes beyond to the heavens and dies, his feathers becoming sacred objects.

## ⟬⟭ MOVING TRIGRAMS ⟬⟭

The two trigrams that make up a hexagram are often in a positional relationship with each other when being described by the Image Statement or other commentary. The top trigram can be "on top," "over," or "above." In other hexagrams, the lower trigram can be "within" the upper trigram.

The unbroken line and broken lines have characteristics based on the Yin-Yang Principle. The yang line is light and firm, and the yin line is dark and receptive. The yang line wants to rise, and the yin line wants to fall or be a barrier to rising. Rising and falling lines give a different interpretation than one might expect from the interaction of the Heaven and Earth trigrams. *The Great Treatise* describes the interaction of lines:

> *The strong [yang] and the weak [yin] (lines) displace each other, and produces changes and transformations*[12]

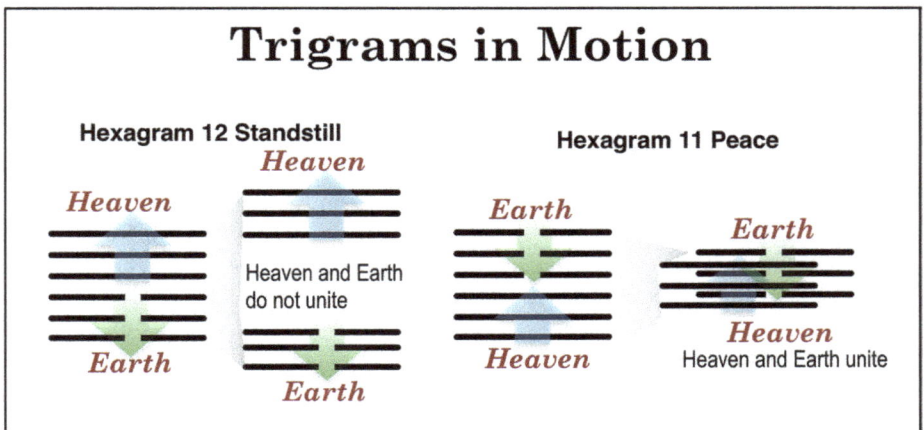

**Trigrams in Motion**

Trigrams in Motion Hexagram 12 and Hexagram 11

Since Heaven is made up of light lines that want to rise and Earth of dark lines that want to fall, when Heaven is above Earth they separate, the Image of Standstill; when Heaven is below the Earth, they come together, Peace.

Another example shows moving lines moving upward toward a promising future. For Hexagram 19, *Approach*: "The organization of the hexagram is altogether favorable. The two lines (light yang lines) entering from below and pushing upward give the structure of the hexagram its character."[13] On the other hand, Hexagram 23, *The Abysmal,* has yang lines that are "trapped" between yin lines, like water flowing in a narrow ravine.[14]

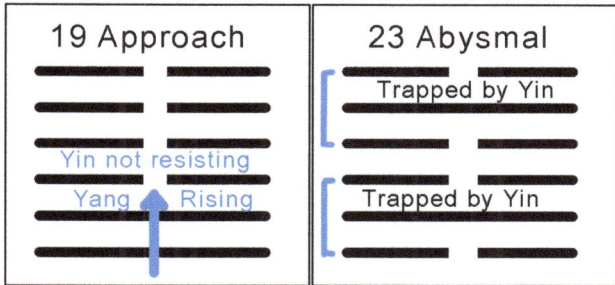

Yin and Yang Line Interaction within a Hexagram

### ⟫⟨ TRIGRAM IMAGERY ⟫⟨

Figure 6.4 illustrates how Thunder, ☳, and Water, ☵, combine. Thunder over Water, for Hexagram 40, provide deliverance. Why deliverance? For a farmer, deliverance from one of his greatest fears, drought, is rain — thunder announces the coming of rain, the coming of deliverance. In Hexagram 40, Thunder is *above* Water, *precedes* Water. The release of pent-up tension, the water held in the gray clouds suddenly released as rain creating, "the bud of the plants and trees that produce the various fruits begin to burst. Great indeed are the phenomena in the time intimated by Deliverance."[15] For other hexagrams, such as Hexagram 24, Thunder, ☳, laying below Earth ☷, lies *inside/within* the earth — the roar of a volcano about to erupt.

The Interior or Nuclear Trigrams, which overlap in Hexagram 40, are Water and Fire. (Discussed in the additional commentary in Book III of Wilhelm.) The top and bottom line drop away, the two lines in the center shared.[16]

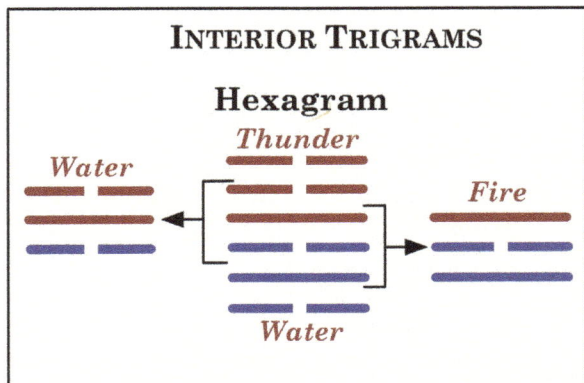

Interior/Nuclear Hexagrams — Hexagram 40

Over time Chinese philosophers have matched trigrams to family members, body parts, animals, directions, and the cosmology prevalent in middle-ages China. In addition to the Image Statement, the commentaries may deal with other correlations with the trigrams. There are also correlations of family relationships, compass directions, animals, and parts of the body that will sometimes come into play.[17] These are shown in Figure 6.5. The particular correlation which is brought forth to a hexagram depends on the context of the hexagram.

As you read the *I Ching*, in your time, place, and circumstances, the long-standing tradition in Chinese scholarship is that your understanding arises both through the text and the imagery. Wang Bi says that images are for comprehending the idea, words explain the images — but don't get stuck on either the words or the image — keep searching for the idea.[18]

~~~

*When images seen in Nature,*
*Meet mean.*
*Our mind then dances,*
*We know.*

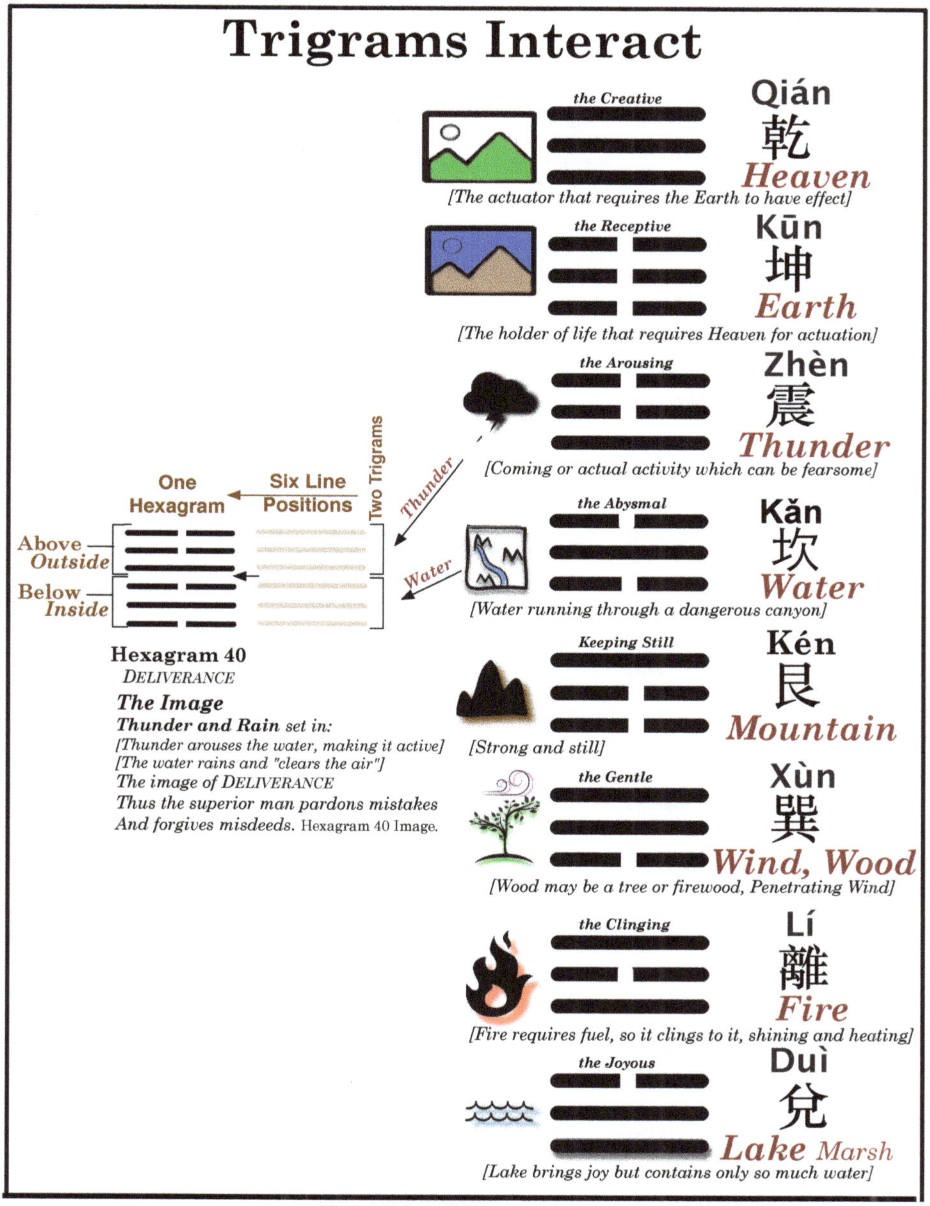

# Trigrams Interact

**the Creative**

**Qián**

乾

*Heaven*

[The actuator that requires the Earth to have effect]

**the Receptive**

**Kūn**

坤

*Earth*

[The holder of life that requires Heaven for actuation]

**the Arousing**

**Zhèn**

震

*Thunder*

[Coming or actual activity which can be fearsome]

**the Abysmal**

**Kǎn**

坎

*Water*

[Water running through a dangerous canyon]

**Keeping Still**

**Kén**

艮

*Mountain*

[Strong and still]

**the Gentle**

**Xùn**

巽

*Wind, Wood*

[Wood may be a tree or firewood, Penetrating Wind]

**the Clinging**

**Lí**

離

*Fire*

[Fire requires fuel, so it clings to it, shining and heating]

**the Joyous**

**Duì**

兌

*Lake* Marsh

[Lake brings joy but contains only so much water]

**One Hexagram**    **Six Line Positions**    **Two Trigrams**

*Thunder*

*Water*

Above — *Outside*

Below — *Inside*

**Hexagram 40**

DELIVERANCE

**The Image**

**Thunder and Rain** set in:
[Thunder arouses the water, making it active]
[The water rains and "clears the air"]
The image of DELIVERANCE
Thus the superior man pardons mistakes
And forgives misdeeds. Hexagram 40 Image.

Figure 6.4 — Trigrams Interact

# Eight Trigrams Bā guà 八卦

| | Qián* the Creative | South |
| | 乾 Ch'ien** *Strong attibute* | Horse |
| | *Heaven* *Father relationship* | Head |
| | Kūn *the Receptive* | North |
| | 坤 K'un *Devoted, Yielding* | Ox |
| | *Earth* *Mother* | Stomach |
| | Zhèn *the Arousing* | NE |
| | 震 Chên *Inciting Movement* | Dragon |
| | *Thunder* *First Son* | Foot |
| | Kăn *the Abysmal* | West |
| | 坎 K'an *Dangerous* | Pig |
| | *Water* *Second Son* | Ear |
| | Kén *Keeping Still* | NW |
| | 艮 Gèn *Resting* | Dog |
| | *Mountain* *Third Son* | Hand |
| | Xùn *the Gentle* | SW |
| | 巽 Sun *Penetrating* | Cock |
| | *Wind, Wood* *First Daughter* | Thigh |
| | Lí *the Clinging* | SW |
| | 離 Li *Light-giving* | Pig |
| | *Fire* *Second Daughter* | Ear |
| | *Lightening* | |
| | Duì *the Joyous* | SE |
| | 兌 Tui *Joyful* | Sheep |
| | *Lake Marsh* *Third Daughter* | Mouth |

* Pinyin - Used in newer translations
* * Wade-Giles Romanization - Used in Wilhelm/Baynes and older translations

Figure 6.5 — Trigram Attributes

Hexagram Astrology Design

Calligraphy and Dictionary

# 7

# WORDS OF LAYERED MEANING

*The Master said —*
*The written characters are not the full meaning of words,*
*And words are not the full expression of ideas;*
*The sages made their images to bring forth their ideas;*
*Created hexagrams to apply them to your circumstances;*
*Appended their explanations*
*To give the full expression of their words*
So Says *The Great Treatise*[1]

The ancient words used in the Judgments were as understandable to the people of Zhou as "It was just a walk in the park" to an American today. But, upon closer examination, the meaning of this metaphor would be lost on "the man from Mars" who was using an English dictionary as his only guide. The meaning could be made clearer if you explained: "It was as *easy to accomplish* as a walk in the park." But the Martian might have to flip the pages and look up "park" with its multiple meanings:

1) a green area in a city town, used for recreation and relaxation,

2) an area set aside for a specific kind of use such as an industrial park,

3) to bring a vehicle to a stop where it can be left,

4) a gear shift position in which the gears are locked.

It might be helpful to the Martian that "park" refers to the first definition because everyone knows that a park is almost always flat, has nice paths, and grassy areas and is easy to walk in.

## ⊷ THREE LAYERS OF MEANING ⊷

Fortunately, like most ancient texts, the *I Ching* has a history of scholarship that helps in getting a sense of what it meant and what it means today. The words and phrases below are commented upon at three time periods of the *I Ching*'s philosophical development:

**1.** *Zhouyi* The period around between 1000 B.C. and 300 B.C., when only the oldest layers of the *I Ching* were part of the text;

**2. Ten Wings:** The period 300 B.C. through the beginning of the twentieth century, when the Confucian philosophy arose, Ten Wings were composed, and Neo-Daoists developed more sophisticated meanings for the words and images.[2]

**3. Self-Awareness:** The period when the *I Ching* was thought about and used in light of modern science and psychology.

The assignment of meanings to words, phrases, Judgments, and Line Statements evolved continuously; so these three categories are *rough approximations*[3] presented to give a sense of the layers-of-meaning that exist on each page of the *I Ching* today. The bold step of assigning specific books to each of these three categories is a step the authors of those books may well not agree with — it is only done to aid in giving a sense of the layers-of-meaning and is definitely *not* a comment on the literary or developmental history of the *I Ching*.

### How I Use the Three Layers

My experience with the *I Ching* is that a reading can be directed at the material world, my activities in society, relationships with people, business projects, and the like. It can also be directed at my internal life, dealing with emotions, striving for the right mind set. It can also be dealing with my spiritual quest, for the calm and generous, for the connection with the divine.

The three levels that in a gross way represent major steps in the development of the *I Ching* are, to me, three possible contexts for the Sage to be speaking, beginning with practical solutions to day-to-day problems.

The Ten Wings added an ethical interpretation to the *I Ching* that has helped me deal with day to day problems in an ethical as well as a practical way. The Meditative has helped with my inner life. It dawned on me that I could interpret the *Zhouyi's* original focus on appropriate sacrifice as a way at the time for people to attempt to have a relationship with the Divine. Now, I can replace "sacrifice" with "attempt to understand the will of the Divine."

The assignment of texts and the layout of the three categories are:

1. ***Zhouyi***. The *Zhouyi*'s literal meaning in the Old Chinese in which it was written and what the words meant at the time.

   The sources for the meaning of the characters is the Doctor of Philosophy Dissertation by Richard Alan Kunst, *The Original Yijing: A Text, Phonetic Transcription, Translation, and Indexes, with Sample Glosses*.[4] Also used are translations of Received Text of the *Zhouyi* by Richard Rutt and of the *Mawangui* text by Edward Shaughnessy, titled, *I Ching, The Classic of Changes*.

   An example of the presentation that will be used for the word-by-word commentary:
   - **Superior Person:** 君子 *jūnzǐ*　　　　君 Noble person 子 Son/child
     ***Zhouyi***
     *Noble [Kunst]* • *Gentleman [Shaughnessy]* • *Prince [Rutt]*.

2. **Ten Wings**. The meaning of the *I Ching* in the context of the Ten Wings as a synergy of Daoist relationship with nature and Confucian morality and outlook.

   The sources used include Legge's translation. Legge translated the *I Ching* as a scholarship exercise using the advice of late nineteenth-century Chinese scholars. *The I Ching* by Wilhelm. Wilhelm was a fan of Chinese culture and the *I Ching*, and was a friend of Carl Jung, who probably influenced some of his translation choices and his commentary. Lynn's *The Classic of Change* brings in Wang Bi's commentary.

   Example:

   **Ten Wings:**
   *Superior Man [Wilhelm]* • *Superior Man [Legge]* • *Noble [Lynn]*.

3. **Self-Awareness:**
   The psychological meaning of the *I Ching* with an emphasis on its use in conjunction with mediation or a modern outlook.

   The sources used are primarily Carol Anthony's books especially her 1988 *Guide to the I Ching*; *I Ching, Walking Your Path Creating Your Future* by Hilary Barrett, and Margaret Pearson's *The Original I Ching*, one of the most recent translations by a scholar who understands Chinese and has studied the history of the *I Ching*. Carol Anthony is the only reference in which the author did not do a translation, but an interpretation. Carol, and later her co-writer Anna Moog, based her books from an extensive diary based on using the Wilhelm *I Ching*. The words I chose for her are my interpretation of her commentary.

Example:

**Self-Awareness:**
*Superior Self [Anthony]* • *One Worthy of Power [Pearson]* • *Noble One [Barrett]*

## WORD-BY-WORD

In the list below the first line will begin with common terms found in the I Ching, followed by the Chinese characters, followed by Pinyin Romanization.

- **Superior Person:** 君子 *jūnzǐ*          君 Noble person 子 Son/child

    ***Zhouyi:***
    *Noble [Kunst]*[5] • *Gentleman [Shaughnessy]* • *Prince [Rutt].*
    when the *Zhouyi* was written a *jūnzǐ* was an inherited position — at least after the surviving warlord who started the inheritance line. Thus, *junzi*, the son of a ruler came to mean a descendant of the ruler. Rutt commented on his choice of the word *prince*: "prince as in old Russia, implying no more than a general, rather than a particular claim to blue blood and high ideals."[6]

    **Ten Wings:**
    *Superior Man [Wilhelm]* • *Superior Man [Legge]* • *Noble Man [Lynn]*
    Confucius and followers redefined the term *junzi* as a person of virtue, with comments such as "If the superior man abandons virtue, how can he fulfill the requirements of that name."[7] *Junzi*, the superior person, is found in all of the Image Statements, saying what the Superior Person, that is a person who embodies the Confucian virtues, would or should do in the situation at hand.

    **Self-Awareness:**
    *Superior self [Anthony]* • *One Worthy of Power [Pearson]* • *Noble One [Barrett]*

Anthony used the Wilhelm translation and often refers to his rendition of "Superior Man." Pearson notes Chinese pronouns are gender neutral and that 子 as with most, but not all, Chinese words are gender-neutral. After much debate for a pronoun such as s/he, she ended up with a gender neutral phrase with variations that reflect, although she does not state it, the Confucian meaning.[8]

Anthony describes the person as one who serves the high and the good, and is obedient to the Sage.[9]

The superior person can also be Freud's Super-Ego which he described as the ego-ideal, the ideal will, the conscience.[10] Or, it can be tapping into Carl Jung's Collective Unconscious.[11]

The superior person in Judaism, Christianity, and Islam traditions is obedient to the Will of God. A Daoist could interpret it as obediently following the Dao. A Buddhist superior person is a sincere follower of the Eight-fold path, the path for this specific situation, time, and place revealed by the Sage, the *I Ching*.[12]

- **Great Person:** 大人 *dà rén*　　　　　　　　　大 Big 人 Person

### *Zhouyi:*
*Big Man [Kunst]* • *Great Man [Shaughnessy]* • *Great Men [Rutt]*.
The meaning of "Great Person" is uncertain, probably the diviner, the sage interpreting the reading, also may be one of high social status.[13]

### Ten Wings:
*Great Man [Wilhelm]* • *Great Man [Legge]* • *Great Man [Lynn]*.
The Great Man may be someone in authority or an impartial advisor. Also, they could be someone not of the ruling or educated class, but good and generous, embodying the Confucian virtues.

### Self-Awareness:
*The Sage [Anthony]* • *Advisor Greater Than You [Pearson]* • *Great People [Barrett]*.
Anthony: Here you are seeking the wisdom of the Universe [or the Divine] by consulting someone wiser than yourself, some other person, or your higher self when that self is intent being in synchronicity with the grand plan of the Cosmos.

Pearson: Seek advice from someone wiser than yourself even if you are a king.

- **Inferior Person:** 小人 *dà rén*                        小 Small 人 Person

  *Zhouyi:*
  *Small Man [Kunst] • Little Man [Shaughnessy] • Small Men [Rutt].*
  A peasant, uneducated person.

  **Ten Wings:**
  *Small Man/Inferior Man [Wilhelm] • Small Man [Legge] • Petty Man [Lynn].*
  A self-serving person not driven by a moral compass.

  **Self-Awareness:**
  *Inferior Man [Anthony] • Petty Person [Pearson] • Small People [Barrett].*
  The ego, the ego-driven impulses.

- **Supreme Success:** 亨元 *hēng yuán*                亨 Treat 元 Grand

  OR [Hexagram Name] 十 元

  *Zhouyi:*
  *Grand Treat [Kunst] • Beneficial to Determine [Shaughnessy] • Supreme Offering [Rutt].*
  Success is in the context of choosing correct sacrifice (a grand treat) and the right time to sacrifice, a critical issue 3,000 years ago when the outcome of the action being contemplated depended upon the effects of hidden forces, the sacrifice being a means to influence those forces. Kunst states that there is evidence that 亨 hēng (treat) is a specialized divinatory term. Grant Treat means a sacrificial offering has been accepted or will be accepted by the heavens.[14]

  **Ten Wings:**
  *Supreme Success [Wilhelm] • Great and Penetrating/Great Progress and Success [Legge] • Fundamentally and Prevalence [Lynn].*[15]
  亨 *hēng* has come to mean prosperous. Success will be in your contemplated endeavor, or you will have success materially and financially. Success depends upon following the advice given in the hexagram reading.

  **Self-Awareness:**
  *The time is right for change and growth [Anthony] • Supreme Success/Progress that Flows[Pearson] • Creating Success [Barrett].*
  Success in personal growth is possible — it has not happened in most instances, but the Universe around you — and you — are ready to un-

dertake the journey. Success in your inner journey is likely if you follow the advice in the hexagram reading.

- **Success:** 亨 *hēng*                                        亨 Treat

  ***Zhouyi:***
  *Treat [Kunst] • Beneficial to Determine [Shaughnessy] • Favorable [Rutt].*
  Success can be about an offering that is accepted or the achievement of your contemplated endeavor.

  **Ten Wings:**
  *Success [Wilhelm] • Success [Legge] • Prevalence [Lynn].*
  Achievement of your contemplated endeavor.

  Also, Wilhelm sometimes used the word "success" to translate phrases that did not include *hēng* — but the phrases he is translating have the same prognosis as "Achievement of a contemplated endeavor."

  **Self-Awareness:**
  *The time is right for change and growth [Anthony] • Supreme Success/ Progress which Flows[Pearson] • Creating Success [Barrett].*
  Inner calmness and truth will bring success.

- **Favorable:** 利 lì                                       利 Favorable

  ***Zhouyi:***
  *Favorable [Kunst] • Beneficial [Shaughnessy] • Favorable [Rutt].*
  A moderately good situation, but less so the Good Fortune.

  **Ten Wings:**
  *Furthers [Wilhelm] • Advantageous [Legge] • Beneficial [Lynn].*[16]
  Doing what is suggested by the reading will move things in a beneficial direction.

  **Self-Awareness:**
  *Steady and Quiet [Anthony] • Effective [Pearson] • Fruitful [Barrett].*
  A calm mind moving in the direction suggested by the reading is useful.

- **Good Fortune:** 吉 *jí*                                 吉 Auspicious
  吉 *jí may be preceded by characters* 元 *yuan (Supreme) or* 大 *dà (Big/ Very) or* 終 *zhōng (Ultimate).*

*Zhouyi:*
*Auspicious [Kunst]* • *Auspicious [Shaughnessy]* • *Auspicious [Rutt].*
As a matter of luck or timing, things will go your way, sometimes conditioned on having taken some action.

**Ten Wings:**
*Good Fortune [Wilhelm]* • *Good Fortune [Legge]* • *Good Fortune [Lynn].*
Good Fortune is yours given the current situation or some action that is about to occur.

**Self-Awareness:**
*Maintain the Correct Path [Anthony]* • *Good Fortune [Pearson]* • *Good Fortune [Barrett]*
The idea of luck all but disappears. It is time to focus on maintaining the middle path and getting rid of ego-inspired narratives.

• **Misfortune:** ⚠ *xiōng*                                    ⚠ Ominous

*Zhouyi:*
*Ominous [Kunst]* • *Inauspicious [Shaughnessy]* • *Disaster [Rutt].*
Rutt notes that in the levels of misfortunes, *xiong* is the worst, which is why he chose *disaster* and reserved *inauspicious* for a less severe omen.

The situation is such that difficulties are unavoidable and that adverse outcomes are certain — although the reading may show that change will quickly follow that passed by the bad times.

**Ten Wings:**
*Misfortune [Wilhelm]* • *Evil [Legge]* • *Misfortune [Lynn].*
Misfortune and difficulty will be your lot even if you do the correct things.

**Self-Awareness:**
*The correct path in the face of adversity [Anthony]* • *Misfortune [Pearson]* • *Pitfall [Barrett]*
When engaged with another or in some situation, and there is no progress on their part or in the situation at hand, it is time to detach your ego from insisting someone else behave as you think they should. The adversary could be internal, the construct of your own ego.

- **No Misfortune/No Blame: 無咎** *wú jiù*          無 No 咎 Misfortune

    *Zhouyi:*

    *No Misfortune [Kunst] • No Trouble [Shaughnessy] • No Misfortune [Rutt].*

    A somewhat negative indication. There is difficulty that is overcome or likely to be overcome. *Wú* implies to not take the contemplated action.

    **Ten Wings:**

    *No Blame [Wilhelm] • No Mistake/No Error [Legge] • Misfortune [Lynn].*

    A somewhat negative indication. Things go wrong, but they are overcome if the reader acts as the Superior Person. As *The Great Treatise* says, you are in the position to correct mistakes in the proper way.[17]

    **Self-Awareness:**

    *Detach from engaging another ego [Anthony] • Without Blame, implying a misstep or misunderstanding for which you will recover [Pearson] •No Mistake [Barrett].*

- **Distress/Humiliation: 吝** *lìn*                              吝 Distress

    *Zhouyi:*

    *Distress [Kunst] • Distress [Shaughnessy] • Distress [Rutt].*
    The situation at hand causes distress.

    **Ten Wings:**

    *Humiliation [Wilhelm] • Distress [Legge] • Distress [Lynn].*
    The situation at hand causes distress. *The Great Treatise* says this is a minor imperfection.[18]

    **Self-Awareness:**

    *Situation where it would be easy to go in the wrong direction [Anthony] • Dangerous situation [Pearson] • Shame [Barrett]*

- **Perseverance: 貞** *zhēn*                                   貞 Determined

    *Zhouyi:*

    *Determined [Kunst] • Determination [Shaughnessy] • Augury [Rutt].*
    A determined effort to see things through.

    **Ten Wings:**

    *Perseverance [Wilhelm] • Firmness [Legge] • Determination [Lynn].*
    貞 zhēn also developed the meaning of chaste, pure. Perseverance becomes seeing things through with pure motives.

**Self-Awareness:**

*Maintain a detached attitude [Anthony] • Persisting [Pearson] • Constancy [Barrett].*

Seeing things through with pure motives is accomplished with a detached attitude.

- **Perseverance Furthers:** 利貞 *lì zhēn*    利 Favorable 貞 Determined

  ***Zhouyi:***

  *Favorable determination [Kunst] • Beneficial Determination [Shaughnessy] • Favorable Augury [Rutt].*

  A determined effort to see things through should produce good results.

  **Ten Wings:**

  *Perseverance Furthers [Wilhelm] • Advantageousness depends upon being Firm [Legge] • Beneficial Determination [Lynn].*

  貞 *zhēn* also developed the meaning of chaste, pure. So, Perseverance with pure motives should produce good results.

  **Self-Awareness:**

  *A detached attitude is beneficial [Anthony] • Persistence Effective [Pearson] • Constancy Bears Fruit [Barrett].*

  Maintaining a detached attitude and a determination to see self-development through will yield benefits.

- **Nothing that would further:**    無攸利 *wú yōu lì*
                                      無 No 攸 That for which 利 Favorable

  ***Zhouyi:***

  *There is nothing for which this is favorable [Kunst] • There is no place favorable [Shaughnessy] • Nothing favorable [Rutt].*

  The situation or contemplated plan to act has no favorable outcome.

  **Ten Wings:**

  *Nothing that would further [Wilhelm] • In no wise advantageous [Legge] • Nothing that is fitting [Lynn].*

  The situation or contemplated plan to act has no favorable outcome.

  **Self-Awareness:**

  *Maintain individual loyalty to the truth [Anthony] • In these circumstances, nothing will prosper [Pearson] • No Direction Bears Fruit [Barrett].*

  A situation which should be avoided before getting into it. If one is stuck in an unfortunate situation, one should maintain loyalty to their inner truth.

- **Captive/Trust:** 孚 *fú*                                                  孚 Capture

   孚 fú — Fu meant captive in the time of the *Zhouyi*, but came to mean trust: merging *Ren*, 人, to the character 孚 for 俘, also pronounced fú means captive in modern Chinese.[19] This is probably the most extreme change in meaning it as trust, sincerity, or confidence instead of captive. The *Mawangdui* Text replaces 孚 fú from the Received Text with the merged character 復, which Shaughnessy translates as "return."[20]

   ### *Zhouyi:*
   *Captive [Kunst] • Return [Shaughnessy] • Captives [Rutt].*

   ### Ten Wings:
   *Truthfully [Wilhelm] • Sincere (& honest appeal) [Legge] • Sincere [Lynn].*
   Trust, truth, and sincerity sometimes in the context of an appeal from a captive or someone appealing to someone in power.

   ### Self-Awareness:
   *Correct Attitude. True, as in authentic [Anthony] • Sincere [Pearson] • Truth [Barrett]*

- **Helper:** 侯 *hóu*                                                   侯 Feudal Prince

   ### *Zhouyi:*
   *Feudal Prince [Kunst] • Lord [Shaughnessy] • Lord [Rutt].*
   Seen from the viewpoint of a King or Emperor, this is the time to appoint Nobles that are loyal to you to control and expand territory.

   ### Ten Wings:
   *Helper [Wilhelm] • Lord [Legge] • Chief [Lynn].*
   The task being performed or contemplated cannot be accomplished successfully without help, which should be done while being willing to participate and lead with an attitude of humility.

   ### Self-Awareness:
   *Help through following the way of the Sage [Anthony] • Helpers to whom responsibility is delegated [Pearson] Help comes from calling upon your higher self in the midst of chaos. • Feudal Lords — helpers human or otherwise [Barrett].*

- **Cross the Great Water:** 涉大川 *shè dà chuān*

涉 Wade across 大 Big 川 River

### *Zhouyi:*

*Wade across a Big River [Kunst]* • *Ford the Great River [Shaughnessy]* • *Ford a Big River [Rutt].*

In warfare and in social situations such as a potential marriage, this indicates a perilous venture and the potential for great rewards. At the time of the Zhou crossing the Yellow River or other large rivers in China involved both the risk of crossing and the risk associated with finding an enemy on the other side, since the river often marked the boundary between kingdoms.

### Ten Wings:

*Cross the Great War [Wilhelm]* • *Cross the Great Stream [Legge]* • *Cross the Great Rivers [Lynn].*

It is time to take action for the benefit of all.

### Self-Awareness:

*Discipline your inferior self [Anthony]* • *Cross the Great Rivers [Pearson]* • *Cross the Great River — Commit to go as far as you can towards transition and take the risk [Barrett].*

This is the time in your inner life to take the next step in your mental and spiritual development, often a risky step that offers great rewards.

## ·───· MEANING OF SOME MYSTERIOUS WORDS ·───·

**Three Days** — A short time.

**Seventh Day** — A new cycle begins (after the six steps of a hexagram have completed)

**Ten Days** — The length of a week in ancient China, the idea of beginning to end. The first day of the week is literally the "to go" day. Some translations such as Wilhelm will use the "starting point" for the first day and for the last day "the change day."[21]

**Ten Years** — A long time.

**Lǐ or Mile** — *Li* is currently 500 meters but has varied over the centuries. It is sometimes translated to mile. A hundred Li is a long distance.

**Western Mountain** — The place of the family shrine.

**Dragon** — The creative force, full of energy, with auspicious powers (from the time of Confucius and onwards).[32]

**Cauldron** 鼎 Dǐng (Ting Wade-Giles) — A sacred cooking vessel. Can be the Sage of the *I Ching* speaking of itself.

**Tail in the Water** — A mistake because of incautious or hurried behavior.

**Pigs and Fishes** — Cannot be convinced of anything if you speak to them, or indication of wealth.

**Geese** — Geese migrating signals the coming of winter, the end of the monsoon season, the time for making war is beginning and the fighting men must leave home. There were songs about this: "The wild geese fly along the land; when the prince goes back, it means that my lord will not return."[23]

**Yellow** — The color of royal garments and within the Five Elements (similar to the Greek Four Elements), the color of the Earth.

## TRANSLATION MATTERS

*I have it in my mind, a thought, with its nuances and feelings; I wish you to know it. Without effort the emotions of my mind announce themselves on my face, but the content I must arrange into symbols. I speak those symbols and call them words. Oh! Are you not present? I must write those symbols called words with the strokes of my pen, hoping you understand the true content of my mind, hence, when you read them.*

This is a note on the issues with translation and to suggest that, with the tools this book has provided:

1. It is unavoidable that the translator's thoughts, wisdom, and decisions will be in the translated text you read.

2. Readers must mentally transform the cultural context of the original ancient author and the translator and the modern commenter to their own culture context.

While it is not necessary to dwell on these points, it will sometimes be helpful to have them in the back of your mind.[24] The *I Ching*, and any ancient text, is best read with an unhurried approach, letting the text settle in your mind before finally concluding what it means. It might be well to think of it as interpreting a dream since you are attempting to interact with the thoughts of the ancient authors or even, as some might say, the numinous world.[25]

Thoughts and wisdom held in an author's mind get onto the written page. The different word choices and meaning interpretations of the *I Ching* are driven by the same issues as other ancient texts such as the Jewish Tanakh; Christian Bible; Hindu Upanishads, Vedas, and Bhagavad Gita; and Buddhist Pāli, Kangyur, and Taishō Tripiṭaka Canons.

#### ⤜∞⤛ USING WRITTEN LANGUAGE TO COMMUNICATE THOUGHTS AND WISDOM ⤜∞⤛

Ancient philosophical and religious texts have the limitations inherent in written language as well as challenges due to the distance in culture and era from our own.

Language and Culture

There is a difference in speaking to a person and writing. Speech usually occurs when people communicating share a mutual context, the culture they live in, the history of their relationship, common idioms, references to events with which they are both familiar. Further, the emphasis in spoken language and indeed the style of language differs from written language.[26]

For example, if someone says, "Will you please get the orange juice out of the refrigerator," the "mutual context" is the speaker assuming the listener knows there is only one refrigerator, that the orange juice is in the refrigerator, and the listener knows where to put orange juice when they retrieve it, which might be to hand it to the speaker, put in on a counter, or put it some other place which both people know is the intention. The written word seldom has this kind of context outside of a novel.

Then there is the matter of emphasis, "Will you PLEEEASE get the orange juice out of the refrigerator," resulting in a whole different social interaction when the word "please" is emphasized and stretched out. This difference would not be evident in the written sentence.

On the other hand, written language can be reread and studied. Writing usually includes a richer vocabulary and is more syntactically complex, allowing writing to more easily express complex ideas.

Written Chinese consists of ideograms. The modern Chinese language combines pictograms, symbols, and sound symbols, which evolved from the ancient Chinese in which the *I Ching* and its commentaries are written.

In Chinese culture the written language is not only related to expressing ideas, but it is also art. The act of writing a character, the calligraphy, is considered an important art form. Further, there is a symbolic connection of characters with nature and everyday objects: "The first characters were very much like primitive pictures representing those things necessary for the divination of oracles and for day-to-day transactions in a primitive culture: the animals owned or hunted; the protection of territory; the weather; the body; the land; the family." Of course as the language got richer, the language began "joining words" for example, joining words for "speak" and "pen" became "book."[27]

Specifically, Chinese characters can be:

1. pictures,

2. symbols [For example, 1 or the word "one"],

3. sound-loans [a character with the same sound that has a different meaning. For example, if you used Tail for the word Tale],

4. sound-meaning compounds, [Joining two characters where one has the right sound and the other the right meaning. For example, Knight = Night + Armored-Horseman],

5. meaning-meaning compounds [made by joining two symbols and together create the meaning. For example, Saw + Blade],

6. and reclarified compounds [Joining two characters where one clarifies the other one. For example, Pen + Ball Point].[28]

Old Chinese Script

A homophone is the same written symbol to represent two words that sound the same but mean different things like "I" and "eye."A homograph is a homophone that is the same word as well, such as "band" [as in rubber band] and "band" [as in a group of musicians]. Chinese has many more homophones than the English language. Sometimes with a fairly long list of possible English words attached to a Chinese character.

The Chinese language was evolving when the *I Ching* was written, with the "Old Text Version" being transmitted in the first century B.C. The language became more organized later. 540 common semantic "categories" were codified in the second century A.D. with further simplification in A.D. 1615 to the 214 common semantic radicals used in modern Chinese. The thrust of all of this is that the Chinese from which the English texts were translated had:

1. Several possible English translations that, because of the concise text, often does not provide enough context to resolve the meaning. Indeed, several commentators note the dense nature of the text encourages the use of imagination, self-knowledge, and the interaction with the text to the situation at hand — in some cases ambiguity was the original author's intent.

2. Homophones (puns) and Joined Words create connections that are specific to the language and affect *I Ching* Judgment or *Commentary*. A pun in English would not make sense in another language since they are only connected due to the spoken English language — so it is with Chinese homophones and joined words.

But, so far, we have only dealt with the original written text. Other factors need to be considered about what was "meant" by the authors.

What is our current understanding of how the authors of the ancient texts formed their thoughts and transmitted them to written text? The cultural context can be critical even with a common language. The meaning of words changes with time. If I said that I saw a movie called *Gay Divorcee*, it would be good to mention the year since in 1934 the word meant "carefree" or "promiscuous," not necessarily sexual orientation as it does today. "Gay" was introduced into the English language in the twelfth century but suddenly changed meaning in the late twentieth century. We have already seen this as "captive" became "trust" in Chinese.

*The cultural context and even the meaning of words change as history progresses.*

The *I Ching* uses rhyming, puns, and references to common sayings, such as "step on a crack, break your mother's back" to enhance the emotional impact of words — a device called word-magic.[29] Particular to divination systems, to present intentional ambiguity by its original authors to the use of rhyme to connect seemingly meaningless connections to lead to an omen-symbol.[30]

The enhanced emphasis on works in popular music is a similar device to make memorable philosophical statements such as, "Freedom's just another word for nothin' left to lose," belted out by Janis Joplin in *Me and Bobby McGee.*

—∞— TRANSLATING THE WRITTEN WORDS TO ANOTHER LANGUAGE —∞—

Translation starts with the Chinese language in both its words and syntax. Translation involves the translator deciding, "How far to go." Does the translator translate word-for-word, which can often end up with a strange syntax that does not conform to the rules of the translated language? Does the translator take the word-for-word and change the word order to meet syntax rules?

Even for word-for-word, does the translator need to add or remove "articles" such as "the"? Or does the translator begin to decide what the author meant and to what extent? Something as simple as deciding if a Chinese noun is singular or plural based on its context may be called for. Or, does the translator take it further, focusing on trying to have translated text transmit the "understanding" or "spirit." This may involve changing or adding to the original text to do their own *mental cultural transformation.*

What to translate? The Chinese source documents used for the *I Ching* evolved over a period of one thousand years before it was "canonized" as one of the Confucian classics. It started as a divination manual with just unbroken and broken lines around 3,500 years ago, had text written for each hexagram around 3,000 years ago, and had commentary added during the time of Confucius about 2,000 years ago. Yet, the earliest extant (writing still in existence) is A.D. 249. This means that the source text translation is the result of oral traditions being written, transcribed several times, and possibly modified.

By comparison, there is a 200 to 300 year gap from the events recorded in the Christian New Testament and the earliest copy of anything being written about it. For a long time most translations of the Bible were based on 1) a Greek source, known as *Textus Receptus,* compiled by Erasmus in A.D. 1516, had many typographical errors, and 2) the Vulgate, a Latin translation of Greek texts which were lost in time. This was the case for the New Testament through the mid-twentieth century.[31]

New sources were found in the twentieth century — now there are several New Testament versions which are more carefully translated. Thus, the "scripture" which millions of people believed as a true and accurate account changed over time — not significantly, but in details some thought were important.

Yes, there have been many vigorous and sometimes fatal arguments about some of the text of the New Testament. Even so, when one compares the various versions, the words for Jesus of Nazareth are there for one to contemplate and have a remarkably consistent message as it emerges from the fog of translation and source text variations.

What this means is that most ancient texts go through this kind of retranslation, restudy of its words, but the core messages and themes seem to remain constant through the process. The *I Ching* is such a book.

The *I Ching* is more problematic because it is cryptic compared to many ancient texts that are narratives, such as the Christian New Testament and *Bhagavad Gita*. The narrative form provides more of a context in the text itself for the translator than the short statements in the *I Ching* — and sometimes context is everything.

Added to this, ancient texts were transcribed going through the hands of scribes, which leads to the possibility that a Christian scribe who believes in the Trinity decides it must be an accident that was not made clear in 1 John, and "therefore saw it as his duty to remedy the matter."[32]

Just as with Jesus, Gautama Buddha didn't write anything down that was passed on to his followers. Similar to the New Testament history, it took 400 years before the Pāli canon Buddhist text was agreed upon.

In spite of this, the canon texts for all of these traditions remain potent documents that deliver the teachings of their founders to us.

*The source text used for the translation goes through many hands whose wisdom, thoughts, and mistakes are included in the final text.*

The problem with the multiple translations of the *I Ching* can be illustrated with one of my own casts a year or so ago, a cast for which someone in our culture could do a double take. The roll was Hexagram 54, *Kuei Mei*, "Marrying Maiden" in the Wilhelm translation. But two other translations of *Kuei Mei* are Risema, "Converting Maidenhood," and Pearson, "Coming Home."

Portrayed by all of the translations is a woman who is entering an arranged marriage into a polygamous family as a "Junior" wife or Concubine. The lines show the woman in different positions from slave to princess in the Wilhelm translation. (The commentary suggests "slave" is probably not in the literal sense, even though slavery existed in ancient China.)

Pearson translates "slave" in this line as "concubine," but the meaning of the line is similar in both translations. While the translators' words may be different, the meaning is often the same or similar, although there are occasions when different translators come to opposing conclusions from the same original text.[33]

What is our reaction to the cultural context? Does one protest such an arrangement as the marrying maiden because it is not acceptable in our culture? I chose to recognize such an arrangement as accepted in its time and place and that I need to mentally do a cultural transformation of the situation to my culture and particular situation.

Imagine someone translating the following sentence 1,000 years from now: "Only when the applicant had enough clout would the gatekeeper with a chip on his shoulder give him the green light." Would anyone know about stop lights and their green lights? Would anyone remember what a chip on a shoulder meant, an allusion from the 1930s that is already fading from collective memory? Would they realize that there is no actual gate? A translator of the *I Ching* knows the Chinese language — but also brings their knowledge or seeks the assistance of others to interpret the words to get their correct meaning.

*There is no such thing as a perfect translation; there are always compromises between the literal and the meaning.*

It is unavoidable that the translator's thoughts, wisdom, and decisions will be in the translated text you read.

*The reader must mentally transform the cultural context of the author to his own cultural context.*[34]

A variety of *I Ching* translations can easily be equally valid. The original author is joined during the history of the document by a "Team of Sages." The accumulated wisdom of the final text you read is that of the "Team of Sages." This, in fact, is the case for virtually all canonical texts for all traditions and religions. But, these texts are meant to speak to the heart, mind, and soul, so let the words sink in and roll around in you centered mind.

~ ~ ~

*That which was from the beginning,*
*which we have heard,*
*which we have seen with our eyes,*
*which we have looked upon,*
*and our hands have handled,*
*of the Word of life;*
So Says *The Holy Bible*, 1 John 1, KJV

Lucky Number 88 囍 Becomes a Design

Traveling from Old to New

# CHAPTER 8

# A JOURNEY WITH THE *I CHING*

*The town changes but the Well does not change.*
*The Well Water is never dry, never overflowing.*
*The people come and go in an orderly manner*
*Happily drinking from the well.*
*When the well-rope is about to reach the water,*
*And has not drawn water —*
*The Jug breaks — Disaster.*
*Ah! But when the fifth line changes,*
*There lies the clear, cold spring within the Well,*
*From which you may now drink.*
So Says the *I Ching*[1]

Your journey begins with getting your tools: coins or yarrow stalks, an *I Ching* book or books, and a pen and paper — or better a journal. Of course, you may add guidebooks or ritual elements as you wish.

## ⤞ WHICH *I CHING* BOOK SHOULD YOU BUY ⤝

A translator who knows the Chinese language and who has studied the history and culture of ancient China is important if you are looking for accurate translation. The website, www.iChing.Wiki has a complete list that is kept up to date. In choosing a book, there are other issues to consider. Here are some criteria to consider when choosing an *I Ching* book:

1. How good a translation is it and how much do you care about accurate translations? No translation is perfect. As we have seen, the best scholars chose different words and phrases for the same Chinese characters from the cryptic text.

2. Are you interested in a viewpoint that influences that translation? How much? Are you willing to accept someone's perspective because it is so compelling? Would that persuasive viewpoint be im-

portant to you even if you know that the translation deviated from what a Chinese scholar would call decent translation?

3. Does the book have additional commentary from the author and what is the viewpoint of that author?

4. Is the *I Ching* book a translation or a paraphrase. A translation must be done by someone who knows the Chinese language. On the other hand, there are many paraphrased *I Ching* books which are "inspired by" some other translation, often the James Legge's translation, for which the copyright has expired. In this case, you are getting wisdom, the wisdom of the author of the book, which may be important to you.

5. Does the book have Image Statements? Do you want the wisdom of Confucius, or are you looking for only the *Zhouyi*. Many books that set out to have a "Daoist" viewpoint only translate the *Zhouyi*, leaving out the Confucian Image Statements and commentary, and often getting into to the Chinese cosmology interpretations.

6. Does it include the additional commentary, including line relations and interior trigrams? Are these further explanations important?

#### ⸻ TRANSLATIONS BY SCHOLARS AND PEOPLE ⸻ WHO ARE LITERATE IN CHINESE[2]

This list includes scholars who have a body of literature on the *I Ching* and related issues, plus some others who know the Chinese language — there are other translations available which are not listed. *Indicates that the book or author is often cited in other works.*[3]

#### ⸻ *I CHING* BOOKS — INCLUDES CONFUCIAN IMAGE STATEMENT ⸻

**Wilhelm/Baynes, *The I Ching*** (German 1923); English Translation, Baynes, 1950.*

The book that made the *I Ching* a best seller is still one of the most accessible translations by a scholar. Many people find this an excellent place to start; many people find that dealing with the full commentary right away is too daunting; some start by only using "Book I." Even if your favorite book were some other book, the Wilhelm translation might be a good addition to your library.

The Wilhelm *I Ching* was the first to put the parts of the Ten Wings together in a single Hexagram reading. In what he labels as "Book I," he provides the Judgment, Line Statements, and Image Statements into a single reading organized by Hexagram number. Wilhelm then repeats these in Book III, adding the other Commentaries collected and organized from across the Ten Wings. Figure 2.2 in Chapter 2 illustrates how these layers of text and commentary are laid out on Wilhelm's *The I Ching*.

Wilhelm added his own commentary — bringing his knowledge from instruction by Neo-Confucian Chinese Scholar, Lao Naixaun (Nai-hsuan) and the influence of his friend Carl Jung. Wilhelm, a Protestant missionary, came to his task as an admirer of Chinese culture[4] with the goal of making the *I Ching* accessible to the Western reader.

Thus, the reader will get all of the *Zhouyi* and the Ten Wings related to a hexagram by reading the hexagram in Part I, and then turning to Part III and reading it. The translated text is mixed with Wilhelm's commentary.

The difference between Wilhelm's commentary and the translation of the Received Text is indicated by the layout, the translation being indented blocks of text.

Like many people, I got used to this book — using others to bounce against it as needed. But, I know other devotees of the *I Ching* who have a different favorite.

Book II contains a discussion of the Ten Wings and translation of the *Trigram Commentary*, *The Great Treatise*, and the *Structure of a Hexagram* (including line relationships). These also include Wilhelm's commentary, the translated text again being indented.

The Wilhelm translation is rooted in the tradition of the late Neo-Confucian philosophy of China with a nod to Jung's ideas of synchronicity on which Jung expounds in his foreword to the book. This is the book I use most.

**Legge,** ***The YÎ KING or Book of Changes***, 1882.* Vol. 16 of *Sacred Books of the East, The Sacred Books of China, The Texts of Confucianism,* Part II, Project founder and editor, F. Max Müller. It can be found online on Internet Archives and the Sacred Texts[5] as part of the sacred book series.

Since the Legge translation is out of copyright, it is republished in several print and ebooks. His work is found on many internet sites, occasionally with no attribution to Legge.

This was the first accurate translation of the *I Ching* — there had been a few other attempts, including one by Legge himself, which he admits needed revision. Legge had to begin by developing his own Romanization system as part of the project, accounting for the *Yi King* title. Later versions published by others that use Legge's work substitute the Wade-Gilles system or Pinyin. For example, the Yellowbridge website uses Legge's translation along with Pinyin as does the website for the Chinese Text Project.[6]

Legge, a missionary, approached the *I Ching*, as well as several other Chinese classics such as the *Daodejing*, as a project for missionary work: ministers needed to understand the Chinese philosophy so they could convert them to Christianity.[7]

Legge's translation is in the order of each of the Ten Wings separately, requiring flipping through different parts of the book to get the complete reading for a given hexagram. Authors of books and websites that provide the Legge translation have reorganized his translation in ways similar to what Wilhelm did. I often will look at Legge's translation to see if there is a different take on a hexagram or line compared to Wilhelm.

I use a version — *I Ching Book of Changes* translated by James Legge, edited with introduction and study guide by Ch'u Chai with Winberg Chai, 1969. It preserves the Legge Romanization. It is still available. But, this book *does not* integrate the Ten Wings, they are printed separately.

A Legge translation that is easier to use (and uses Pinyin) than the book above can be found on https://www.yellowbridge.com/chinese.

**Pearson, *The Original I Ching*, 2011.\*** The first translation of the *I Ching* by a female scholar begins with a reminder that the Chinese language pronouns and nouns (with a few exceptions) are gender neutral. She also reminds the reader that the attachment of Yin and Yang to the lines was a much later invention and that the "Female as Yin" and "Male as Yang" were not intended by the text.

Wilhelm and Legge were products of Western languages and customs that forced a choice of gender pronoun using the rule: Male, choose he; Female, choose she; could be either gender, pick he. The debate about how to make English gender-neutral when it should be neutral began as early as the 1960s and continues to this day. Many modern books continue this tradition even though the Chinese pronoun or noun does not specify gender. Some, such as Lynn, point to the male dominated society in Wang Bi's time, but this is not uniform in the history of China.

This book could be considered as a first book, or in combination with Wilhelm, if you will have difficulty reading past the male-default translation of other books.

I use this book often.

**Lynn, *The Classic of Changes*,** 1994.* Lynn provides both a translation of the *I Ching* and Wang Bi's commentary along with other Chinese scholars' commentary, along with his own commentary for each hexagram. The book is excellent scholarship and laid out for personal use — and Wang Bi is still considered one of China leading scholars for his era.

I use this book to get a different take on readings compared to Wilhelm and Legge.

Readers might be set back by Wang Bi's remark that may appear unnecessarily misogynous on Line 5 of the Hexagram 23 dismissing the court ladies as inherently petty.[8]

I use this to get a different interpretation from other translations.

**Minford, *I Ching*,** 2014. Minford produces a translation with word choices that are close to Kunst and Legge, with an occasional surprising twist, such as the name of Hexagram 3 as "difficult birth." He adds extensive commentary from other Chinese sources as well as poetry apparently of his own.

**Cleary, *The Buddhist I Ching*,** 1987. This is a translation of the *I Ching* and a commentary from Chih-hsu Ou-I (1599–1655) — a Buddhist scholar.

**Cleary, *I Ching, The Book of Change*,** 2006. The Judgment/Decision in this translation is untitled and is the text right under the name. The supplemental commentary on the Judgment is under the title "Overall Judgment."

**Huang, Alfred.** *The Complete I Ching: The Definitive Translation by the Taoist Master Alfred Huang*, 2003. Translation is similar to Wilhelm. The author's commentary is based on an oral tradition passed down to him.

**Ritesma and Karcher,** *I Ching, The Classic Chinese Oracle of Change*, 1994. The book does not translate Judgments into English phrases per se, but simply lists translated words, then in the "fields of meaning" gives the Pinyin words and a meaning. Its stated purpose is a psychological tool.

**Karcher,** *I Ching; The Classic Chinese Oracle of Change*, 2002. An update to the previous book with some changes.

**Ritesma and Sabbadini,** *The Original I Ching Oracle*, 2007. The book does translate Judgments into English phrases but also includes "fields of meaning" that were in an earlier book — Ritesma and Karcher, *I Ching; The Classic Chinese Oracle of Change*, 1994. Significant differences with Wilhelm and Legge translations.

### ZHOUYI BOOKS — NO IMAGE STATEMENT

**Shaughnessy,** *I Ching The Classic of Changes*, 1996.* This is a translation of the *Mawangui Zhouyi* texts as opposed to the Received Text of most translations. The original Chinese text in the *Mawangui* differs in places from the Received Text — Shaughnessy includes both sets of Chinese texts for each hexagram on the page facing the translation of the *Mawangui* text.

The hexagrams have a different order and numbering scheme, so matching the number from other books to the *Mawangui* text involves looking in a table provided by Shaughnessy. He also includes a translation of another text found at the *Mawangui* sites, "The Several Disciples Asked," "The Properties of the Changes," "The Essentials," and "Mu He and Zhao Li."

For a person already familiar with the *I Ching*, Shaughnessy's book is a source of additional insight into *I Ching* in a historical context, written and translated by a leading scholar.

I often use this book to help resolve ambiguities.

**Shaughnessy,** *Unearthing the Changes*, 2014.* This is a translation of several archaeological finds of the *Zhouyi* most dating from around 300 B.C. Unfortunately, all of these finds are missing some or a lot of the text. Of course, these did not get canonized, so there is little literary history that marches forward in time. It was not written to be useful as the only book for consulting the *I Ching* because of the missing hexagrams.

**Kunst, *The Original Yijing: A Text, Phonetic Transcription, Translation, and Indexes with Sample Glosses* 1985.\*** A PhD dissertation that is not widely published, but the standard for a thorough scholarship in translating the *Zhouyi*. I use this often when the meaning of a translated word is in question.

**Ni, Hue-Ching, *The Book of Changes and the Unchanging Truth*, 1983.** This book by "Taoist Master Ni, Hua Ching," introduces the reader to Daoist concepts, cosmology, and spirituality in Part I of the book. Part II contains translation of the Judgment and Lines along with "specific guidance" for Personal Fortune, Marriage, Housing/Familty, Childbirth, Looking for Help, Social Governmental Position, Trade/Business, Search for Someone, Waiting for Someone, Looking for Something Lost, Hunting for Thieves, Lawsuit, Climate, Travel, Disease, and Personal Wish.

After being introduced to this book by a devotee, I found this book a very insightful addition.

**Rutt, *Zhouyi*, 2002.\*** The translation seeks to preserve the early interpretation of readings, removing metaphors of later interpretations, regarding punishment of prisoners and sacrifices of war captives, including cutting off body parts.

**Wincup, Gregory, *Rediscovering the I Ching,* 1986.\*** Provides distinctly different interpretations of several hexagrams, often by translating the name literally and building the theme around that. It appears to be as accurate an interpretation as more traditional interpretations.

**Redmond, *The I Ching (Book of Changes),* 2017.** The stated purpose of this book is a "translation of the early text, with the later overlays that completely altered how it was read. I have tried to present it as accurately as possible in plain English."[9]

**Cleary, *The Taoist I Ching,* 1986.** This is a translation of the *Zhouyi* and a commentary from Liu I-ming (A.D. 1734–1821) — a Neo-Daoist scholar. The Judgment and Lines are in Book I, the Images are in Book II, and

Mixed Hexagrams (Pairs in the Received Order) are in Book III.

This book provides a different perspective — not in the translation of the *Zhouyi* so much as in the commentary.

**Karcher.** *Total I Ching,* 2003. An interesting translation in that Karcher's purpose is poetic, which means that he stays close to the Received Text as the source of his word choices as he poetically interprets them. My view is that it is a more mystical interpretation. He appears to go back to some of the more sexually explicit implications of heaven and earth's relationship that is present in some ancient literature.

**Jing-Nuan, Wu,** *Yi Jing,* 1991, Includes Chinese characters and the English translation. It is a *Zhouyi* translation said to be with a Daoist outlook.

**Wu, Yi,** *The Essentials of the Yi Jing,* 2003. The book places an emphasis on line relationships and transformations. Includes commentary, such as trigrams representing family members that are not found in most books.

**Huang, Kerson and Rosemary,** *I Ching,* 1987. This is translated by physicists. Concise, with short author commentaries. Some interesting twists in translation. The *I Ching, The Oracle,* by Kerson in 1984 is its predecessor, and shows the Chinese version across from the English translation. There is also a 2014 edition by Kerson Huang.

**Field,** *The Duke of Zhou Changes,* 2015. Field presents the translation in tables that separate Omen, Counsel, and Fortune. Commentary relates reading to ancient divination practices. For example, Hexagram 1, which Kunst translates as "Grand Treat," in which he says that "treat" is a sacrificial offering.[10] Field translates it as "Your primary plea is heard," relating it in his commentary as a sacrificial offering.

#### ━━━ KNOWLEDGEABLE USERS ━━━

Books which were not translated directly from Chinese may be very valuable resources. Someone who has used *The Book of Changes* for a long time can present an authentic version of the book. Two which are in the tradition of self-awareness advices are:

**Anthony and Moog,** *I Ching, The Oracle of the Cosmic Way,* 2002. Carol Anthony has written several guides on the *I Ching* based on the Wilhelm translation of her own journey and journals. She uses Buddhist-like metaphors that on the interior life. This book, coauthored with Anna Moog, builds upon the Wilhelm translation with their insight.

**Barrett, *I Ching, Walking Your Path, Creating Your Future*,** 2010. The author has an active forum in England. She has been active in studying the *I Ching* for decades, is familiar with the scholarship, and comments on  translations in addition to her own.

**Schorre. *Yijing Wondering and Wandering*,** 2003. The book has a long introduction, explaining concepts such as yin-yang and has a Daoist orientation. It has a focus on hexagram imagery and transformation: hexagrams in pairs, with beautiful calligraphy with a discussion of some. It is interlaced with quotes for Daoist classics.

*See www.iching.wiki for more book reviews.*

⚹⚹⚹ **PARAPHRASES** ⚹⚹⚹

Many *I Ching* books are not translations, but paraphrases, with people from many different outlooks and levels of experience. It is the book's author who provides whatever insights are to be found in the book. There are several books which contain Legge's translation.

Someone such as Swami Anand Nisarg, *The Magician's I Ching*, is one who acknowledges what he is and is not and goes forth to provide his insight into *The Changes* providing his interpretations in the Judgments, etc. His note begins:

> This work is not an academic work. It is not the product of a professional sinologist. Those who are engaged with serious Chinese historical study … will no doubt find that while this book delves far more into the Chinese context of the *I Ching* than many others on the popular market, there will be a number of things missing from what would constitute a properly "academic" work. Likewise, they may find that some of the concepts and choices in the material seem unusual, that certain things may … not fit the traditions … appears radical, if not to say "wrong." In order to clarify: this book is written from the point of view of a mystic and magician.[11]

This would be a good introduction for many books on the market. You may find some of these books useful and inspirational — the author being the one who brings most of the wisdom. As one long-time user commented af-

## TREES

*Autumn's beauty lines the highways*
*Then in the umber shades of late October*
*Their leafless limbs stood in gloom*
*Waiting in their helpless nakedness*

*The shroud of comforting falling snow*
*Covering them with luxurious coats of ermine*
*Laden them to test their strength*
*Insulating against the north winds*

*So that in spring's renewing breath*
*Their vigor once more stirs anew*
*Bursting forth from deep within them*
*Flowing to their trembling tips*
*Sprouting buds of tender newness*
*Bursting forth with springtime green*

*Until at last their cycle finished*
*Then return once more to sleep*
— Barbara Olsen

Forest Path

ter a discussion of how to interpret a particular reading, the ultimate test for anyone using divination is, "Does it work?" Use what works for you.

## ══ WEBSITES ══

There are a ton of websites, some offering on-line readings — primarily the Legge translation but some Wilhelm and others. Two that include the Chinese characters are Yellow Bridge (www.yellowbridge.com/onlinelit/i-ching.php) and the Chinese Text Project (ctext.org), both of which have been around for years and are dedicated to presenting the Chinese classics and other literature. Two other sites contain the products of Max Muller's Project — including the Legge *I Ching*:

1. Sacred Books East. https://archive.org/details/SacredBooksEastVariousOriental-ScholarsWithIndex.50VolsMaxMulle
2. Sacred Texts: http://www.sacred-texts.com/sbe/index.htm.

## ══ AN *I CHING* READING AND HOW IT WORKED OUT ══

The lawsuit had been filed, an accusation of fraud; there was no fraud — not even close. My lawyer said that losing would mean being hounded for life. It seemed to be an attempt to drive my family and me into poverty. Our answer was due.

I set up my space for interacting with the *I Ching*. A 6-inch statue and a few other artifacts at the head of the table, the *I Ching* book in front of it, my journal to the right.

I took 50 yarrow stalks and placed one of them in front of the book.

I opened my journal to the next blank page. I wrote "Saturday" followed by the date. I then wrote what was on my mind. That day it was cryptic, just one word, "Response."

I manipulated the remaining 49 stalks, grasping them in my left hand, using my right hand to grasp half the bundle and place it on the table, picking one stalk from the pile on the table and holding in my left hand with my pinky, counting off 4 stalks at time and putting them on the table to the left of the pile ready there, and so on…resulting in three piles arranged so that their tops rested on the stick lying in front of the book: 5 stalks (Heads), 4 stalks (Heads), 8 stalks (Tails). Its 3 +3 + 2: an 8. I drew a broken line on the page.

I picked up the 49 stalks and manipulated them again, resulting in three piles. 5 stalks (Heads), 8 Stalks (Tails), 8 Stalks (Tails). Its 3 +2 + 2, a 7. I drew an unbroken line above the broken line.

I manipulate the 49 stalks a third time, resulting in three piles. 9 stalks (Tails), 4 Stalks (Heads), 8 Stalks (Tails). Its 2 +3 + 2, a 7. I draw an unbroken line above the other two and get ☴ drawing in my journal.

What trigram did I get for the bottom? I looked it up. Its wood and wind — could be either one.

I continue to the fourth line: a broken line, then I am in the fifth line, the line that is usually most beneficial: Five stalks (Heads), 4 stalks (Tails), 4 Stalks (Tails).

A Nine! I draw an unbroken line with a circle in the middle to show a changing line.

Finally, at the top, a broken line. The trigram at the top is ☵: water running through a dangerous canyon — dangerous. This is usually bad news. But, it depends on how it interacts with the other trigram.

I picked up the *I Ching* book looked up the hexagram number by opening the chart in the back of the book, looking up ☵ across the top, and ☴ down the side: 48.

I turned to Hexagram 48 in Part I of Wilhelm's *The I Ching*: 井, The Well. I read the Judgment:

> The WELL. The town may be changed,
> But the well cannot be changed.
> It neither decreases nor increases.
> They come and go and draw from the well.
> If one gets down almost to the water
> And the rope does not go all the way,
> Or the jug breaks, it brings misfortune.

It was apparent to me that the jug was already broken. What was the advice? Just live with the coming misfortune — destined to become an aggressive litigation. I turned to Part III of Wilhelm's book, turning to number 48 to find The Appended Judgment:

> The WELL shows the field of character. The WELL abides in its place, yet has influence on other things. The WELL brings about discrimination as to what is right.

The appended Judgment seemed to say we would prevail in the lawsuit, but that seemed a long way off. But, it also said, "abides in its place." What did that mean? The WELL that remains in its place, unchanging, always ready to provide water — if the rope and jug can just get down to it?

There was also a Commentary that begins:

> Penetrating under water and bringing up water:
> this is the WELL.
> The well nourishes and is not exhausted.

It seemed that there was something else being said beyond the litigation situation — that's broken, and I am in for a bad ride full of setbacks. But, the water that nourishes — there is hope yet.

Then I read the changing line:

> Nine in the fifth place means:
> In the well there is a clear, cold spring
> From which one can drink.

With a description of a disaster, the Judgment seeming to say it wouldn't go away anytime soon, this line said that there was something else here — it seemed to be talking about nothing less than holy water.

I took it to mean to develop spiritually while all the nasty lawsuit stuff was going on. But, I would quickly come to realize that reading about it was not the same as "getting it." That didn't keep me from reading, but there had to be more, faith in something greater than myself.

As the months passed, I consulted the *I Ching* about once a week. My informal rule was to wait for the meaning and progress from the previous consultation to manifest itself, both as events unfolded and thinking about what it means. I still had work to do.

I resisted the misfortune of litigation, its financial and other consequences. I wanted it to be over. But, when I tried to take a shortcut out of the mess, I got The Well again.

I certainly could have become angry, disillusioned, vengeful, given it all up, thrown away my ethics — and all those thoughts crossed my mind. I added my simple mantra to my *I Ching* ritual: "The Universe has a purpose; my purpose is to align myself with the purpose of the Universe." Sometimes adding: "And God's Will be done." The anxious agitation fell away as I said it, as I consulted the *I Ching*: my well-being need no longer be married to the cycle of misfortune in the litigation process.

There were cycles within the cycles, the ups and downs; I started to feel I was in the yin-yang cycle of change, but it seemed more like I was in the world's cosmic wave, somehow being battered by random events, asking, as each decision was forced upon me, what the superior person would do. I got it right most of the time — not winning-right — although I did have to think about that — but morally right — never wavering from the truth; most of the time, but not every time, not blaming; not angry, most of the time. I realized that what happened did not need to force some emotion into my heart, I could choose to be calm, detached — sometimes I actually pulled that off.

After a year I finally got The Cauldron — I was getting there, but it came with changing lines 3, 4, and 5 — more work to do. Another year, again, The Cauldron, this time with one changing line, line 3.

Another year. Trial finally happened. Another Cauldron as we were waiting for a decision. Changing line in the 6th place. There was no doubt of the outcome — maybe I had made some progress at spiritual growth. Then Hexagram 16, line 1 changing, warning — "enthusiasm that expresses itself brings misfortune" — no bragging — we knew we had a good case.

Then it was 37 Family, then 31 Joy, that 31 Joy again.

Then the Court made a decision. It appears that old roll: "The WELL brings about discrimination as to what is right" came in the form of a decision — it wasn't even close — we prevailed. But, my very imperfect search, my ever stumbling search, my sometimes forgotten search for "clear, cold water spring" from which I could drink had become even more important than the outcome. The next roll was Hexagram 11 — Peace.

Peace: changing lines in the first and second place — I should have paid closer attention to Line 2 — it turned out I still had a lot of work ahead of me.

So, I continue to try to walk Matthew 7:13's narrow path, to trod Zhuang-zi's path of untroubled ease, to stay on the straight path of the Confucian Dao. I know when I finally "get it" for longer than a fleeting moment, that all three paths will be the same path.

*From what I have learned so far*
*I offer to you in this book.*

The Well

Pen Drawing a Line

# LETTER TO THE READER

I began my experience with the *I Ching* with the belief that the Christian religion, in which I was raised, holds a good part of the answer to what I should do in this life. I have not lost that belief. I am no judge of any church's theological beliefs, but for me, the compelling words of The Christ Jesus of Nazareth when he gave a sermon on a mountain, goes straight to my soul. I believe a strong faith or ethic can stand being informed by other traditions, which will inevitably have differences in theology or theories that underlie its ethics.

Like the authors Carol Anthony and Hanna Moog who have written several books on the *I Ching*, it was a crisis that led me to the *I Ching*. But I wish I had not waited for a crisis, realizing that I could have used the insight provided by the *I Ching* much earlier.

I had tried the *I Ching* briefly a few decades ago and thought it might help me. In fact, when I was looking through my bookshelves, I found a forty-year-old printed version of Legge's translation published in 1964.

**Sermon on the Mount**

When he saw the crowd, he began to teach them.
Blessed are the poor in spirit,
  for theirs is the
    kingdom of heaven.
Blessed are they who mourn,
  for they shall be comforted.
Blessed are the meek,
  for they shall inherit the land.
Blessed are they who hunger and
  thirst for righteousness,
  for they shall be satisfied.
Blessed are the merciful,
  for they shall be shown mercy.
Blessed are the pure of heart,
  for they shall see God.
Blessed are the peacemakers,
  for they shall be called
    the children of God.
You have heard it said,
  An eye for an eye,
  A tooth for a tooth.
But I say to you,
  Offer no resistance
  to one who is evil.
When someone strikes you on
    your right cheek,
  Turn the other one to him
    as well.

~ ~ ~

But I say to you,
Love you enemies
And pray for those who
  persecute you.
— From Matthew 5, KJV & NABRE

So, I was inspired to walk into a bookstore and bought the Wilhelm/ Baynes translation of the *I Ching*. The bookseller handed me a copy of Carol Anthony's Guide to the *I Ching* and said, "This might help." It did.

The book that inspired me to walk into the bookstore in the first place was *The Man in the High Castle*, by Philip K. Dick. Among other things, this book was, for me, an instruction manual on how to approach the *I Ching* because the characters in the book frequently consult the *I Ching* while having an internal dialog of their thought process.

*The Man in the High Castle* is rated the best or one of the best of the genre of Alternate History. The premise is that Roosevelt is assassinated in 1933, changing the historical timeline and the outcome of World War II. The Pacific States of America became a puppet government of Japan. Faced with this reality, many Americans had to adapt to the customs and tastes of the Japanese to make a living. "The *I Ching* is prominent in *The Man in the High Castle*; having diffused it as part of their cultural hegemony overlordship of the Pacific Coast US, the Japanese — and some American — characters consult it, and then act per its replies to their queries."[1] I found it instructive to have American characters who needed to "translate" Asian ways of thinking into American thought processes when they used the *I Ching*.

I learned that an *I Ching* reading could be about my internal psyche, external events, or both. The challenge for me was that my ego wanted to see it as confirming its wants and desires, but Carol Anthony's *Guide* always pulled me back into the world of self-awareness. That does not mean that my readings did not help me sort out decisions about this-world dramas. The lesson is that just reacting to an understanding of the external events is never the whole meaning, or even the most significant part of the *I Ching*.

It is a book that attempts to mirror nature's dynamic behavior as it affects relationships between you and your inner mind, family, other people, nature, and sometimes the Divine.

I realized I was getting the advice of the *I Ching* in my own ethical framework, as well as the context of the *I Ching* in its own history and culture. That made me want to learn more.

Over the years, I would take up a book to familiarize myself with the history of the Christian movement and faith. For example, the New Testament story of the Good Samaritan gets a much more insightful meaning when the reader realizes that Jesus of Nazareth's audience despised Samaritans because they viewed Samaritans as heretics who cut any connection with the Holy Temple of Jerusalem. Yet, Jesus constructed a story where this was the one person who helped a beaten and robbed stranger, making the point that what you do is more important than what you profess. Indeed, think how this story applies to today's world, politics, and conflicts.

Then I was inspired by the autobiography of Mahatma Gandhi who believed that a Hindu should acquaint himself with all of the world's religions. He read the The Holy Bible from cover to cover and, like me, was particularly moved by the Sermon on the Mount. So, I began to read other religious texts and acquaint myself with their history, to learn about ancient China; read the books written by Daoists, Confucians, Buddhists; read the books written by unknown authors.

This book emerged as a project to motivate my self-study. As I studied, I began to give some classes on the *I Ching* and its relationship with religious, philosophical, scientific, and psychological thought. The teacher became the student: the people who showed up taught me as much as I taught them. I am not an expert in any of these subjects, although my engineering degree provides a grounding in some of the sciences. This book can only claim to be a humble attempt to share what I have learned so far.

As I began drafting the book, I decided to ask the *I Ching* about it. When I asked the *I Ching* about the wisdom of doing this project, I rolled the *Ting* (The Cauldron, Hexagram 50) with a changing line at the top. This seemed to be a firm caution to listen carefully to the Sage but seemed to encourage continuing the project. The Changing Nine at the Top gave me pause. It lies outside the development of the idea and at the place where "everything is completed." In this case, it seemed to be a caution from the Sage that nothing should be added, only explained, to tell the *I Ching*'s story as it is, not as I would wish it to be.

Yes, strange as it seems, I did indeed cast the Ting, as did Carl Jung when he undertook to write the forward of the Wilhelm translation of the *I Ching*. And, I believe for the same reason: that the *I Ching* "was testifying for itself." As I embarked on this path, it seems Modesty (Hexagram 15) is appropriate as well.

Of course, there is a lot written on the subject, so one can delve as deep as they wish. But, I think anyone and the *I Ching* can interact no matter what level of depth they go, as long as their mind is open to realizing that authors from another era and culture created the text.

When I started reading *The Great Treatise* and the Image Statements about what a Superior Person might do, I realized that the *I Ching* was built on a foundation of Daoist metaphysical concepts and Confucian ethics. Any discussion of the *I Ching* would be lacking without examining them both. This book includes a chapter on Daoist ideas and one on Confucian ethics.

The *I Ching* continued to grow. After all, *The Great Treatise* was written over two millennium in the past. Buddhism, Neo-Daoism, Neo-Confucianism, philosophies, religions, psychology, and even quantum mechanics added their wisdom to how the *Book of Changes* is understood and used. The only thing to do was to present the *I Ching* as a living document that can be approached from many viewpoints, as if it were a castle with a Thousand Doors.

So, the title, *I Ching of a Thousand Doors,* ends up presenting a grand tour of many of the world's belief systems, each with a rich scripture and literature, which provides an amazing amount of material, beautifully written, that goes to the heart of what the *I Ching* has to teach — each presenting us with rational narratives, emotional experiences, and a call to spirituality in many different ways. Does one understand it as dry scholarship, a heart-felt engagement, or a mystical experience. I took what some told me was the bold step to attempt all three in one book — Mind, Heart, and Spirit — narrative that transitions to poetry and poetic prose from the ancient scriptures to some of my own.

It seems that nearly all of our "self-development" programs and books strive to "make us happy." Is the best they can do is deliver temporary relief? In my explorations, I discovered that every religion, most psychological therapies, and many philosophies have the same goal: happiness, but not a temporary satisfaction that wears off, but as a final and continuing state of being.

> *I seek the happiness,*
> *Knowing the pleasures of this earth do not last.*
> *Sublime happiness,*
> *Beyond the reach of words and ego's grasp.*
> *The paths are endless,*
> *Path's climbed,*
> *I seek nevertheless,*
> *The sublime.*

The I Ching is universal in its advice. So, I offer this book as an aid to the seeker of its wisdom. I offer this book to the reader in the hope that it is an aide to your spiritual path, in whatever tradition that path may take.

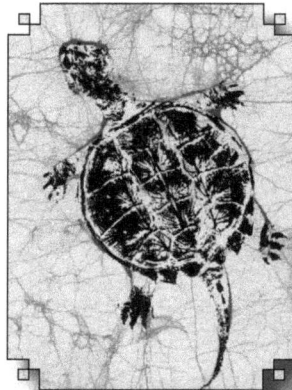

Gyotaku Turtle by Mary Byers

# Notes and Acknowledgments

## Common Cultural Beliefs Versus Historical Consensus

Every culture has a common set of beliefs and stories associated with the foundation of their traditions. In some cases, historical research will differ from the traditional story. However, the culture stories serve as a primary motivation for the culture and the motives and context cannot be understood without them. In many of these cases I will keep the narrative flowing without getting into the historical analysis, but use the word "story" or "tradition."

In many cases there is a main view by historians and minority views. Generally, if the majority view matches the cultural belief being written about, I will present the majority view as a simple statement of fact. I sometimes include the minority views in footnotes or in commentary within the text.

## Honorifics and Capitalization

This book presents, in part, what I have learned so far about many of the world's religions and cultures. It attempts to honor each of them. If I fail in this attempt, it is not intentional but due to my lack of learning, for which I humbly beg forbearance.

Thus, when a tradition has an honorific for their text, I will use it. For example, the *The Holy Bible* and the *Noble Qur'an,* where "holy" and "noble" are honorifics used by the followers of the traditions that consider the books their scripture. Indeed, the Chinese classics are traditionally referred to this way when the word *Jing (or Ching)* is used: the word means *great book*, a *classic*, and is applied to imported scriptures such as the Bible (*Sheng Jing*), Koran (*Gulan Jing*) and Buddhist Canon (*Dàzàng Jing*).

While I avoid technical words, one exception is the word "text," which I often use to avoid confusion with the word "book" because ancient documents were often not in books, but in China were often written on bamboo

strips tied together — which accounts for the vertical writing. "Text" is used
per the following definition:

> A written or printed work regarded in terms of its content
> rather than its physical form.

Capitalization is used for Heaven and Dao (and the translation, The Way)
when they are referring to a metaphysical concept. This is the case for *Qi*
*(Chi)*. Chinese Pinyin for words that are well known, such as yin, yang, and
Dao are not italicized.

## ⟶⟵ DATES ⟶⟵

Terminology for dates will honor the historicity of the Western dating system. Calendars are culturally important to nearly every tradition.[1] It was
common in ancient and medieval Europe and China to count years from the
date of the ascension to throne of an Emperor — the "fifth year of Augustus"
for example in Rome.

Thus, it made sense for the people in Europe during the age of Christen-
dom, which got underway around A.D. 500, to begin using the birth of Jesus
of Nazareth, who was to Christians, The Christ. Christ comes from a series
of translations of the Hebrew word מָשִׁיחַ (messiah) which means "anointed
one," which referred to a ceremony reserved for the King and High Priest.
The Greek translation is Χριστός, which was rendered phonetically in Latin — as the Greek word sounded — *Christos*, in English becoming Christ.
As the concept of the Trinity took hold, Jesus was the Son of God, he also
become one with "The Lord," which was a term used often in the Old Testament to refer to God. This idea runs deeply through European, and later,
American history.

For the system for counting dates, I have used "B.C." (before Christ) and
"A.D." (*anno Domini* — year of Our Lord) strictly to honor the historic context of the Western dating system passed down to us. This book retains the
tradition of an accurate grammatical translation, in which A.D. precedes the
year, for example A.D. 525, for "the year of our Lord 525" — although it is
not uncommon to find, 525 A.D.

The equivalent terms BCE (Before Common Era) and CE (Common Era) are often used because some wanted to secularize the dating system. The use of B.C./A.D. for counting years began in Europe and was meant to mark time from the birth of Jesus of Nazareth, which is an important event that affected much of Europe and the Americas' history.[2]

The use of BCE/CE is viewed as a way to recognize the secular and diverse nature of our society, which this author also recognizes. But, some would claim that even recognizing this, the historicity of our dating system would be lost and serves no good effect. Indeed, our months and weekday names are also named after Roman gods and emperors, so the attempt to eliminate historicity from our timekeeping seems problematic. We cannot avoid our own history.

### ⸺ CHINESE CHARACTERS ⸺

Another term I use is "Romanization," which simply means that the Roman alphabet is substituted in a systematic way for another alphabet. The Roman alphabet is the same alphabet as English, but with more diacritics (accents). Scholars developed a Romanization system for Chinese characters, called logograms by linguists. 道 for example, is the logogram that is Romanized as *Dào* in the now international Romanization standard, Pinyin. I call Chinese logograms "characters" to differentiate them from Pinyin Romanization or translated English words.

Three Romanization systems have been used to translate the *I Ching*:

1. The "Legge" standard was developed by James Legge in the mid-1800s when he translated the *I Ching* and numerous other Chinese classics and texts. The title *Yi King* was used for the *I Ching*, for instance.

2. Wade-Giles (developed by Thomas Wade and Herbert Giles) was the English-speaking academic "standard" starting in the early 1900's.

3. *Hànyǔ Pīnyīn*, or simply Pinyin (developed by Zhou Youguang), was sponsored and adopted by the Peoples' Republic of China to make teaching English easier and was adopted by the International Standard Organization (ISO) in 1982.[3] The Romanization system has another use as well — load the right keyboard software, type Pinyin, get the Chinese character.[4]

Some terms that are well known in the West are from the Wade-Giles system: *I Ching, Tao,* and *Tao Te Ching.* There are still many books and websites that use the Wade-Giles system. Pinyin is used throughout this book, often omitting the Pinyin accents (diacritics), except for *I Ching*, because of the longstanding popularity of the title.

Many readers are familiar with *Chi* or *Ch'i*, which is from the Wade-Giles system. This book uses, *Qi,* omitting the diacritic of the Pinyin, *Qí.* This is probably the one change from Wade-Giles to Pinyin that may make a reader stumble. Most of the others, such as Dao/Tao, will more easily pair themselves in a reader's mind. The world is moving toward Pinyin and will not go back. When a Wade-Giles spelling is familiar, the Wade Giles will be included in parentheses. For example. *Tiān (T'ien)* where *Tiān* is Pinyin and *T'ien* is Wade-Giles, which is usually translated as Heaven.

Remember, while the transcription may be different between Wade-Giles and Pinyin, making it seem like they are somehow different sounding, the Chinese character(s) and spoken words are exactly the same. For example, some people thought the Chinese changed the name of Peking to Beijing, but, in fact, it is the same name in two different Romanization systems, Beijing being the Pinyin transcription. The other thing about Romanizing Chinese is that Chinese Characters for a name or title are written with no spaces. For example, the characters, 道德經, can be Romanized as *Dao De Jing* (one word for each character) or *Daodejing.*

When referencing the numbers related to a hexagram, such as the six line positions or number of trigram, I use the Arabic number instead of the English word to reflect the Chinese characters used in the same context.[5]

Another complication is that a simplified-character movement resulted in many Chinese characters having a traditional and simplified form — the simplified being easier to write since it has fewer pen strokes. For example, the traditional character for yīn which this book uses is 陰, while the simplified character is 阴. While simplified characters are most commonly used, this book uses the traditional character for the purpose of giving a sense of the language used by past scholars and *I Ching* users in China.

## CAPITALIZATION

Various traditions include capitalization rules that distinguish religious or metaphysical meanings from the ordinary meaning of a word. The most familiar is *god* and *God*, where *god* means *a god, one of many gods* and *God* means *the one and only God*. *Allah,* الله, is the Arabic word for God, the one and only God. When dealing with religious ideas of terms for God or attributes that are only associated with God, or in other belief systems a universal form, these will be capitalized — Love, Truth, Mind. When the English translation of the *Dao* is used to designate *Dao* in its metaphysical meaning it will be capitalized, i.e. The Way or Way.

Finally, I have included Chinese characters in places to remind the reader of the original source text. I have selected the traditional character because of the ancient nature of the text.

## ACKNOWLEDGMENTS AND CREDITS

Art and Graphics: Graphics by James R. Olsen include icons and photo licensed from Flaticon and Shuttertock.com. Credits for other work:
- *I Ching* text Song Dynasty. Wikimedia.Public Domain Uploaded by EdescasReijiYamashina.Frontmatter
- Figures 1.1 and 1.2, retyped for review and comment from *Original I Ching* by Margaret Pearson. Pages 2 & 3.
- Western Zhou Gui Vessal, Freer and Sackler Galleries of Washington D.C. Wikimedia Commons, Photo by PericlesofAthens.Creative Commons Attribution-Share Alike 3.0 Unported. Page 17.
- Fuxi and Nuwa, Hanging scroll — Color on silk, Tang Dynasty. Wikimedia CommonsPublic Domain. Uploaded by Stout256. Page 18.
- Portrait of King Wén of Zhou — Ming Dynasty painter unknown. Wikimedia.Public Domain Page 19.
- Tortoise plastron with divination inscription from the Shang dynasty, dating to the reign of King Wu Ding: Wikimedia, Photo by BabelStone/ Wikimedia.CC-BY-SA-3.0. Page 19.
- Yin-Yang/Trigram Octagon: Benoît Stella alias BenduKiwi/Wikimedia Commons/license CC-BY-SA-3.0. Page 20.
- Amitabha Buddha and Bodhisattvas, Hangzhou, Zhejiang province, China. Wikimedia. C CC0 1.0 Universal Public Domain Dedication Photo by Tengu800. Page 26.
- Luncheon of a Boating Party — Philips Collection. Wikimedia. Public Domain. Page 29.

- Wilhelm/Baynes I Ching Book. Photocopy of four pages The I Ching by Wilhelm marked up by James R. Olsen. Page 33.
- Zhuangzi and a Frog. Wikimedia.Public Domain. Page 64.
- Loazi Statue: Photo by Thanato. Wikimedia.CC-BY-SA-3.0 Page 66
- Wu Xing,schematic diagram incorporated in Five Agents, by Parnassus. Wikimedia. Creative Commons Attribution-Share Alike 3.0 Unported Page 69.
- Dao Small Seal: by Erin Silversmith/Wikimedia. Public Domain.
- Immortal Land Yuan Jiang-Penglai Island by Yuan Jiang (袁江) A.D. 1708 Palace Museum, Bejing. Photo by Zhongguo gu dai shu hua jian ding zu (中国古代书画鑑定组). Wikimedia.Public Domain. Page 80.
- Zhou Dunyi Ultimate Principle diagram. Uploaded by Edescas2. Wikimedia.Public Domain  Page 81.
- Moon — da Vinci Moon "The Codex Arundel," Catalogue, The British Museum, New Series, 1 vol. in 3 parts (London: British Museum, 1834–1840), I, part I: The Arundel Manuscripts, 79. Page 82.
- The Wave and Solar by Walter Russell, University of Science and Philosophy, Waynesboro, VA — used with permission. Page 82–83.
- Web of Life Mandala — original art of Mary Byers, silk screen and batik on cotton — used with permission. Page 84.
- Confucius by Wu Daozi, modified. Wikimedia.Public domain  Page 87.
- Ru Seal by Rintojiang. Wikimedia.Public domain. Page 88
- Analects Text. Photo by AlexHe34 (AndyHe829)/Wikimedia CC-BY-SA-3.1. Page 92.
- Portrait of Xunzi — Spring and Autumn Period. Wikimedia Public Domainuploaded by AmaryllisGardener. Page 99.
- Sanxing Dieties. Roof Takdekoration med Sanxing vid Magong Beiji-temple, Taiwan. Photo by 雲角. Wikimedia. RightforCommericalUseByCopyrightHolder. Page 102.
- Gyotaku Turtle. Silk Screen and Batik on Cotton by Mary Byers, with permission. Page 165,
- Map of China 500 B.C. by Hugo Lopez, Wikimedia CC-BY-SA-3.0. Page 175.

There is a group of English language scholars who have brought the rich Chinese philosophical history related to the *I Ching* to the English-speaking world and added much insight to it. This book would not have been possible without a lifetime of study by Richard Smith, Edward Shaughnessy, John Lynn, James Legge, David Keightly, Joseph Alder, and others. Richard Kunst's dissertation and translation of the *I Ching* along with a thorough commentary on the meaning of the ancient Chinese language and characters is a baseline which has been very helpful.

The Western world owes much to Friedrich Max Müller, Max Muller as he is commonly known. His project, *The Sacred Books of the East*, resulted in the translation of numerous ancient texts in the late nineteenth century. His project includes the James Legge's translation of the *I Ching,* which is still very prevalent to this day. Muller's project remains relevant as a rich on-line source for the sacred texts of Daoist, Confucian, Hindu, Buddhist, and other traditions, some of which are still the only English translation.

Of course, Richard Wilhelm and Cary Bayne's masterful and accessible translation of the *I Ching* must be recognized. Carol Anthony who has written several books on the *I Ching* (some coauthored with Anna Moog) wrote the *pioneering guide* for helping the English reader interpret *I Ching* in her *A Guide to the I Ching.*

While this book depends upon a wide variety of literature about Chinese history and the world's religions, philosophy, science, and psychology, it is hard not to mention three books which were very helpful in capturing what I hope is the essence of Confucianism, the history of psychology, and the intellectual and developmental history of the *I Ching*:

1) Herbert Fingarette's *Confucius, The Secular and the Sacred,* is often cited in the literature and is a wonderfully subtle book on the *Analects of Confucius* in comparison with Western ways of thinking. Without this, one could fall into the trap of thinking Confucius taught a Western style of humanitarianism — which is far from the truth.

2) I have a long history of interest in perception, especially as it relates to artificial intelligence and the way subconscious thought interacts with conscious symbols and language. Danial Robinson's *An Intellectual History of Psychology* puts it all into context from Aristotle to today's latest neuroscience. When I found his Great Course on the same subject, I found it to be an even more elegant review of a very complex subject. It was a great help in sorting out how the theoretical models developed by Freud, for example, as it relates to other models of the mind. I will note that Robinson does not deal with Carl Jung, so putting Jung's thoughts into the context of psychology was "left to the student" as my professors would say.

3) While I cite several books regarding the history and development of the

*I Ching*, the book that deals with it directly is Richard Smith's *Fathoming the Cosmos and Ordering the World.* Added to this is Shaughnessy's *Before Confucius*. His translations, and histories further the cause of seeking to understand how the Chinese understood and used the *changes*. Of course, the *I Ching* grew up in the midst of a religious people. Julia Ching's, *Chinese Religions* provides a very accessible short history — a good place to start.

My mother, Barbara (Street) Olsen, was quite the poet. When she passed away, my sisters found her poetry in almost every drawer they opened, written on notepads, scraps of paper, and even napkins. Some of them are included in this book.

My wife, Mary Byers, who pressed me to explain what an *I Ching* meant to me. She has a created a large body of original fabric art; one of her several designs that have a yin-yang theme appears in this book.

Finally, my sister, Valarie Anderson, for her encouragement and editorial critique as this book took shape. Thanks so much Val.

### ⸻ Poetry and Poetic Prose ⸻

Italicized, indented text will be followed by an attribution citation if they are quotes. If no attribution is present, it is the author's own work.

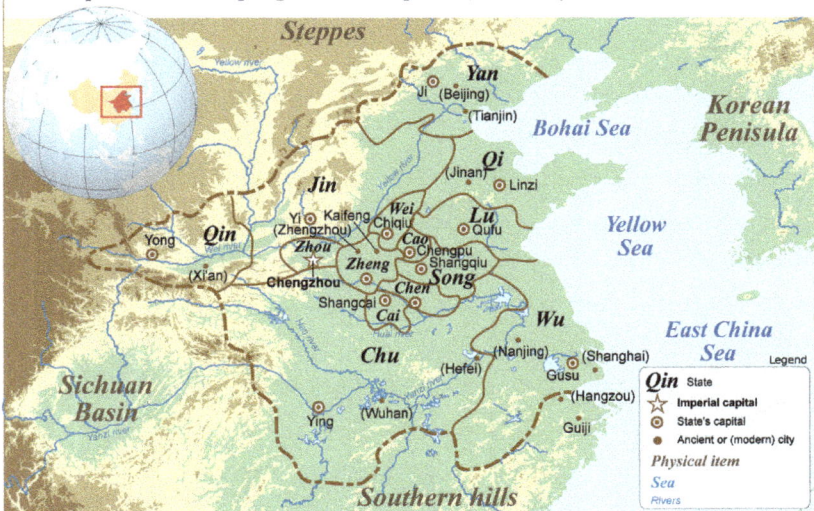

*Chinese plain in the late Spring and Autumn period (5th century BC)*

# TIMELINE OF CHINESE HISTORY

ANCIENT

Neolithic ...................c. 8500–2070 B.C.
Xia ...........................c. 2070–c. 1600 B.C.
Shang........................1600–1046 B.C.
Zhou ........................1046–256 B.C. — *Zhouyi* written
   *Western Zhou*
   Eastern Zhou
   Spring & Autumn .. 771 to 476 B.C. — Confucius, Laozi
   Warring States .......475–221 B.C. — Zhaungzi, Mecius, Great Treatise

IMPERIAL

Qin............................221–207 B.C.
Han...........................202 B.C.–A.D. 220 — Buddhism, Celestial Masters
Three Kingdoms...........220–280 — *I Ching* Canon with 10 Wing*s*
Jin.............................266–420
North South dynasties...420–589
Sui............................581–618
Tang..........................618–907
   (Wu Zhou 690–705)
5 Dynasties, 10 Kingdoms 907–979
Liao..........................916–1125
Song..........................960–1279 — Neo–Confucianism
Yuan.........................1271–1368
Ming..........................1368–1644
Qing..........................1636–1912

REPUBLICS and CONFLICT

A republic was founded in 1912, but by 1916 fell into what is known as the War Lord Period. A communist movement arose and civil war ensued. In the 1930s the Japanese invaded, the combatants in the civil war formed a fragile truce to fight the invaders — this became bound up in World War II. After WW II, the civil war resumed resulting in the Peoples Republic of China (PRC) ruling China in 1949 with the island of Taiwan being governed by the Kuomintang party as the Republic of China (ROC). This became bound up in the Cold War, with various blocks recognizing the two entities. The PRC became a member of the United Nations in 1972. The civil war was never formally concluded between the PRC and the ROC.

Goose in Flight

# ENDNOTES

## Front Matter - Notes

1. {Old Chinese} Kunst, *The Orginal YiJing,* 1.

## Chapter 1

1. {Chapter introduction quote} Yinglin, *Three Character Classic,* Verse 15. The *Three Character Classic* 三字經 has a three character title: 三 is the number 3; 字 means character; and 經 is the same *Ching* as in *I Ching.* This classic contains simple statements of Confucian ideas and Chinese history, used primarily to teach children. Written in the early 1200's A.D., it was usually the first book of a child's formal education through the latter part of the late nineteenth century.
2. {*I Ching* title} "The Classic of Changes" — Smith, *The I Ching A Biography,* xix; For "The Book of Changes" — Wilhelm, *The I Ching,* xxi.

    Regarding "The Easy Classic," the character 易 also means "easy," possibly because using the *I Ching* was easier that divination using turtle shells or on shoulder bones, heated with a red-hot poker so that the resulting cracks in the divination results. This method was used in early China, sometimes being used in conjunction with yarrow stalk manipulation for *I Ching* — Redmond, *Teaching the I Ching,* 8.

    Since Chinese characters are often ambiguous as to singular or plural if there not a sufficient context, the question is unsettled as to whether 易, *Yi,* (*I* — Wade-Giles) of the *I Ching* title should be singular or plural.

    Smith articulated his choice to translate 易 as "Changes" because it implies several different types of change, but notes that at least one other scholar renders it as "Change" because it is a single philosophical concept — Smith, *Fathoming the Cosmos and Ordering the World,* xvii.

    Shaughnessy, *The composition of the Zhouyi,* 106: notes that Zheng Xuan (A.D. 127–200) first articulated the notation that *Yi* 易 has three equal simultaneous meanings: Changing, Unchanging, Easy.

    See also: Cammann, "The Eight trigrams: Variants and Their Uses."
3. {I pronounced "ē"} Legge's late nineteenth century translation and Romanization scheme used "Yi." When Wilhelm translated the title to German, he used "I Ging." "I" is pronounced "ē" in German. When Cary Baynes translated the German to English she retained part of Wilhelm's title, "*I Ching.*"
4. {Different *I Ching* Titles} Smith, *The I Ching A Biography,* xix.
    周易 zhōu yì is another name sometimes used for the *I Ching* — *ibid.*
    Wade-Giles (Chou I) — Balkin, *The Laws of Change,* 3.
    yì jīng — "Mandarin Chinese Dictionary," Yabla Chinese.
5. {*Zhouyi*} Rutt, *Zhouyi, the book of changes,* 44; Ristsema, *The Original I Ching,* 2. Balkin, *The Laws of Change,* 3; Zhu, *Introduction to the Study of the Classic of Change (I-hsüeh Ch'i-meng),* i; Shaughnessy, *Unearthing the Changes, Preface,* viii – first page, not page numbered; Smith, *Fathoming the Cosmos and Ordering the World: The Yijing,* xvii.
    See also Wade-Giles dictionary, Chan, *A Concise English-Chinese Dictionary: With Romanized Standard Pronunciation for pronunciation of words used in Wilhelm.*

    The title *I Ching* (*Yi Jing*) first appeared in the Han Dynasty (Founded 206 B.C.) and the word Jing (Ching), "Great Book", was not used before then. The title, *I Ching,* corresponded with the writing of the ten wings. In fact, Zhou refers to the Dynasty and not the utility of the text, so what the book was originally called is a matter of speculation, with the logic that it was simply called *Yi* (*I*), Shaughnessy, The composition of the *Zhouyi,* 106.
    *Zhouyi* 周易 which is translated "The Changes of Zhou," is specifically used by Shaughnessy to refer to the Western Zhou Empire (circa 1100–770 B.C.) — Shaughnessy, *Before Confucius,* 27.

*Notes to pages 6 to 10*

"Western" refers to the location of the capital (Goajing — currently west of Xi'in in the Henan Province) compared to a new Zhou empire with a capital to the East, King Wen strengthened the Zhou clan and his son King Wu when his father died and overthrew the Song Dynasty in 1100 B.C. — Ye, *China, Five Thousand Years of History & Civilization*, 30–31.

King Wen is credited with writing the Judgments and the Duke of Zhou, King Wu's younger brother, the Line Statements — Smith, F*athoming the Cosmos and Ordering the World, the Yijing*, 9.

6.   {Yi symbol} Shaughnessy, *The composition of the Zhouyi*, 106.
7.   {Different English spelling} Further, spaces are often omitted in Pinyin and capitalization varies compared to other systems since the rule for running words together are different than in English. Generally, a pair of words with the same meaning are linked  with exceptions. See Swafford, "Pinyin.info a guide to writing of Mandarin Chinese in romanization," http://www.Pinyin.info/reading/xyg/rules.htim#x4.
     {Dao}: Also Romanized as "Tao," from the Wade-Giles Romanization system, which is how the word commonly seen in the English. Tao, and then the Pinyin Dao, have made their way into the English Language (See Oxford Dictionary).
     Dao means "way," "path," or "principle." See Hansen, "Daoism," 37;
     {Confucianism}: Ye, *China Five Thousand Years of History*, 220–236; Legge; *The Chinese Classics*, "Confucius and His Doctrines," 55–263; Peterson, "Commentary on the Attached Verbalizations of the Book of Change." 72.
8.   {So simple a child} Based on a statement from Diao Bao (Tiao Pao), "A child can practice it. But, a white-haired man cannot fathom it," Henderson, *Scripture, Canon and Commentary*, 134 quoting Tiao Pao, I-cho hsu (*Preface to the Deliberations of Changes*).
     Ch'ing-uju Hsueh-an 15.2b-3a (Vol. 1). Also quoted in Smith, Fathoming the Cosmos and Ordering the Word, 2; Hendson uses this quote to compare with similar quote regarding Homer and the Bhagavad Gita.
9.   {Synchronicity} Wilhelm, *The I Ching*, xxiv; Jung, *Synchonicity*, 105; Aziz, *Jung's Psychology of Religion and Synchronicity*; Cambray, *Synchronicity*, 28.
10.  {History of scholarship} Smith, *The I Ching, A Biography*, 7.
11.  {*I Ching* statecraft and philosophy} Wilhelm, The *I Ching*, liii, xviii, xlvii, lx.
12.  {Divination} Raphals, "Divination in the Han Shu Bibliographic Treatise," 47–48.
13.  {Points of View} Smith, "The Book of Changes Mirrors The Mind," 2;
     {Cosmology} Redmond, Teaching the *I Ching*, 19–20; Raphals, "Divination in the Han Shu Bibliographic Treatise," 48–49; Anthony, *The Philosophy of the I Ching*, Chapter 2, 23–76; Anthony, *The Psyche Revealed through the I Ching*, Chapter 14.
14.  {Predict the future every day} There is a significant body of evidence that the mind, in particular, on a subconscious level, lives in a world of anticipation, both and the point of perception, and in the more complex framework of subconscious higher-level memory/perception analysis.
     The popular books on the subject are Blink and The Signal and The Noise which are backed up by numerous academic papers — Gladwell, *Blink: the Power of Thinking without Thinking*; Silver, *The Signal and the Noise: Why Most Predictions Fail — but Some Don't*;
     A more technical look can be found in — Montagne, "What is visual anticipation and how much does it rely on the dorsal stem?"; Dozolme, "The neuroelectric dynamics of the emotional anticipation of other people's pain."; Mathews "Visual anticipation biases conscious decision making but not bottom-up visual processing."
15.  {Perform and religious rites} Anthony, *The Philosophy of the I Ching*, 83; Anthony, *I Ching, The Oracle of the Cosmic Way*, xii.
16.  {Quote} Smith, "The Psychology of Divination in Cross-Cultural Perspective," 1: See also Smith, "Knowing the Self and Knowing "Other": The Epistemological and Heuristic Value of the Yiching," 467.
17.  {As long as we reach the same goal} Gandhi, "Hind Swaraj or Indian Home Rule," Chapter X. Quote from a 1910 newspaper
18.  {Dominant mode of thinking} His Holiness The Dali Lama, *True Kinship of Faiths: How the World's Religions Can Come Together*. Kindle Locations 2020–2025.
19.  {Being the end of actions} Aristotle (Taylor trans.), *Nicomachean Ethics*, 24 [1097b21] — "Felicity" replaced with "A State of Happiness."
20.  {Authentic state of happiness} See for example — Augustine, *Confessions*, Book IV, Chapter

7, Book 5, Chapter 4; *Kath-Upanishad*, Part Four, II; *Buddhiprakāśa*, Dhammapada 21 (290; The Noble Koran 10:1. *Daodejing*, 58; *Confucius Analects*, Book 16; *The Holy Bible*, Isaiah 52:7.

21. {compatible with Christian beliefs} "Matteo Ricci," "Richard Wilhelm," "Richard Rutt," Wikipedia accessed March 2019.; Rutt, *Zhouyi*, Kindle Location 958; Smith, *Fathoming the Cosmos and Ordering the World*, 141.
{When you first read them} Hardy, *Sacred Texts of the World Lectures — Transcript*, Lecture 1, 9.
22. {Science ruler} Wilhelm, *The I Ching*, 280.
23. {Beatific Vision} Augustine, Chadwick (Trans.). *Confessions*, 123–124.
24. {Might of Truth} Eddy, *Science and Health*, vii, 25.
25. {Bodhi tree} Thich Nhat Hanh, *The Heart of Buddha's Teaching*, Kindle location 155; Bahm, *Philosophy of the Buddha*; Nārada. *The Buddha and His Teachings*.
26. {Charioteer} *The Bhagavad Gita*.
27. {Gabriel} *The Nobel Quran*, 53:4–9.
28. {Golden plates} *Book of Mormon for Latter-Day Saint Families*, Testimonies of … Witnesses, Kindle location 413
29. {Mandate of Heaven} Schwartz, *The World of Thought in Ancient China*, 39.
30. {Tightly to the truth} Gandhi, *Satyagraha*.
31. {Women's status when the original text — the *Zhouyi* — was written} Redmond [and Hon], *Teaching the I Ching (Book of Changes)*, devote a chapter this subject, Chapter 3, 72–94.
{Patriarchal slant} Lynn, The Classic of Change, 9.

~~~

Lynn uses Wang Bi's (A.D. 226–249) commentary, while recommending that one accepts the historic reality of Wang Bi's time, then "bracket them and put them aside." But, the Chinese characters in the text use the Chinese characters for the numbers 6 and 9 for broken and unbroken (See Shaughnessy, *I Ching*, The Classic of Changes, 42–43). Yin and yang being associated with the lines later.

○✦══════✦○✦○═══◀◀○

# Chapter 2

1. {Have and have not...Daodejing} Taoteching Verse 2; Lao-Tzu, Lao-tzu's Daoteching: With Selected Commentaries from the past 2,000 Years, 4. Traditional title and author: 道德經 by Lǎozi 老子.

~~~

The author is also called Lao Tzu, Laozi, which is an honorific title meaning "Old Master" attributed to a man named Li Tan, circa 550 B.C. or, some scholars maintain, Loa Tan circa 350 B.C., ibid. xv. Other scholars contend that Laozi was not a historical person and the *Daoteching* was the work of several authors.
2. {Fu Xi and mythical origin of trigrams} Smith, *Fathoming the Cosmos and Ordering the World*, Fu Xi is both the Pinyin and Wade-Giles Romanization.

~~~

Two-character expressions and names are generally run together with no space in Pinyin as in Fuxi. The name is Romanized Fuhsi in some texts using another Romanization system called Gwoyeu Romatzyh.
3. {Trigrams preceded hexagrams} Smith, *Fathoming the Cosmos and Ordering the Earth*, 9; Nielsen, *A Companion to Yi jing Numerology and Cosmology*, Kindle location 356.
{Fúxī} Qian, *Records of the Grand Historian*, 42; Ching, *Chinese Religions*, 23; "Fuxi," Wikipedia — accessed July 2017.
4. {Writing} Earliest pictographic written characters go back to at least 3000 B.C.
5. {Oracle bone divination} Creel, *The Birth of China*, 197–203; Redmond, *Teaching the I Ching*, 47–49; Smith, *Fathoming The Cosmos and Ordering the World*, 11, 55.

~~~

Sacrifice included war captives, sometimes in large numbers during the Shang Dynasty and before. The practice continued into the Zhou at diminishing frequency until if disappeared as a practice. However, the ritualistic meaning remains in the *Zhouyi*.
6. {Turtle shell and bone divination} Smith, *Fathoming the Cosmos*, 1–30 gives an easy to read scholarly account. Keightly, *The Ancestral Landscape*, gives a scholarly but accessible

*Notes to pages 19 to 24*

account of how the people of the time saw time, space, and community.

7. {Lunar cycles} Smith, *Fathoming the Cosmos and Ordering the World*, 9.
8. {Tian} Probably derived from great man — Zhang, *Key Concepts in Chinese Philosophy*, 3.
    人 Man –> 大 Great Man –> 天 Heaven — "great man in heaven" by adding the top line
9. {Historians doubt} Shaugnessy, *The Composition of the Zhouyi*, 49 — based both on historic/ literary analysis.
10. {Hunting Quote} Keightley, *The Ancestral Landscape*, 21, 30.
11. {Superior person in the *Zhouyi*} Redmond, *Teaching the I Ching*, 111–113.
12. {Other Asian Countries} Smith, *I Ching, A Biography*, xix.

     {Japan} Ng, *The I Ching in Tokugawa Thought and Culture*, 3; Ng, "Study and Uses of the *I Ching* in Tokugawa Japan," 24, 35; Smith, *I Ching*, A Biography, 132–139).
     {Korea} Ng "The *I Ching* in Late-Chosŏn Thought."; Smith, *I Ching, A Biography*, 114–149.
     {Vietnam} Ng, "Yijing Scholarship in Late-Nguyen Vietnam."; Smith, *I Ching, A Biography*, 150–158.
     {Tibet} Smith, *I Ching, A Biography*.
13. {Hundred Schools of Thought} Schwartz, *The World of Ancient Thought In China*, 59, 135; Jones,*The Great Qing Code, Qing Dynasty*, 1644–1911; Kohn, "Lao-tzu and the Tao-te-ching."; Wong, *Taoism*, 22.
14. {Yin-Yang symbol} The origin of the symbol seems to be uncertain. The symbol appears on Roman Shield designs circa A.D. 400 as well as Celtic art in circa A.D. 100. Of course, European contact with China was centuries old by that time — Wilhelm, *The I Ching*, lv, liii, 280 (Ta Chuan— The Great Treatise section); Rubin, "The Concepts of Wu-Hsing and Yin–Yang," 130, 140.
15. {Tian — Dao used by Confucius} Specifically, Confucius saw the ideal way as that ancients reconstructed from stories about the founders of the Zhou Dynasty, Waley, *The Analects*, Kindle Location 329.
16. {Correlative Cosmology} Som, *Comprehensive Discussions in the White Tiger Hall*, 75–81; Retsima, *The Complete I Ching Oracle*, 52–53; Rutt, *Zhouyi*, Kindle Location 619.
17. {Doing for nothing} Yu-Land, *A Short History of Chinese Philosophy*, 45.
18. {Judgments/ Lines in circulation 300 B.C.} Redmond, *Teaching the I Ching*, 111–113.
19. {Confucius Canon} Lynn, *The Classic of Changes*, 25; Smith, *The I Ching A Biography*, 5, 11, 22; Ye, China, *Five Thousand Years of History and Culture*, 156.

20. {Current text little change from Recived Text} Historians agree that there was more than one version, as evidenced by late twentieth century archeological finds, but the versions that are known are very similar — Redmond, *Teaching the I Ching*, 14, 93.

     Most English translations up until the 1990s, including Wilhelm's and Legge's, are translations of the Received Text, which is the Imperial Edition first published in 1715 — Legge, *The I Ching (The Yi King)*, Preface, xxi; Wilhelm, *The I Ching*, Introduction, lxi.
     Since then, some translations take into account late twentieth century archeological versions of the *I Ching* or present other philosophic schools.
21. {Rounded out ... political and moral} Redmond, *Teaching the I Ching*, 156; Smith, *Fathoming the Cosmos and Ordering the World*, 32; Wilhelm (Hellmut), *Understanding the I Ching*, 85–86.
22. {Synergy of Daoism/Confucianism} Daoism is a term that can refer to either a Philosophy or Religion. The works of Daodejing attributed to Laozi 老子 and Zhuangzi 莊子 attributed to an author of the same name, are viewed as philosophical works written during the Hundred Schools of Thought, whereas Daoism as a religion was organized in the second century A.D. as a salvation religion, with a heritage of Daoist Philosophy and ancient Chinese religions, being influenced by, and in reaction to, the arrival of Buddhism to China, (Ching, Chinese Religion, 85–85, 102–103)
     {Dates of Ten Wings} Smith, *Fathoming the Cosmos and Ordering the World*, 37–38.
23. {Gentleman} Waley, *The Analects of Confucius*, See 27–29, Chün-Tzu (Wade-Giles), Jūnzǐ (Pinyin), "Gentleman" ruling class.

     However, Waley's commentary appears to miss a critical difference. The English class system was based on inheritance, with ways to move up the class structure (Enter the Warrior Caste and Marriage in the earlier history). This existed in China as well, but Confucius insisted that the character of Junzi could be achieve though education. China developed a merit system where Government officials and indeed being a member of the noble class required passing examinations in Confucius thinking. See Fairbank, *China A New History*, 95.

Whereas England required inherited membership noble class at least until the industrial revolution and Gentry, "The English Class System in the Early 1800s (Class Report)"; See also "Junzi," Wikipedia — accessed July 2018.

24. {Orderly laws of change} Redmond, Teaching the *I Ching*, 167.
25. {Focus on human relationships} Waley, The Analytics of Confucius.
26. {Unlearning} Ibid., 73.
27. {When I cast the *I Ching* Legge, *I Ching*, Appendix III, Section I, Chapter 12, Verse 76, 376–377. Paraphrased. The "Master" refers to Confucius.
28. {Pure Land Buddhism} One advantage of Pure Land Buddhism in its spread to commoners is that it does not require literacy or rigorous meditative practices to reach the "Pure Land" paradise. The Buddhist movement throughout East Asia had an effective network of monasteries for spreading the belief system — Ebray, *Cambridge Illustrated History of China,* Chapter 4, pages 86–107; Benjamin, *Lectures: Foundations of Eastern Civilization*, Especially Lectures 19 and 20); Ou, "The Successful Integration of Buddhism with Chinese Culture: A Summary."
29. {Buddhism's spread into China} Ebray, Cambridge Illustrated History of China, Chapter 4, pages 86–107; Benjamin, *Lectures: Foundations of Eastern Civilization,* Lectures 19 and 20.
30. {Pure Land and Chan taught together} Ye, *China Five Thousand Years of History & Civilization*, 386, 395–396; Benjamin, *Lectures: Foundations of Eastern Civilization*, Lectures 19, 20, and 45.
31. {Buddhism influence on the *I Ching*} Lai (editor), *The Yijing <易經> and the Formation of the Huayan 華嚴 Philosophy: An Analysis of a Key Aspect of Chinese Buddhism* — Chapter by Cheng, *Philosophy of the Yi 易: Unity and Dialectics*, 101–111.

The Huayan school was a major influence on Chan Buddhism and is considered part of its historic development. The Huayan movement did not really recover from the purges of A.D. 841; Translations that are "Buddhist" *I Ching* texts are a reinterpretation of the *I Ching* written well after the Received Text — Ou-i, The Buddhist *I Ching*, vi – first page of Introduction.);

{Buddhism incorporating the *I Ching*} Smith, *Fathoming the Cosmos and Ordering the World*, 90.,153, 165–167.
32. {Four Books} Gardner, *The Four Books*, Kindle location 30, 102.
33. {Legge translation} The *I Ching* was translated into Latin earlier by a Jesuit Missionary Jean-Baptisti Régis in the 1730s. Smith, The *I Ching*, A Biography, 180; The Legge translation is Vol. XVI of The Sacred Books of the East, published in 1899.

~~~

Legge was a great scholar but not a believer in much of the Chinese viewpoint including the divination utility of the *I Ching* — Legge, *I Ching*, Introduction, 21. The translation was part massive undertaking organized by F. Max Müller, *Sacred Texts of the East*, to translate the religious books of the East including the Hindu, Buddhist, and Chinese classics.
34. {Out of copyright} Legge's translation used his own Romanization system; the transliteration table is found at the end of the second edition of the Legge translation. His title was Yî King. Publications using Legge's translation will be titled *I Ching* and use the Pinyin or Wade-Giles Romanization because of its popularity.
35. {Wilhelm translation} Smith, *The I Ching A Biography*, 188–189.
36. {Carl Jung} "About Jung." The Jung Page; Wilhelm, *The I Ching*, Forward; Jung, *Man and His Symbols* — Part 5 Symbols in an Individual Analysis by Jonade Jacobi, Kindle location 4827. Jung, *Psyche & Symbol, A Selection of Writings*; Jung, *Synchronicity: An Acausal Connecting Principle*; Jung, *On Synchronicity and the Paranormal*.
37. {As a tool of self-awareness} Smith, *The I Ching A Biography*, 198.
38. {1960s ideas} Smith, *The I Ching A Biography*, 194–210.
39. {Dao of Physics} Capra, *The Tao of Physics*, 107–108; Smith, *The I Ching A Biography*, 195.
40. {Psychology} See Jung, Synchronicity, §986; Jung, *Archetypes and the Collective Uncon-*

*Notes to pages 28 to 36*

*scious*, §82.

41. {Lunch Party Painting} White, *Renoir, His Life, Art, and Letters*, 110–111.

42. {Quote} "Impressionism," Wikipedia (CC BY-SA-3.0; Kapos, *The Impressionists and Their Legacy*, "An Impressionists View."

43. {Gua} These are referred to as Guá, which is the same term for each of the eight trigrams, although they called Ba (eight) gua.

44. {Yin and Yang; Female and Male} Pearson, *The Original I Ching*, 19–21.

> The gender assignment to Yin and Yang occurs in Wang Bi's commentary. This and the "received text" — the imperially sanctioned version has been used for most English translations. In contrast, the late twentieth century discovery of an older version *I Ching* called the Mawangdui text has gender neutral associations with broken and unbroken lines.
>
> Smith, Fathoming the Cosmos and Ordering the World, 12–13 notes that the association of male and female with Yang and Yin developed in the Han Dynasty (206 B.C. to A.D. 200) as part of the correlative cosmology that was developed, most notably by Dong Zhongshu 董仲舒 (179 B.C.–104 B.C.), who had much to do with convincing the emperor to canonize the Confucius Classics. Here Yin and Yang are seen as male and female cosmic forces, not simply animal or human genders. While the attachment to Yin-Yang evolved, the idea of male and female cosmic forces, including sexual union, is an old idea, found in many creation stories throughout the world including China.

45. {Original Chinese text} *The Zhouyi*.

46. {Chinese scholars made the connection} The translations almost always use the imperially sanctioned "received text" unless specifically translated recent archeological finds, the most complete being from the Mawangdui texts. Yin is found in the *Zhouyi* in Hexagram 61, Line 2.

47. {Hexagram number} The numbering is standard for nearly all translations for what is called the "received text" — although recent archeological finds have different orderings, most notably the version the *I Ching* called the Mawangdui Texts. The translation by Edward Shaughnessy lists the hexagrams in a different order. Shaughnessy's translations include a table that matches the Mawangdui order to the received order.

    The received order organizes the hexagram in pairs, pairs cycling their trigrams upside down — with some exceptions. The order of the pairs is the subject of much discussion and speculation. Another ordering is a binary arrangement in some graphics but is not used in translated texts. The binary order was the result of later thinkers trying to tease out numerology meanings from the text with some claiming an early instance of binary counting. The Mawangdui order is a systematic ordering using trigrams as the basis for the sequence.

48. {Statement for each of the six lines} The first two hexagrams, the first with all unbroken lines, Heaven, and the second with all broken lines, Earth have a seventh statement that is read in the rare event that all lines are changing — Wilhelm, *The I Ching*, 10, 15.

49. {Books of the Bible} For example, the Torah, the first five books of the Hebrew Bible/Christian Old Testament, are traditionally attributed to Moses, most scholars believe that they were a compilation of early books that evolved over a century or two — Thompson, *The Historicity of the Patriarchal Narratives; the Quest for the Historical Abraham*, Chapter 12, Summary and Conclusions, 315–330.

50. {Understand the old poem} Shaughnessy, *Source of Western Zhou History*, 3.

# Chapter 3

1. {Great Treatise} Legge, *The I Ching*, Appendix III, Chapter IX:49, 365.

2. {Ancient divination in China} Redmond, Teaching the *I Ching*, 256–257;

    The examples below are from divination using turtle shells and on shoulder bones (also called oracle bones), using a technique that involved heating and cracking the shell, occurring during the late Shang Dynasty in the period of 1200–1045 B.C. The use on yarrow stalks began to be used in conjunction with this method, eventually replacing it in the following Zhou dynasty.

## Notes to pages 36 to 39

Keightley, *The Ancestral Landscape*, 114 for two examples: We should send men.../ We should not send men; There will be a flood/There will not be a flood.

Ibid. 108–109 for a conditional example: It should be the officers that the King joins, then there will be no disaster with a follow up in the same divination: If the king joins the officers on the hunt, they will succeed.

3. {Divine Mind} Emmerson, *Essential Writings*, "Over Soul," 236–251; Eddy, *Science and Health with Key to the Scriptures*, 77–79; Holmes, *The Science of Mind, A Complete Course in the Science of Mind and Spirit*, "Lesson One: Metaphysical Chart No. 1."; Auge, "Meditation," *Christian Science Sentinel*, 19 March 1921; Turk, "Divine Mind's Control," *Christian Science Sentinel*, 12 July 1950;

~~~

For the American grown religious transcendental movement see: Satter, *Each Mind a Kingdom: American Women, Sexual Purity, and the New Thought Movement, 1875–1920*}.

4. {Positive affirmation} Creswell, "Self-Affirmation Improves Problem-Solving under Stress."; Scheier, "A Model of Behavioral Self-Regulation: Translated Into Action."

5. {Positive Affirmation} Schucman, A Course in Miracles, 102.

6. {Fates} Homer, *The Iliad*, 16, 35, 122;
Called the Norns in Germanic and Nordic mythology — *Poetic Edda*, Helgakvida Hundingsbana Fyrri, Verse 2, 227; Called Μοῖραι in Greek; For Romans it was the Parcae who control one's Fata.
The three Μοῖραι/Fates:
Clotho: spinning the life thread;
Lachesis: Measuring the life thread;
Atopos: Inevitable, cutting the life thread — Plato, *The Republic*, 480.

7. {Subconscious mind — framework} See Eagleman, *Incognito: The Secret Lives of the Brain*.

8. {Person Centered Therapist} Nickerson, "Confirmation Bias: A Ubiquitous Phenomenon in Many Guises," 177, 195.

9. {ELIZA} ELIZA program was written by Joseph Weizenbaum and can still be found on the web, which was also called "DOCTOR." Eliza, Wikipedia (Accessed 10/16/2015).
{Person-Centered Therapy — Seeks to bring congruence of self-concept and emotional experiences,} Cain, *Person-Centered Psychotherapies*, Kindle Location 320, example at Kindle location 1945.

~~~

The therapist is a positive reinforcement, affirming listener who lets the patient guide the therapy, ibid. Chapter 4. When the *I Ching* is in this role, a person's self regard stands in for the therapist.

10. {Confirmation bias} Nickerson, "Confirmation Bias: A Ubiquitous Phenomenon in Many Guises."
See especially page 177 for definition under title "Hypothesis-Determined Information Seeking and Interpretation." On Page 211, the author notes that people only think of one hypothesis at a time, leading to overestimating the accuracy of ones Judgments.

11. {Self-awareness tool} Redmond, *Teaching the I Ching*, 33-34.

12. {Will of the Divine} Hebrew Bible (Tanakh נָביא) /Holy Bible Old Testament: Judges 18:5; New Testament: John 11:22; Noble Qur'an نآرقلا ميركلا: Surah 2:213.

13. {Hud 11:56} Kahn, *The Holy Quran The Qur'an Translation*. Allāh is Arabic for "The God." The notation of "An interpretation" is due to the fact that the English translation of the Qur'an is not considered the revealed scripture and its meaning cannot be entirely accurately transmitted unless it is written and heard in its original language, Arabic.

14. {Faith if the} Lightman, *The Accidental Universe*, 52.

15. {Good} Redmond, *Teaching the I Ching*, 29–30.

16. {Centered self} Anthony, *The Other Way, Meditation Experiences Based on the I Ching*: This book is essentially a journal by subject of Carol Anthony's experiences that seem primarily based on this outlook.

17. {Quote} Papamânanda, *The Upanishads*, 29.

18. {Eight poem} Let 8 and 8 be (the hexagram name) Joy (the hexagram name) Joy so that with Double Joy (the iconic image of) Double Joy can twice be seen. Using Pinyin it reads, Bā [shí] bā be the Duì so that with shuāngxǐ, can twice be seen — the image of Xǐ.

19. {Hexagram 20 quote — Ritual} Wilhelm, The *I Ching*, 82–83.

20. {Forming a questions} See Redmond, Teaching the *I Ching*, 256–257 for example for a focus

*Notes to pages 39 to 45*

on how to formulate a question based on Chinese ancient custom, advising not to ask, "should I," but to ask "what if."

21. {Discussion of ritual} Anthony, The Other Way, Meditation Experiences Based on the *I Ching*, 9–19.

22. {Zhu Wen Kung} Friedman, *Life Magazine*, "The Life Millennium: The 100 Most Important Events and People of the Past 1000 Years,"

23. {Ritual}{Master Zhu}: Smith, *Fathoming the Cosmos and Ordering the World*, 229; {A Pschological process} Xunzi (Watson trans.), Xunzi: *Basic Writings*, 98–108. Circa 300 B.C.
{Ruling Class Ritual}: T'ung. *The Comprehensive Discussions in the White Tiger Hall*, 524– 525;
{The Logogram for East, 東} combines the characters for sun and tree/wood.

24. {Compass Direction} Redmond, *Teaching the I Ching*, 256.

   Chinese ancient maps had South at the top: See Figure 5, Luo Shu Square/Luo River Map diagram, in Wilhelm, *The I Ching*, 310 showing South at the top.
   The tradition in ancient China is that a palace should face South toward the ruler's subjects — Redmond, *Teaching the I Ching*, 52; Benjamin, *Foundations of Eastern Civilization (Transcript)*, Lecture 22, 367.

25. {Development of *I Ching* based on experience} Shaughnessy, *Before Confucius*, 13; Redmond, *Teaching the I Ching*, 68–69.

26. {Rooted in your own tradition} Ritsema, *I Ching*, 18; Redmond, *Teaching the I Ching*, 256.

27. {Formulating a question} Redmond, *Teaching the I Ching*, 256–257; Ritsema, *I Ching*, 18; Wilhelm, *The I Ching*, Introduction, liv.

28. {*I Ching* and Meditation} Anthony, *A Guide to the I Ching*, xx; Anthony, *The Other Way* — A series of journal meditations organized by subject using the *I Ching*; Wilhelm, *The I Ching*, 314: The Great Treatise, Part 1, Chapter X — The Fourfold Use of the Changes, Verses 1 and 2.

29. {Lines and Yin-Yang} The attachment of Yin and Yang to the broken lines (the dark principle) and unbroken lines (the light principle) during the Qin (Ch'in) and Han Dynasties (221 B.C.–A.D. 220) is discussed in Wilhelm's Introduction — Wilhelm, *The I Ching*, iv–lvii (Wilhelm Introduction).

   There are various hypotheses as to the origins of the Lines: segments of single or double segment bamboo sticks used for divination, knotted cords, and representations of sexual organs of the first two hexagrams. Smith, The *I Ching, A Biography*, 23.

30. {Ancient attachment of even and odd numbers to line} Smith, *Fathoming the Cosmos and Ordering the World*, 10; Shaughnessy, *I Ching, Classic of Changes*: See translation of Mawangdui Text beginning on page 39; Shaughnessy, *Unearthing the Changes*, See translations in Chapters 5 and 7.

   Historical records of using the *I Ching* (the *I Ching* text itself not surviving), show using a range of numbers from 1 to 9, before settling down to 6 to 9, but the method being used has been lost. Both the Received Text of the *I Ching* and the oldest extant versions, such as the Mawangdui text, use 6. mith, *Fathoming the Cosmos and Ordering the World*, 26.

31. {Three types of components} Ibid. 138.

32. {He has fish} Ibid. 139.

33. {Auspicious, inauspicious, danger, no blame } Shaughnessy, *The composition of the Zhouyi*, 152–153.

34. {Image Statement} Paraphrase of Legge, *I Ching*, 316 (Appendix II, XL).

35. {Yarrow stalks} Achillea millefolium — Also referred to a Milfoil stalks.
{Divination methods} Smith, *Fathoming the Cosmos and Ordering the World*, 8–9; Smith, *The I Ching, A Biography*, 21; Redmond, *Teaching the I Ching*, 257.

36. {Date of Coin Use} Huang, *The Complete I Ching*, xxiv.
   This is an approximate date for the early Tang Dynasty (A.D. 618–907) when most scholars date the beginning of coin use, although Kartcher, (*I Ching*, 21) claims that it became popular in the Southern Song (Sung: Wade-Giles) period (A.D. 1127–1279).
   {Ease of Use} The coins are easier than the yarrow Stalk method. It should be noted that Yi (I) in the title of the Yijing (*I Ching*) can also mean, "easy." Some scholars speculated that

the yarrow stalk method began as an easier alternative to cracking more expensive turtle shell or on cattle shoulder bones —Whincup, *Rediscovering the I Ching*, 217 (Appendix B).

37. {Yarrow} Also referred to as Milfoil in the literature. Latin name: *Anchillea millefolium.*

38. {Recreated by Zhu Xi} Zhu Xi (Chu Hsi) — Adler, *Introduction to the Study of the Classic of Change*, x.
{Yarrow Method described} Ibid. 33–47.
{Early Divination} Smith, *Fathoming the Cosmos and Ordering the World*, 15–16; Shaughnessy, *Before Confucius, Studies in the Creation of the Chinese Classics*, 26–27.
{Translated text used by Zhu Xi} Wilhelm, *The I Ching*, 308 — Da Zhaun 大傳, (Ta Chuan), Book II, Chapter IX, Verse 1.

39. {Changing Lines} The original method of selecting which lines to read is a subject of controversy. The idea of one hexagram changing to another was a later invention. The original method of manipulating yarrow stalks to get numbers from 1 to 9, using an unknown method, resulted in only one line reading — Shaughnessy, *The composition of the Zhouyi*, 84, 102.

40. {Great Expansion} Legge, *I Ching*, 365: *The Great Treatise or Great Commentary, Dazhuan* 大傳, Section 1, Chapter IX, Verse 51. Author's paraphrase.

This verse was the one used by Zhu Xi to reconstruct the yarrow Stalk method. The verse combines numerology and key theme of the correlative cosmology to provide meaning to the divination method used as part Confucian commentaries.
{Use of yarrow stalk — Milfoil — in early Zhou just prior to the birth of Confucius} Smith, *Fathoming the Cosmos and Ordering the World*, 15.
{Association with Correlative Cosmology} — Smith, *Fortune-tellers and Philosophers, Divination in Traditional Chinese Society*, 27.

There is at least one analysis of ancient divination records that suggest that the method was not as stated by Zhu Xi — Chen, "How To Form a Hexagram and Consult the *I Ching*."

⊶═══⊷⊶⊷═══⊷⊷○

# Chapter 4

1. {Heaven and Earth} Legge, *I Ching*, 348: *The Great Treatise* or *Great Commentary*, Dazhuan 大傳, Section 1, Chapter 1, Verse 1. Author's Paraphrase.

2. {Science of the Concrete} Levi-Strauss, *The Savage Mind*, 13–15.

3. {Written character for hill} ß is a radical, a part of a Chinese character that has a meaning or phonic clue. See Glossary for Radical,

4. {Yin-Yang} Yu-Lan, *A Short History of Chinese Philosophy*, 138; Wang, "Yinyang (Yin-Yang)."; Wilhelm, *The I Ching*, lvi; Wang, *Yinyang*, 1; Rubin, *The concepts of Wu-hsing [Wu Xing] and Yin-Yang*, 139–140.

Note that the Yin-Yang earliest reference to a the two characters 陰陽 appears to be reference to a a Dynastic Poem — Waley, *Book of Songs*, Song 239, 243–244; Legge, *The Book of Poetry*, Part II, VI, Verse 5, 314). The verse is about a victorious ruler marking off land to give to his army. It clearly did not have the philosophical meaning here that it acquired later. However, philosophical concept is clearly present by the end of the Warring States Period (476–221 B.C.) and was philosophical term for many of the schools of thought including, School of Naturalists or Yin-Yang, Taoist Philosophy, and Confucianism.

5. {Yin-Yang Principle} Wilhelm, *The I Ching*, lvi;
{Yang-Yin-Cycle three aspects of Yin-Yang} Chen, *Bain (Change): A Perpetual Discourse of I Ching*, 10–11.

6. {The Creative actuates} Legge, *I Ching, The Great Treatise*, Appendix III, Section 1, Chapter 1, Verse 5, 349.

7. {Heaven is High...} *The Great Treatise*, Part 1, Chapter 1, Verse 1, Legge, *I Ching*, Appendix III, 348; Wilhelm, *The I Ching*, 280. Included authors interpretation of some phrases.
{Deep Ecology} Næss, "The Shallow and the Deep, Long-Range Ecology Movement. A Summary," 95. Næss essentially repeats essence of the Confucian/Doaist dialog (*See Page*

*Notes to pages 64 to 71*

*21*) using the terms "man-in-the-environment" (Confucian) "in favour of" "the relational, total-field image" (Daoist). Finding resonance with Baruch Spinoza, Næss has to take a different tact than Laozi and Zhuangzi: to start from the religious/ethical proactive Wesstern philosophies and work back similar to where the Daoists began.

8.  {Quote} Legge, *Zhuangzi*, Book II, Part 1, Section II.2, Kindle Location 157 replacing "Let us Stop" with "Leave it be" by Author using Zhuangzi, and Watson, *Zhuangzi,* 33 as a guide.

9.  {Daodejing 2} Laozi and Legge, *Daodejing*, 2; Laozi and Red Pine, *Daodejing*, 2. Author's interpretation.

10. {superficial reader... throught full reader} Smith, *Fathoming the Cosmos and Ordering the World*, 2.

11. {Wu Wei} Theodore, *Sources of Chinese Tradition*, 78; Littlejohn, "Daoist Philosophy," Paragraph 5; Schwartz, *The World of Thought in Ancient China*, 216–217; Ye, *China Five Thousand Years of History and Civilization*, 248; Smith, *Fathoming the Cosmos and Ordering the World*, 104; Shaughnessy, *Before Confucius*, 207.

12. {Quote} Legge, *Zhuangzi*, Kindle location 1501.

13. {Yin-Yang and the *I Ching*} Smith, *The I Ching A Biography,* 31; Lynn, *The Classic of Changes*, 15.

14. {Correlation of Three Powers, Heaven, human, and nature/Earth} is part of what is known as a Correlative Cosmology.

    {Yin-Yang and Human Events} *Smith, Fathoming the Cosmos and Ordering the World,* 32; Schwartz, The World of Though in Ancient China, 350; *The Great Treatise*, I 5:7, Wilhelm, *The I Ching*, 300; Rubin, *The Concepts of Wu-Hsing and Yin-Yang*, 141; Example of a Han Dynasty interpretation of an circa 800 B.C. divination attaching Yin-Yang principle to *I Ching* lines — Shaughnessy, *Before Confucius*, 207.

    {Tendency to correlation Heaven and Human} Schwartz, *The World of Though in Ancient China*, 351; Levi-Strauss, *The Savage Mind*, Chapter 6 provides several examples of correlative knowledge that provides useful and comprehensive understanding of nature in various tribes, 161–177; See also Nostradamus, Century I:56 for an example

15. {Three powers} Wilhelm, *The I Ching*, 264–274; Redmond, *Teaching the I Ching*,152.

16. {Correlative Cosmology and Medicine} Smith, *Fathoming the Cosmos and Ordering the World*, 32–36; Theodore, *Sources of Chinese Tradition*, 274; Littlejohn, "Wuxing (Wu–Hsing) [Five Agents]."

    See Pregadio, "The Seal of the Unity of Three for both the Wuxing and Yin Yang" as a source of medicine and the Daoist Religious search for longevity. A brief history of the development of the Five Agents is in, Dainian, *Key Concepts of Chinese Philosophy*, Chapter 12, 93–103.

    The Five Elements and Yin Yang are central to acupuncture and other Chinese medicine. For example, see Liao, "The Origin of the Five Elements in the Traditional Theorem of Acupuncture: A Preliminary Brief Historic Enquiry," 7–14.

    You can see the idea of five forces expressed 2000 years later by Walter Russell as the five octaves of yang and five octaves of yin in the Ten Octaves — Russell, *The Universal One*, Kindle Location 715.

17. {Quote} Fransesco of Assisi, *The Canticle of the Sun*. Quoted in part. Note the alternation of male and female references.

18. {Dhammapada Quote} Muller, *The Dhammapada*, Chapter 15 Happiness, Verses 197–200.

19. {Description of offering} Black Elk, *Black Elk Speaks*, 117. See also, Black Elk, *The Sacred Pipe*, 112, Hunkapi rite, the making of relatives — where the chanters turn in the four directions,... where the sun goes down, where the Giant Lives, where the sun comes from, the power ... the heavens, the earth, all relatives, all one.

20. {*Qi* meaning} Major, *Heaven and Earth in Early Han Thought*: Chapters Three, Four and Five of the Huainanzi, xxxv.

21. {Matter and Energy} For *Qi (Ch'i)*, see Dianian, *Key Concepts of Chinese Philosophy*, 45 and the "Treatise on the Patterns of Heaven," Section 1 of the Huainanzi, "Spacetime produced the original *Qi*"; Major, *Heaven and Earth in Early Han Thought*: Chapters Three, Four and Five of the Huainanzi, 31.

    For the Western Science, see Penrose, *The Road to Reality*, 433–435. The Newtonian laws of Conservation of Matter and Conservation of Energy become unified in Einstein's Equation for matter at rest in relation to the observer: $e = mc^2$ — energy and matter are the same thing, where if one assumes units of the speed of light (Warp 1 in Star Trek or, for the physicist, a Planck Units), then e = m.

22. {*Qi* (Ch'i) meaning over time} Schwartz, *The World of Thought in Ancient China*, 181–183; Smith, *Fathoming the Cosmos and Ordering the World*, 115–116. Simplified Chinese is 气. 氣 also means vapor, anger, and pronounced differently, *xì*, to present food. Qi, Wikipedia. — accessed March 2018.
    {Timing of *Qi* as a cosmic force} Zhang, *Key Concepts in Chinese Philosophy*, 53–53; Roth, *The Original Tao*, 41: The approximate date of *Qi* becoming thought of as a cosmic force is prior to 139 B.C. when Hauinanzi wrote his essays on Yin-Yang and *Qi*.

23. {Doctrine of Mean Quote} Zisi and Legge, *Doctrine of the Mean* 315–316; Zisi and Muller, *Doctrine of the Mean*.

24. {德 De translation} Author translated and substituted the quoted text De (德) as Inner Power of Virtue, which is also translated as Inner Power: Roth, *The Original Tao, 42. Current definition of Dé includes morality, virtue, and character, See Linnell, "G*uanzi, Number 49 : Study of Inner Cultivation"; Yabla Chinese, "Mandarin Chinese Pinyin English Dictionary." — accessed April 2018.
    If both ideas are embodied in De of Power and Virtue, one arrives at what Mahatma Gandhi called "soul-force," Gandhi, *Non-Violent Resistance (Satyaaraha [insistence on truth])*, 17, 34–35.

25. {Nie Ye}See Roth, *The Original Tao* ; Linnell, *Guanzi*, Number 49: "Study of Inner Cultivation [Nei Ye]".

26. {Zhu Xi Commentary} Commentary on: Gardner, *Zhu Xi's Reading of the Analects: Canon, Commentary and the Classical Tradition*, Kindle location 921: This is in response to the Confucian Analects where The Masters said he was born not knowing — referencing back to loyalty, truthfulness, and love of learning.

27. {Mysticism and the Dao} Schwartz, *The World of Thought in Ancient China*, 193–194.

28. {Zhuangzi} *Zhuangzi*, Legge (trans.), Kindle location 91 — inserted *Qi* where Legge used, "spirit-like powers."

29. {Character scripts/styles} The earliest Chinese characters were written in a collection of sytles called Zhaun Shu (Seal Style). Since this was difficult to write with a calligraphy brush resulting in a series of standards including that used in most modern publications including this book, the Kai Shu (Standard Style). https://en.wikipedia.org/wiki/Chinese_script_styles — accessed June 2019.

30. {The Way} The Dao 道 character is used for both the mundane, a principle, and metaphsical term in the same text, such as the Confucian Analects were it will be translated as "road" or "path" in the mundane sense to walk on and be combined with *Ren* (a good hearted person) to become a principle of virtue or *Tien* (of the heavens) to become a metaphysical term to act in accord with the workings of Heaven. One can see this as a somewhat similar concept to acting in accord with the Will of God in the Abrahamic Religions (Jewish, Christian, and Islam).

31. {No name and shape} Wilhelm, *The Secret of the Golden Flower*, Chapter 1, Heavenly Consciousness (The Heart), 21.

32. {Sound} Here Legge is using a nautical term for finding the bottom of the sea: "Sounding the Depths" by tossing a weighted rope over the side of a ship and recording how much rope was let out when the weight hits the bottom (King, *A Sea of Words*, 410) — keeping in the spirit of the poetry of the *Daodejing* while translating the word/character Guān 观 defined in current dictionaries as: to watch, to observe, to behold, concept.

33. {Daodejing Quote} Legge, *Sacred Books of the East — Vol 34, Part 1, Daodejing*, 47. See also, Pine, *Tao te ching*, 1. Replaced Legge's transliteration of Tâo with Dao.

34. [Fish in water} See *Zhuangzi*, Book IV. Part 1, Section VI, Verse 11 "The Great and Most Honored Master", Kindle location 690 — Fishes breed and grow in the water; man develops in the Tao. Growing in the water, the fishes cleave the pools, and their nourishment is supplied to them. Developing in the Tao, men do nothing, and the enjoyment of their life is secured. Hence it is said, Fishes forget one another in the rivers and lakes; men forget one another in the arts of the Tao.

35. {"Gives life"Pregaido, *The Routledge Encyclopedia of Taoism*, Vol. 1, 305.

36. {Field} Feynman, "Space-Time Approach to Quantum Electrodynamics," 770–771; Penrose, *The Road to Reality*, 60; Bell, "Speakable and unspeakable in quantum mechanics."
    See also Misner, *Gravitation*, 431–434 (History of Einstein's gravitational field equations. Gravitational Waves in Gravitational Fields: ibid. 444–445. The math is difficult in this book, but some of the illustrations, particularly in Chapter 1, are informative and

*Notes to pages 75 to 82*

can be followed without working through all of the math.
37. {Daodejing verse 19} Legge, *The Text of Taoism*, 62.
38. {"if one puts their ego aside"} Author's interpretation — Wilhelm, *The I Ching*, *The Great Treatise*, Part 1, Chapter 1, Verse 287: Legge, *I Ching*, Appendix III, Section 1, Chapter 1, Verse 349.
39. {De and Dao} Schwartz, *The World of Thought in Ancient China*, 76, 197.
40. {Logos...Divine logic of the Universe} Plotinus, *The Enneads*, First Ennead, Second Tractate, 3rd Chapter; Philo, *The Works of Philo Judaeus of Alexandria*, Kindle location 5, 96; *The Holy Bible*, John 1:1–5, 1:14–15.
Of course the Jewish (and since they have the same scriptural heritage: Christian and Muslim) tradition of Philo was that God Created the Universe by an act of Divine Will or by the act of speaking the creation into existence (See Genesis Chapter 1 and note that God is actually speaking — the creative power of the spoken word is shared with other ancient traditions). On the other hand, Plotinus belived the Universe was simply a consequence of God's existence; Morwood, *The Pocket Oxford Classical Greek Dictionary*.
The comparison gets more remote, however, when this was carried further in Christian thought to include the personification of Logos as embodied in the living, loving, presence of Jesus Christ that is believed to be available to the faithful of the Christian tradition to this day.
{Embodied in Jesus Christ} i.e. Incarnation — the Divine taking on flesh, which in most Christian traditions is unique to Jesus Christ.
41. {God came quote} Meyer, *The Nag Hammadi Scriptures,* Generation of the Son, 22:31 (Translated by Einar Thomassen), 667.
42. {Brahman} See: Swami Paramananda, *The Upanishads*, Katha Upanishad, Part 6, Verse 1, 41.
{Wu wei} Lynn, *The Classic of the Way and Virtue: A New Translation of the Tao-te Ching of Laozi* as Interpreted by Wang Bi, 16; Schwartz, The World of Though in Ancient China, 189–190.
43. {Cosmic consciousness} Binder, *In The Waves Lies the Secret of Creation*, Introduction.
44. {Flashes of insight} Binder, "Consciousness is the Key to the 'Dawn of a New Era.'"
45. {Wu and You table} Smith, *Fathoming the Cosmos and Ordering the World*, 93 — in reference to Lynn, The Classic of Changes, 297–299, 310, 318, 202 footnote; Noumenon is a Kantian term: "a posited object or event that exists independently of human sense and/ or perception." Wikipedia — accessed July 2018.
46. {Without effort} Loy, David. "Wei-wu-wei: Nondual Action," 73–87 examines Wu-wei as a paradox when seen through a Western lens.
{Never, Negative Imperitive, Do Nothing} Kunst, *The Original Yijing,* 132.
{Wu in Hexagram 48} Legge, *I Ching*/Yellowbridge.com; Wilhelm, *The I Ching*, 185.
47. {"When the sun disappeared..."} Lalla Ded, *The Wise Sayings of Lal Ded*, Verse 9. Changed some punctuation. Used alternate translation for "Then wihter…".

~~~

Lalla Ded was a fourteenth century mystic in northern India whose work is claimed by both Hindus and Muslims as part for their mystic tradition.
48. Saint John of the Cross, Peers translation, *Dark Night.*
49. Saint John of the Cross, Starr translation, *Dark Night of the Soul,* 109.
50. {Early Religious Daoism} Wang, *Taoism*, 14, 40.
51. {Elixirs and out-of-body} Wang, *Taoism*, 61, 74.
52. {Spiritual world,... such as Tai Chi} Ni, *The Book of Changes,* 188, 200, 231.
53. {Unity Diagram} Wang,. "Zhou Dunyi's Diagram of the Supreme Ultimate Explained," 309–317.
54. {Father as one while being the many} Meyer, *The Nag Hammadi Scriptures*, Tripartite Tractate, 51:8 (Translated by Eirnar Thomassen), 62.
55. {da Vinci Moon} "The Codex Arundel," Catalogue of Manuscripts in The British Museum, New Series, 1 vol. in 3 parts (London: British Museum, 1834–1840), I, part I: The Arundel Manuscripts, 79.
56. {Universal Mind} Holmes, *The Science of Mind,* 30; Eddy, *Science and Health*, 109.
The Western tradition tends to conceive of the Universal or Divine Mind in a subtle way as more "active" than the Chinese descriptions which characterize the idea that implies an ultimate "stillness." Holmes and others tend to describe the human relationship as a connection, Mary Baker Eddy, who uses the term "Divine Mind" and is rooted firmly in the Christian tradition tends to emphasize it as a submission.

57. {but one mind} Russell, *The Universal One,* Kindle location 644. Russell emphasizes that the Universal Mind is the source of all consciousness, it is a thinking consciousness, and is the source of what Dunyi would call the multitude of things.
58. Legge, *The Book of Poetry*, 136.

◦━◆━━◆━━◇◆◇━━━◆◦

# Chapter 5

1. {Heaven and Earth} Legge, *I Ching*, 393: *The Great Treatise or Great Commentary,* Dazhuan 大傳, Section 2, Chapter 5, Verse 44. Author's Paraphrase.
2. {Confucius} The term "Confucius" was coined by Jesuit Missionaries in the 16th Century (Probably Father Matteo Ricci at a Latinization of "Kong Fuzi." Confucius' given name is 孔丘 Kǒng Qiū, where the family name Kong comes first and his given name second, as is still the case in China today. His courtesy name, given upon achieving adulthood is, 仲尼 Zhòngní — Morton, China Its History and Culture, 33–34.
3. {Translation of Confucian Classics} Camus, "Jesuit's Journeys in Chinese Studies," 7.
4. {Teachings carried on by disciples} Morton, China, *Its History and Culture*, 34.
5. {Little change since the received text} Fairbank, *China A New History*, 49–51.
6. {Ruled by moral individuals} Henderson, *Scripture, Canon, and Commentary, A Comparison of Confucian and Western Egesis*, 39; Smih, The *I Ching*, A Biography, 5; Schwartz, *The World of Thought in Ancient China*, 62.
7. {Confucius and students codified the morality found in the *Zhouyi*} Smith, *Sung Dynasty Uses of the I Ching*, 13.
8. {Carl Jasper and Axial Age} Bellah, *The Axial Age and Its Consequences*, 1–3.
9. {Egyptian Poem} Parkinson, *The Tale of Sinuhe and Other Ancient Egyptian Poems*.
10. {Greek golden rule} Laertius, *The Lives and Opinions of Eminent Philosophers*, Kindle Location 289.
11. {Zoroaster golden rule} West, *Pahlavi Texts,* Part II, *Dadistan-I Dinik and the Epistles ofManuskihar*, Chapter 94, Verse 5, 272.
12. {Confucian golden rule} Author's translation informed by review of Waley's translation and Confucius/Legge, *The Analects of Confucius: Bilingual Edition, English and Chinese:* 論語, Kindle location 1736.
13. {Reciprocity Quote} Legge, *The Analects of Confucius*, 84.
    Reciprocity, the character, 恕, shù, is literally, "forgiveness," a word used in the only Christian prayer attributed to the Christ Jesus. Known as the Our Father, it includes a reference God the Father, And forgive us our debts, as we forgive our debtor — Matthew 6:12, KJV.
14. {List of virtues} Confucius/Legge (trans.). *The Analects of Confucius: Bilingual Edition, English and Chinese*, Kindle Locations 2770–2771 and{Courtesy as the first virtue in lieu of Legge's translation, "Gravity" and "Diligence" in lieu of Legge's "Earnestness" This also seems to correlate with the Greek Virtue of Courage} Waley, The Analects of Confucius, Kindle Location 3828.
15. {"Earnest in practicing...} Mencius/Legge, *Doctrine of the Mean: Bilingual Edition, Englishand Chinese* 中庸, Kindle Locations 130–132.
16. {Excess and deficiency...}Aristotle/Peters, *Nicomachean Ethics*, 46.
17. {Avoid extremes} Bhikkhu (Trans.), "Dhammacakkappavattana Sutta: Setting the Wheel of Dhamma in Motion"
18. {Hexagram Image Statement} Used the Legge translation except for 安, for which Wilhelm translation uses "fortifies{the thinking]" and Legge uses "settlement [to the aims]" where I use "gives contentment" which is implied by the current definition of the character.
19. {Ren human-heartedness} Zhang, *Key Concepts in Chinese Philosophy*, 287.
20. {Ren/Jen described in relation the ancient Chinese historical documents} Waley, *The Analects of Confucius* (Introduction), Kindle location 292;
    {Ren/Jen described in relation to Western philosophy} Schwartz, *The World of Ancient Chinese Thought*,75–85.
21. {One of three virtues practiced daily} Legge, *Doctrine of he Mean: Bilingual Edition, English and Chinese,* Kindle Location 264.
22. {Way of the Good Hearted Person} Rén 仁 paired with Dáo 道.

*Notes to pages 92 to 99*

23. {Superior person} Theodore, Sources of Chinese Tradition, 42;
    {Gentleman} English Scholars have noted Junzi could be translated as "Gentleman" in the true European sense of the cultivated, virtuous, educated man Waley, *The Analects of Confucius*, Kindle location 402.
24. {Love of wisdom...} Author's interpretation: Waley, *The Analects of Confucius*, Kindle location 3840; Legge, *The Analects of Confucius*.
25. {The superior man...} *Mencius*, Legge (Trans.), *Mencius*, Kindle locations 1549–1552.
26. {Choice and Free Will} There is a centuries long tradition of thinking about free will and its relationship with determinism or fate, especially in the presence of an omnipotent God who, by definition is all Good, but somehow evil exists in the word. For if a person has not choice, then there can be no blame, and if there is no blame, then there can be no sin, that is no evil-doer. Thus, humans must have free will, the choice to good or evil, and in the Christian Tradition, the choice to accept God's truth — Augustine, *Of Free Choice and Free Will*, 70–74.
    The basic idea continued in secular philosophy, with, for example, "Universal Laws" being the objective good in lieu of divine will — Kant, *Fundamental Principles of the Metaphysic of Morals*, 117.
27. {Choice} Fingarette, *Confucius The Secular and the Sacred*, 35–36.
28. {Author modified Quote} Aristotle, *Nicomachean Ethics*, Book IV, Verse 14. .
29. {Quran quote} http://corpus.quran.com/translation.jsp?chapter=11&verse=56 Open source license. http://corpus.quran.com/license.jsp;
30. {Straying from the path} Fingarette, *Confucius The Secular and the Sacred*, 34.
    {Following the path} Fingarette, *Confucius The Secular and the Sacred*, 32–33, discusses how Confucius uses judicial imagery advise that a person emulated the superior person, but not judge the inferior person, that is to avoid "litigation," getting to the idea of: And judge not, and ye shall not be judged: and condemn not, and ye shall not be condemned, Luke 6:37 ASV.
31. {Mencius quote}, Legge translation, *Mencius*, Chapter 23, Verse 7, Kindle location 2316.
32. {Free Will} The idea of Free Will in Christian thought was developed by Saint Augustine of Hippo (A.D. 354–430) and others in a quest to explain how evil can exist in a Creation by an Omnipotent and Loving God — Augustine & Schaff (Editor), *Complete Works of Saint Augustine: On Grace and Free Will*, Kindle location 167577.
    The Greek philosophers, particularly the Stoics, examined the relationship between a deterministic universe and human free will without appealing to the divine. "Truth," in the Christian tradition is "God's Truth." The Chinese tradition during the same time as the beginning of the Christian movement "means the authentic expression of the 'real' person of the author" — Lynn, "Truth and Imagination in China: Opposition and Conciliation in the Tradition," 3.
    {The Way and Free will} The Way of Nature in which humans are imbedded operates in the Yin-Yang cycle and the cosmology that is in common with Daoist Philosophy. While complex, it can be seen as a deterministic Universe in a Western sense, since it operates according to "rules," even though the mathematical precision of those rules may not be known.
33. {Virtue} Fingarette, *Confucius The Secular and the Sacred*, 7.
34. {Poem} Author's poem inspired by Fingarette, *Confucius The Secular and the Sacred*, 79.
35. {Ethical rule of a kingdom} Bellah, *The Axial Age and Its Consequences*: Heiner Roetz, "The Axial Age Theory," 248; David Martin, "Axial Religions and the Problem of Violence," 249; Ingolf, Dalferth, "The Idea of Transcendance," 146.
    {Scholarly class} Lewis, *China Its History and Culture*, 35. See Schwartz, *The World of Thought in Ancient China*, the first half of Chapter 3, 56–70 for a discussion of Confucius in relation to Greek philosophers and their different outlooks.
36. {Spin} Selective presentation of facts to back into a preconceived conclusion, often ignoring some words and selecting others for the purpose of influencing the audience to reach the preconceived conclusion. As on popular talk show's byline says. "The no spin zone." — O'Reilly Factor show, http://www.urbandictionary.com/define.php?term=The%20No%20Spin%20Zone.
37. {Names have no intrinsic value} Xunzi, Watson (Trans/), *Xunxi Basic Writings*, 15.
38. {Joyous *I Ching* Quote} Legge, *I Ching*.
39. {Confucian and Women sidebar} Blake, "Foot-Binding in Neo-Confucian China and the Appropriation of Female Labor."

40. {Buddhist influence on Neo-Confucianism} Chang, *The Development of Neo-Confucian Thought*, 129 — Buddhists stimulated Confucians to and build their own philosophical system that matched all of the disciplines brought by Buddhism, some of which were seen as needing work or reinterpretation.
41. {Rationalistic Wing and Classic Greek Philosophy} Chang, *The Development of Neo-Confucian Thought*, Chapter 1; Bowker, *The Oxford Dictionary of World Religions*, 691.
    {Idealistic Wing} Yang-Ming, *Instructions for Practical Living*, xi.
42. {At ease} From the Analects — Gardener, *The Four Books*, 28.
43. {He will keep all these...} Legge, *Book of Odes*, Kindle Location 9186.
44. {Meal quote} Watson, *The Analects of Confucius*, 32W.

# Chapter 6

1. {Heaven and Earth} Legge, *I Ching, The Great Treatise or Great Commentary,* Section 2, Chapter 1, Verse 1.
2. {Concepts discussed in this chapter} Risema, *I Ching*, 13 — These concepts were developed during the Han Dynasty (206 B.C. to A.D. 220).
3. {Number used for changing lines} This is why the sums coins and yarrows stalks have 2 and 3. 1 is the supreme polarity and is not counted. 2 is the heaven, the creative, and 3 is earth, the receptive.
4. {Figure 5.1 Quote} Legge, *I Ching Book of Changes*, 373; See also Wilhelm, *The I Ching*, 318–319.
    {Development of images using the terms Yin and Yang} Xhuxi/Chu Hsi, Introduction to the Study of the Classic of Change, 22.
5. {Hexagram 40 translation} Combined from Wilhelm, *The I Ching*, 156 and Ni, *The Book of Changes*, 445.
6. {Hexagram 40 translation} Legge, *I Ching*, 145 — replacing male terms with gender neutral.
7. {Finally, everything is in order} Wilhelm, *The I Ching*, 709.
8. {Then follows its opposite} Wilhelm, *The I Ching*, 715.
9. {The second and fourth lines are of the same quality} Legge, *I Ching*, 400–401.
10. {Hexagram 4} Author's interpretation from Wilhelm, *The I Ching*, 408 and Legge, *I Ching*, 65.
11. {King and Ministers} Som, *The Comprehensive Discussions of the White Tiger Hall*, Vol I, 603.
12. {strong and weak lines — Great Treatise quote} Legge, *The I Ching*, 350.
13. {Hexagram 19} Wilhelm, *The I Ching*, 482.
14. {Hexagram 23} Wilhelm, *The I Ching*, 28.
    In this chapter commentaries on hexagrams are based on Wilhelm's *I Ching* translation unless otherwise noted.
15. {Deliverance} Legge, *I Ching*, 245.
16. {Interior Trigrams} Wilhelm, *The I Ching*, 359–359.
17. {Correlations with the Eight trigrams} There are also many more including time of day and calendar correlations which has a long history of development in Correlative Cosmology thinking — the School of Images. This will be explored in Chapter 6.
18. {Wang Bi commentary on how to approach the *I Ching*} Lynn, *The Classic of Changes*, 31 (Translating Wang Bi); Smith, *Fathoming the Cosmos and Ordering the World*, 93.

◁━━━◁◆◇◆◇━━━━◆◁

# Chapter 7

1. {Great Treatise Quote} From Legge, *I Ching*, 377 modified with reference to Wilhelm, *The I Ching*, 323 and Karcher, *Ta Chuan*, 106. The translation from Legge is modified to change "speech" to "words"; "emblematic symbols" to "images"; Omitted: Is it impossible... The Master said; "set forth fully" changed to "bring forth"; "appointed..." changed to "Created Hexagrams to apply them to your circumstances."
2. {Date of Ten Wings} 300 B.C. is a bit arbitrary. The ideas and some of the text of the Ten Wings were in circulation by 300 B.C..
3. {Wu} Wang Bi's commentaries would be recognizable to many practicing Buddhist's and people practicing variations of Buddhist meditation practices today.
4. {References} Doctor of Philosophy Dissertation by Richard Alan Kunst, 1983, University of California at Berkeley: *The Original Yijing: A Text, Phonetic Transcription, Translation, and Index, with Sample Glosses.*
   Kunst's prodigious work examines the historical context of the *Zhouyi*, the meaning of key words used, and includes a word by word transcription of the Judgment and Line Statements followed by his translation.
5. {Noble} Kunst, *The Original Yi jing*, 400–401 has a discussion of Wilhelms translation of Junzi to "der Edle," the noble in German, saying Baynes gave it the Confucian interpretation when she chose, Superior Man. Kunst final take is that its primitive meaning Noble [by birth] in the Judgments of hexagrams 12 and 13 but with the "secondary" meaning of noble minded.
   Of course, Superior Person, when used in the Image Statement (which Kunst does not deal with), was written by Confucians and should be read in as it was defined by Confucians — noble minded.
6. {Superior Man} Rutt, *Zhouyi*, Kindle location 3987.
7. {Superior Man} Waley, *The Analects*, Kindle Location 316.
8. {Superior Man} Pearson, *The Original I Ching*, 37–39.
9. {Superior Man} Anthony, *A Guide to the I Ching*, Second Line, 33.
10. {Superior Man — Super Ego} Freud, *The Ego and the Id*, Kindle location 365.
11. {Superior Man} Jung, *Archetypes and the Collective Unconscious*, Kindle locations 930.
12. {Superior Man} Walsh, *The Long Discourses of the Buddha*,146;
    {Eight-fold path} Tuffley, *The Essence of Buddhism*.
13. {Great Man} Kunst, *The Original Yi jing*, 396–397.
14. {Grand Treat} Kunst, *The Original Yi jing* 372.
15. {Prevalence} Lynn explicitly gives Fundamentally for yuan and Prevalence heng as his translation in parentheticals in his Judgment Translation — Lynn, *The Classic of Changes*, 129 for example.
16. {Beneficial} Lynn explicitly gives Fundamentally for yuan and Prevalence heng as his translation in parentheticals in his Judgment Translation — Lynn, *The Classic of Changes*, 129 for example.
17. {Correct Mistakes} Wilhelm, *The I Ching*, 291.
18. {Correct Mistakes} Wilhelm, *The I Ching*, 291.
19. {Definition of Fu} Yabla Online Dictionary, https://chinese.yabla.com/chinese-english-Pinyin-dictionary.php?define=俘
20. {Fu} Redmond, *Teaching the I Ching*, 131: says孚 stands without the added 人 came to mean sincerity.
21. {10 day week in ancient China} Keightley, *The Ancestral Landscape*, 33; Nielsen, *A Companion to Yi jing Numerology and Cosmology*, Kindle location 2615); Taylor and Francis. Kindle Edition.
    {To Go} Kunst, *The Original Yi jing.*
22. {Dragon} Smith, *Fathoming the Cosmos and Ordering the World*, 22.
23. {Wild geese} Kunst, *I Ching Phonic Translation*, 77 (Used alternate translation by Kunst in his narrative); also Shaughnessy, *I Ching*, 13.
24. {Have in back of mind} Deutscher, *Through the Language Glass: Why the World Looks Different in Other Languages,* 111.
25. {Numinous World} Ritsema, *I Ching*, 14.
26. {Spoken and Written language styles differ} Schallert, "Analysis of Differences Between

Reading and Oral Language (Technical Report No. 29), 2.
27. {Joining words} Aria, *The Nature of the Chinese Character*, 11.
28. {Types of Chinese characters} McNaughton, *Read and Writing Chinese*, 11; Qui, *Chinese Writing*, Chapter 2, 13–59.
29. {Rhymes} Smith, *Fathoming the Cosmos*, 23.
30. {Ambiguity and Rhyme} Kunst, *the Original Yi jing*, 53–55.
31. {New Testament translation gap} Johnson, *A History of Christianity*, 27
32. {Duty to remedy the matter} Ibid.
33. {Different translators sometimes come to different meanings} Wilhelm, *I Ching*, 209, Hexagram 54 Judgment : The Marrying Maiden; "Undertakings bring misfortune; Nothing that would further."; Legge, *I Ching*, 153: Legge on the other hand, in his footnote, thinks the author intended this to express the relationship between the ruler and his minister instead of an actual marriage.
34. {Translation and Language} Translation begins with language itself, and how people attach meaning to words and phrases, and how those words and phrases are organized in a grammar. This is full on nuance, including how thought and language interact and affect each other. Norm Chomsky has a large body of work, particularly grammar — essentially inventing that area of linguistics. Chomsky, *Knowledge of Language: Its Nature, Origin, and Use*; Chomsky, *On Language*.
   Then oral communication and written communication differ. Schallert, "Analysis of Differences Between Reading and Oral Language (Technical Report No. 29)."

◁▬▬◁◦◁◦◁▭▭▷

# Chapter 8

1. {The Well Judgment } Author's interpretation: Modification of Legge, The *I Ching* modified based on Kunst, *The Original Yi jing*.
2. {Translation by scholars} One of the few useful online critiques on *I Ching* translations: Biroco, "A Critical Survey of *I Ching* Books."
3. {* Often Cited} This is strictly an observation of the author and does not necessarily mean that other books are inferior.
4. {Wilhelm} Alleton, "Richard Wilhelm, a 'Sinicized' German Translator."; Redmond, *Teaching the I Ching*, 239.
5. {Internet Archive: Online *I Ching* as part of Sacred books of the East Series} https://archive.org/details/SacredBooksEastVariousOrientalScholarsWithIndex.50VolsMaxMuller
   {Sacred Tests: Online *I Ching* as part of Sacred books of the East Serie} http://www.sacred-texts.com/sbe/index.htm
6. {Yellowbridge Legge translation} https://www.yellowbridge.com/onlinelit/i-ching.php; {Chinese Text Project Legge translation} https://ctext.org/book-of-changes/qian
7. {Legge bio} Legge, *James Legge, Missionary and Scholar*, Chapter 4.
8. {Wang Bi comment dismissing the court ladies as inherently petty} Redmond, *Teaching the I Ching*, 20–21.
9. {Plain English} Redmond, *The I Ching*, Kindle location 285.
10. {Treat} Kunst, *The Original Yi jing*, 374.
11. {Preface on the author's outlook} Nisarg, *The Magician's I Ching* (Kindle location 96.

◁▬▬◁◦◁◦◁▭▭▷

# Letter To The Reader

1. {*Man in the High Castle* quote} Wikipedia, "Man in the High Castle." — Accessed September 2018.

*Notes to pages 166 to 168*

## Notes and Acknowledgments

1.  {Calendar today} International Standard Organization (ISO) 8601 which used the Gregorian Calendar. The book will simply uses the date from text being referenced, but the reader should note that they may be off from each other by a year or so since the standard calendar system being used has a history in from the Western world that reaches back to the Roman Empire.
2.  {AD} Some commenters note that Anno Domini should precede the date, but it seems that the syntax rules of both Latin and English also the use of the more standard form of placing it after the date.
3.  {Romanization} Legge, *I Ching*, 445 (Transliteration table used for translation); Chan, *Concise English-Chinese Dictionary*, vi; "Wade Giles," Wikipedia; "Pinyin," "*I Ching*," Wikipedia — accessed December 2019.
4.  Because Pinyin can march more than one Chinese character, particularly when the accent is left off, menu of possible choices, each the a number pops up. A more efficient system Wubi is used by speed typists, which uses system for the strokes of simplified Chinese and is harder to learn — but faster and less ambiguous than Pinyin.
5.  {Numbers} With some exceptions: The Line Statements in the *I Ching* refer to their position as: 初 "first," 二 "two," 三 "three," 四 "four," 五 "five," 上 "top."

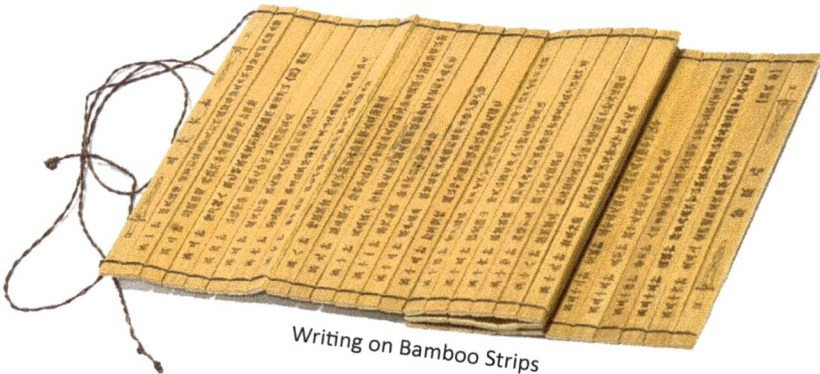

Writing on Bamboo Strips

# REFERENCES CITED

## BOOKS

Adler, Joseph A. *the Confucian Dao. Zhu Xi's Appropriation of Zhou Dunyi*. Albany: State University of New York Press, 2014.

Anthony, Carol K. *A Guide to the I Ching*. Stow, MA: Anthony Pub., 1988. Stow, MA: Anthony Publishing Company, 2002.

————— *The Other Way: A Book of Experiences in Meditation Based on the I Ching*. Stow, MA: Anthony Publishing Company, 1990.

————— *The Philosophy of the I Ching*. Stow, MA: Anthony Pub., 1998.

Anthony, Carol K., and Hanna Moog. *I Ching The Oracle of the Cosmic Way*. 1st ed.

————— *The Psyche Revealed through the I Ching*. Stow, MA: Anthony Publishing Company, 2009.

Aria, Barbara, Russell Gon. Eng, and Lesley Ehlers. *The Nature of the Chinese Character*. New York: Simon and Schuster, 1991.

Aristotle, and F. H Peters (Trans.). *The Rhetoric , Poetic, and Nicomachean Ethics of Aristotle*. London, UK: Kegan Paul, Trench & Co. Ltd, 1983. http://lf-oll.s3.amazonaws.com/titles/903/0328_Bk.pdf.

Aristotle, W. D. Ross, and J. A. Smith (Trans. & Editors). *The Works of Aristotle: Oxford Edition*. Republished Kindle Edition: Catholic Way Publishing 2015. London, UK: Clarendon Press, 1928–1952.

Augustine, and Henry Chadwick (Trans.). *Confessions*. Oxford: Oxford University Press, 1998.

Augustine, and Thomas Williams (Trans.). *On Free Choice of the Will*. Indianapolis: Hackett Pub., 1993.

Aziz, Robert. *C.G. Jung's Psychology of Religion and Synchronicity*. Albany: State University of New York Press, 1990.

Barret, Hilary. *I Ching*. Arcturus Publishing, London, 2016.

Bahm, Archie J. *Philosophy of the Buddha*. Originally Published Harper and Bros. 1959. Fremont, CA: Jain Publishing, 1993.

Balkin, J. M. *The Laws of Change: I Ching and the Philosophy of Life*. Branford, CT: Sybil Creek Press, 2009.

*Bible, Revised Standard Edition, King James*. New York, NY: Thomas Nelson and Sons, 1952. Revised [American] Standard Version" as of 1952 with minor revisions in 1959. Division of Christian Education of the National Council of Churches of Christ in the United States of America. According to the Preface, the translations heritage subject to further scholarship is the King James Bible.

*Bible: The Great News, The New Testament New International Version (NIV)*. Colorado Springs, CO: International Bible Society, 1984.

Binder, Timothy. *In The Waves Lies the Secret of Creation*. Waynesboro, VA: The University of Science and Philosophy, 1995.

Black Elk, and John Gneisenau Neihardt. *A Full Length Black Elk Speaks*. Chicago: Dramatic Pub., 1976.

Black Elk, and Joseph Brown (Recorded and Edited). *The Sacred Pipe*. New York, NY: Penguin Books, 1971.

Blofeld, John. *I Ching = The Book of Change: A New Translation of the Ancient Chinese Text with Detailed Instructions for Its Practical Use in Divination*. First Published in 1968. New York: Arkana, 1991.

*The Book of Mormon for Latter-day Saint Families*. General Editor Thomas R Valletta, Salt Lake City: Deseret Book Co., 2012. Kindle Edition

Brennan, J. H. *The Magical I Ching*. St. Paul, MN: Llewellyn Publications, 2000.

Buddhiprakāśa, Acharya (Trans.). *The Dhammapada: The Buddha's Path of Wisdom*. Kandy, Sri Lanka: Buddhist Publication Society, 1985.

Cain, David J. *Person-Center Psychotherapies*. 1st ed. Kindle. Washington, DC: American Psychological Asscoation, 2012.

Cambray, Joseph. *Synchronicity: Nature and Psyche in an Interconnected Universe*. Pdf Version Available on Http://www.jung.org (Nov. 15, 2014). College Station: Texas A&M University Press, 2009.

Capra, Fritjof. *The Tao of Physics: An Exploration of the Parallels between Modern Physics and Eastern Mysticism*. Berkeley: Shambhala, 1975.

Chan, Shau Wing. *A Concise English-Chinese Dictionary: With Romanized Standard Pronunciation [Wade-Giles]*. Stanford, CA: Stanford University Press, 1955.

Chang, Carson. *The Development of Neo-Confucian Thought, Vol. 1*. 1963 Paperbound ed. New Haven, CT: College and University Press, 1957.

Chang, Jung, and Jon Halliday. *Mao the Unknown Story*. New York: Anchor Books, 2005.

Ching, Julia. *Chinese Religions*. Maryknoll, NY: Orbis Books, 1993.

Chomsky, Noam. *Knowledge of Language: Its Nature, Origin, and Use*. Praeger, 1986.

————— *On Language*. The New Press, 1991. Three pages: Originally published *Reflections on Language* 1975, *Language and Responsibility* 1979.

Cleary, Thomas (Trans.). *The Book of Changes*. Boston, MA: Shambhala, 2006.

Confucius, and A. Charles Muller. "Doctrine of the Mean." Doctrine of the Mean 中庸. Accessed September 20, 2014. http://www.acmuller.net/con-dao/docofmean.html.

Confucius, and Arthur Waley (Trans.). *The Analects of Confucius*. Vol. V–173. New York, NY: Vintage Books, 1938.

Coward, Harold G. *Sacred Word and Sacred Text: Scripture in World Religions*. Maryknoll, NY: Orbis Books, 1988.

Creel, *The Birth of China*, Frederick Ungar Publishing Company, New York, 1937.

Dainian, Zhang, Edmund Ryden (Trans. Editor). *Key Concepts of Chinese Philosophy*. New Haven, CT: Yale University, 2002.

Deutscher, Guy. *Through the Language Glass: Why the World Looks Different in Other Languages*. New York: Metropolitan Books/Henry Holt and, 2010.

Dick, Philip K. *The Man in the High Castle*. Originally Published by G. P. Putman's Sons, New York, 1962. Boston: Mariner Books, 2011.

Eagleman, David. *Incognito: The Secret Lives of the Brain*. New York: Pantheon Books, 2011.

Eddy, Mary Baker. *Science and Health with Key to Scripture*. Boston, MA: Christian Science Board of Directors, 1875.

Fairbank, John King, and Merle Goldman. *China: A New History*. Cambridge, MA: Belknap Press of Harvard University Press, 2006.

Fingarette, Herbert. *Confucius: The Secular as Sacred*. Long Grove, IL: Waveland Press, 1998.

Freud, Sigmund, Joan Riviere (Trans.), and James Startchy (Editor). "The Ego and the ID." The Colby College Community Web (W. W. Norton, New York, NY, 1962 in Print Form). Accessed August 7, 2014. http://web.colby.edu/wg217/files/2010/07/freud-ch.3.pdf.

Gardner, Daniel (Trans.) K. *The Four Books: The Basic Teachings of the Later Confucian Tradition*. Kindle Version. Cambridge, UK: Hackett Publishing Company, 2007. The Four Books: Zhu Xi: Compiled with comments circa A.D. 1190. Great Learning - Zenzi Analects (of Confucius) - Confucius and his students Mencius - Menus Maintaining Perfect Balance (Doctrine of the Mean) Zisi.

Gladwell, Malcolm. *Blink: the Power of Thinking without Thinking*. Little, Brown and Co., 2005

Golding, William. *Lord of the Flies*. London: Faber and Faber, 1962.

Hill, Napoleon. *Think and Grow Rich*. 1st ed. Las Vegas, NV: Alba and Tromm.

Holmes, Earnest in collaboration with Maude Allison Lathem, *The Science of Mind*, 2nd Edition, New York: Penguin Putnam, 1938.

*The Holy Bible*. New York, NY: Thomas Nelson and Sons, 1952 *1. "Revised [American] Standard Version" as of 1952 with minor revisions in 1959. Division of Christian Education of the National Council of Churches of Christ in the United States of America. According to the Preface, the translations heritage subject to further scholarship is the King James Bible.

Huang, Alfred. *The Complete I Ching: The Definitive Translation*. Rochester, VT: Inner Traditions, 2010.

Huang, Kerson. *I Ching The Oracle*. Singapore: World Scientific Publishing, 1984.

Huang, Kerson, and Rosemary Huang. *I Ching*. New York: Workman Pub., 1987.

Saint John of the Cross and E. Allison Peers (Trans.), *Dark Night*. 3rd Revised Edition, with critical edition of P. Siverio de Santa Teresa, Image Books, 1959.

> This electronic edition (v 0.9) was scanned in 1994 from an uncopyrighted 1959 Image Books third edition of the Dark Night. Shared under Creative Commons License, https://creativecommons.org/licenses/by-sa/3.0/ . https://en.wikisource.org/wiki/The_Dark_Night_of_the_Soul_(Peers_translation).

Saint John of the Cross and Marabai Start (Trans.), *Dark Night of the Soul*. New York: Riverhead Books, 2002.

Johnson, Paul. *A History of Christianity*. New York: Simon & Schuster, 1976.

Jones (trans), William. *The Great Qing Code*. Qing Dynasty 1644–1911). Oxford, UK: Clarendon Press, 1994.

Jung, C. G., and R. F. C. Hull. *Synchronicity: An Acausal Connecting Principle*. Princeton, NJ: Princeton University Press, 2010.

Kant, Immanuel and Thomas Kingsmill Abbot (Trans.).. *Fundamental Principles of the Metaphysic of Morals*, a public domain book, *Kindle Edition.*

Karcher, Stephen L. *I Ching: The Classic Chinese Oracle of Change: A Complete Translation with Concordance*. London: Vega, 2002.

————— *Ta Chuan: The Great Treatise*. New York: St. Martin's Press, 2000.

————— *The I Ching Plain and Simple: A Guide to Working with the Oracle of Change*. Hammersmith, London: Element, 2004.

————— *Total I Ching*. London: Piatkus, 2009.

Keightley, David. *The Ancestral Landscape, Time, Space, and Community in Late Shang China (ca. 1200–1045 B.C.)*. Berkeley, CA: Institute of Asian Studies, University of California, Berkeley, 2000.

Kohn, Livia, and Michael LaFargue. *Lao-tzu and the Tao-te-ching*. Albany, NY: State University of New York Press, 1998.

Kunst, Richard. *The Original Yijing: A Text, Phonetic Transcription, Translation, and Indexes with Sample Glosses*. PhD diss., University of California at Berkeley, 1985. , Ann Arbor, MI: UMOI Dissertation Services, A Bell & Howell Company, 1996.

Lalla Ded, Sir George Grierson, and Lionel D. Barnett (Trans.). *The Wise Sayings of Lal Ded*. Vol. XVII. Asiatic Society Monographs. Cambridge, MA: Havard University, 1887. doi:http://babel.hathitrust.org/cgi/pt?id=hvd.32044010300 457;view=1up;seq=1.

Lalla Ded and Coleman Barks (Trans). *Naked Song*. Lalpur Varanasi, India: Epigram Press Pvt., 1992.

Lao-Tzu, and Red Pine [Trans.]. *Lao-tzu's Taoteching: With Selected Commentaries from the past 2,000 Years*. Port Townsend, WA: Copper Canyon Press, 2009.

Legge (Trans.), James, Laozi, and F. Max Muller (Editor). *Sacred Books of the East*. The Texts of Taoism ed. Vol. XXXIV. London, UK: Oxford Millford Press, 1891. doi:http://oll.libertyfund.org/titles/tzu-the-texts-of-taoism-part-i.

Legge, James (Trans.), Ch'u Chai, and Winberg Chai. *I Ching A Book of Changes Ancient Guidance for Contemporary Persons*. Originally Published 1899. New Hyde Park, NY: University Books, 1969.

Legge, James (Trans.). *The Shu King (Sacred Books of the East Vol. III)*. Oxford, UK: Clarion Press, 1879.

————— *The Yi King (I Ching)*. 1st ed. Oxford, UK: Clarendon Press, 1882. https://archive.org/stream/SacredBooksEastVariousOrientalScholarsWithIndex.50VolsMaxMuller/16.SacredBooksEast.VarOrSch.v16.Muller. China.Legge.SacBksChina.TxtConfuc.p2.YiKing.Oxf.1882.#page/n9/ mode/2up. Accessed 9/1/2014.

————— *The Annals of the Bamboo Books (from A Translation, Critical and Exegetical Notes, Prolegomena, and Copious Notes)*. Vol. Vol III Part 1. Pages 105–188. London: Trübner and Company, 1865. https://archive.org/details/chineseclassics07legggoog (Accessed 9/16/2015)

Lévi-Strauss, Claude. *The Savage Mind (La Pensée Savage)*. Chicago, IL: University of Chicago Press, 1966.

Lightman, Alan. *The Accidental Universe*, New York: Vintage Books. 2013.

Linnell, PhD (, Bruce R. R. "Guanzi, Number 49 : Study of Inner Cultivation." Project Gutenberg (License Creative Commons: Creative Commons Attribution-NonCommercial-NoDerivs 3.0 Unported License (CC BY-NC-ND 3.0) . 2011. Accessed January 14, 2016. http://www.gutenberg.org/files/38585/38585-pdf/38585-pdf.pdf?session_id=56e214bed62be7b4b-f88e33e524bb43714bab7ff.

Liu, Yiming, and Thomas F. Cleary (Trans). *The Taoist I Ching*. Translation of a Work Written in 1796. Boston: Shambhala, 1986.

Lynn, Richard John., and Bi Wang. *The Classic of Changes: A New Translation of the I Ching as Interpreted by Wang Bi*. New York: Columbia University Press, 1994.

McNaughton, William. *Reading and Writing Chinese*. Tokyo, Japan: Charles E. Tuttle, 1989.

Mencius, and A. Charles Muller (Trans.). "Mencius (Selections) 孟子." Mencius (Selections) 孟子. originally circa 300 B.C. Accessed September 20, 2014. http://www.acmuller.net/con-dao/mencius.html.

Minford, John. *I Ching*. New York, NY: Viking Penguin, 2014.

Morton, W. Scott, and Charlton M. Lewis. *China: Its History and Culture*. New York: McGraw-Hill, 2005.

Morwood, James, and John Taylor. *The Pocket Oxford Classical Greek Dictionary*. Oxford: Oxford University Press, 2002.

Müller, F. Max, and James Legge (Trans). *The Sacred Books of the East. Vol XXVIII*. Available On: Http://oll.libertyfund.org, Library Fund, Inc. (15 Oct 2014). Oxford, UK: Clarendon Press, 1885.

Muller, Max (Trans.), *Dhammapada*, Sacred Books of the East. https://www.gutenberg.org/files/2017/2017-h/2017-h.htm#link2HCH0015.

Meyer, Marvin W.,Robinson, James M.. *The Nag Hammadi Scriptures*, New York: HarperOne. Kindle Edition.

Nārada. *The Buddha and His Teachings*. Singapore: Singapore Buddhist Mediation Centre, 1988.

*New American Bible, Revised Edition*. Approve by Conference of Catholic Bishops. Washington, DC: Confraternity of Christian Doctrine, 2010.

Ni, Hua-Ching. *I Ching The Book of Changes: And the Unchanging Truth*. 2nd Edition. Malibu, CA: Shrine of the Eternal Breath of Tao, 1990.

Nielsen, Bent. *A Companion to Yi Jing Numerology and Cosmology: Chinese Studies of Images and Numbers from Han (202 B.C.E-220 CE) to Song (960-1279 CE)*. London: Routledge Curzon, 2003.

Papamânanda (Trans. & Commentary), Swâmi. *The Upanishads*. 2nd ed. Boston, MA: Verânta Centre, 1919.

Pearson, Margaret. *The Original I Ching: An Authentic Translation of The Book of Changes*. North Clarendon, VT: Tuttle Pub., 2011.

Penrose, Roger. *The Road to Reality: A Complete Guide to the Laws of the Universe*. New York, NY: A.A. Knopf, 2005.

Philo, Judaeus, Of Alexandria, and C. D. Yonge (Trans.). *The Works of Philo Judae-*

*us of Alexandria*. Kindle Edition: Written circa A.D. 40. Translated in 1984. Saint Ansgar, Iowa: Common Mans Perspective, 2010.

Plato, and Benjamin Jewett (Trans.). *Plato: The Complete Works*. Authored circa 380 B.C. Translation: University of Oxford: 1871. Seattle, WA: Amazon Digital, 2012.

Pregadio, Fabrizio. *The Seal of the Unity of Three, A Study and Translation of the Cantong qi*. Mountain View, CA: Golden Elixir Press, 2011,

Qian, Sima, and Burton Watson. *Records of the Grand Historian*. New York, NY: Chinese University of Hong Kong and Columbia Press Books, 1993.

Qui, Xigui, and Gilbert L. Mattos and Jerry Norman (Trans). Chinese Writing, The Society for the Study of Early China and The Institute of East Asian Studies, University of California, Berkeley. 2000.

Redmond, Geoffrey P., and Tze-Ki Hon. *Teaching the I Ching (Book of Changes)*. New York, NY: Oxford University Press, 2014.

Riseman, Tom. *Understanding the I Ching*. London, UK: Aquarian/Thorsons, 1980.

Ritsema, Rudolf, and Shantena Augusto. Sabbadini. *The Original I Ching Oracle: The Pure and Complete Texts with Concordance*. London: Watkins, 2007.

Ritsema, Rudolf, and Stephen L. Karcher. *I Ching*. Shaftesbury, Dorset: Element, 1994.

Roth, Harold David (Trans. and Commentary). *Original Tao: Inward Training (nei-yeh) and the Foundations of Taoist Mysticism [Nei Ye 內業]*. [Book 49 of the Guanzi 管子]. New York: Columbia University Press, 1999.

Russell, Walter and Louise Russell (Editor). *The Univerasal One, Vol. One First Principles*. (Fourth Printing 2013)Waynesboro, VA: University of Science and Philosophy, 1926.

Rutt, Richard. *The Book of Changes (Zhouyi): A Bronze Age Document*. Richmond, Surrey: Curzon, 1996.

Satter, Beryl. *Each Mind a Kingdom: American Women, Sexual Purity, and the New Thought Movement, 1875–1920*. Berkeley: University of California Press, 2001.

Schwartz, Benjamin I. *The World of Thought in Ancient China*. Cambridge, MA: Belknap Press of Harvard University Press, 1985.

Shakir, M. H. *The Qur'an Translation*. 11th ed. Elmhurst, NY: Tahrike Tarsile Qur'an, 2011.

Shaughnessy, Edward Louis. *The Composition of the Zhouyi*. Stanford University, University Microfilms International, 1983.

———— *Before Confucius: Studies in the Creation of the Chinese Classics*. Albany, NY: State University of New York Press, 1997.

———— *I Ching: The Classic of Changes*. New York: Ballantine Books, 1997.

———— *Rewriting Early Chinese Texts*. Albany: State University of New York Press, 2006.

———— *Sources of Western Zhou History, Inscribe Bronze Vessels*. University of California Press, Berkeley, CA.1991.

———— *Unearthing The Changes: Recently Discovered Manuscripts of The Yi Jing (I Ching) and Related Texts*. New York, NY: Columbia University Press, 2014.

———— *The Composition of the Zhouyi*. PhD diss., Stanford University, 1983. Ann

Arbor, MI: University Microfilms International.

Silver, Nate. *The Signal and the Noise: Why Most Predictions Fail-- but Some Don't.* Penguin Press, 2012.

Smith, Kidder Jr., Peter K. Bol, Joseph A. Adler, and Don J. Wyatt, *S* , Princeton University Press, 1990.

Smith, Richard J. *Fathoming the Cosmos and Ordering the World: The Yijing (I Ching, or Classic of Changes) and Its Evolution in China.* Charlottesville, VA: University of Virginia Press, 2008.

———— *Fortune-tellers and Philosophers: Divination in Traditional Chinese Society.* Boulder: Westview Press, 1991.

———— *The I Ching: A Biography.* Princeton, NJ: Princeton University Press, 2012.

Som, Dr. Tjan (Trans) Tjoe. *The Comprehensive Discussions in the White Tiger Hall (Po Hu T'ung) Two Volumes.* Leiden, Netherlands: E. J. Brill, 1949. Purported to be an Imperially sanctioned official report A.D. 79.

*Tanakh , The Holy Scriptures: The New JPS Translation According to the Traditional Hebrew Text.* Philadelphia: Jewish Publication Society, 1988, 1985.

Theodore, De Bary William, Richard John Lufrano, Wing-tsit Chan, and John H. Berthrong. *Sources of Chinese Tradition. from Earliest times to 1600.* 2nd ed. New York: Columbia University Press, 1999.

Tuffley, David. *The Essence of Buddhism.* 2nd ed. eBook. Australia: Altiora Publications, 2013

Waley, Arthur (Trans.). *Book Songs*, Houghton Mifflin Company, Boston, MA, 1937.

West, E. W. (Trans.). *Pahlavi Texts*, Part II, *The Dandistan-O Dinik and The Epistles of Manuskiha.* Attributed to Zoroaster. Produced by Friedrich Max Müller, Sacred Books of the East and published by Oxford University Press, 1882 — Reprinted by Delhi: Santilial Jain, Shri Jainendra Press, 1962. Can be found at: https://ia801603.us.archive.org/35/items/in.ernet. dli.2015.282556/2015.282556.Pahlavi-Texts.pdf.

Whincup, Gregory. *Rediscovering the I Ching.* New York, NY: St. Martin's Griffin, 1996.

Wilhelm, Hellmut, and Richard Wilhelm. *Understanding the I Ching: The Wilhelm Lectures on the Book of Changes.* Princeton, NJ: Princeton University Press, 1995.

Wilhelm, Richard [Trans. German], and Cary F. Baynes [Trans. English]. *The I Ching: Or, Book of Changes (Including the Great Commentary by Ta Chuan).* 3rd ed. Originally Published in German 1923. Princeton, NJ: Princeton University Press, 1977.

Wu, Chung. *The Essentials of the Yi Jing: Translated, Annotated, and with an Introduction and Notes.* St. Paul, MN: Paragon House, 2003.

Xunzi, and Burton Watson. *Xunzi: Basic Writings.* New York: Columbia University Press, 2003.

Ye, Lang, Zhenggang Fei, and Tianyou Wang. *China: Five Thousand Years of History and Civilization.* Kowloon, Hong Kong: City University of Hong Kong Press, 2007.

Zhang, Dainian, and Edmund Ryder (Trans.). *Key Concepts in Chinese Philosophy.*

New Haven, CT: Yale University Press, 2002.

Zhixu, and Thomas F. Cleary. *The Buddhist I Ching*. Boston: Shambhala, 1987.

Zhu, Xi, and Joseph A. Adler. *Introduction to the Study of the Classic of Change (I-hsüeh Ch'i-meng)*. Provo, UT: Global Scholarly Publications, 2002.

Zhuangzi, and Burton Watson (Trans.). *Chuang Tau (Zhuangzi) Basic Writings*. New York: Columbia University Press, 1996.

Zhuangzi, and James Legge (Trans.). *Zhauangzi*. Amazon Digital Services, 2014.

Zisi 子思, and James Legge (Trans). *Doctrine of the Mean (Bilingual)*. Kindle Edition. Carme., CA: Lionshare Media, 2014. The cover and title page attributes authorship to Confucius

## JOURNALS, ACADEMIC PUBLICATIONS

Bell, J. S. "Speakable and unspeakable in quantum mechanics," *Collected Papers in Quantum Mechanics* 141–158. Cambridge, UK: Cambridge University Press, 1987.

Blake, C. Fred. "Foot-Binding in Neo-Confucian China and the Appropriation of Female Labor," *Signs*, Vol. 19, No. 3,Spring, 1994. 676–712,The University of Chicago Pres. http://www.jstor.org/stable/3174774.

Binder, Dr. Tim. "Consciousness is the Key to the 'Dawn of a New Era'." (Video), The University of Science and Philosophy, 2018.

Cammann, Schuyler V. R. "The Eight Trigrams: Variants and Their Uses." *History of Religions*, vol. 29, no. 4, 1990, pp. 301–317., doi:10.1086/463201.

Chen, Guo-Ming. "Bian (Change): A Perpetual Discourse of *I Ching*." *Intercultural Communication Studies Xvii: 4 2008, University of Rhode Island*, 2008. Accessed November 18, 2014. http://www.uri.edu/iaics/content/2008v17n4/01%20GM%20Chen.pdf.

Chen, Shih-chuan. "How To Form a Hexagram and Consult the *I Ching*." Journal of Oriental Studies, Vol. 92.2, 1972. Pennsylvania State University. 237–249.

Cheng, Chung-yin, and On-cho Ng (Editors). *Philosophy of the Yi 易: Unity and Dialectics*. Supplement to Vol. 39, 2009, Journal of Chinese Philosophy. Chichester, West Sussex, UK: John Wiley and Sons, 2009.

Creswell John D., Dutcher Janine M., Klein William M. P., Harris Peter R., Levine John M. "Self-Affirmation Improves Problem-Solving under Stress." 1 May 2013. PLoS ONE 8(5): e62593. https://doi.org/10.1371/journal.pone.0062593

Dozolme D, Prigent E, Yang Y-F, Amorim M-A (2018) The neuroelectric dynamics of the emotional anticipation of other people's pain. PLoS ONE 13(8): e0200535. https://doi.org/10.1371/ journal.pone.0200535

Hansen, Chad. "Daoism." *The Stanford Encyclopedia of Philosophy*, Summer 2013. Accessed December 18, 2014. https://leibniz.stanford.edu/friends/members/view/daoim/.

Henderson, John B. *Scripture, Canon, and Commentary: A Comparison of Confucian and Western Exegesis*. Princeton, NJ: Princeton University Press, 1991.

Liao, Sung J. "The Origin of the Five Elements in the Traditional Theorem of Acupuncture: A Preliminary Brief Historic Enquiry," 7–14.

Loy, David. "Wei-wu-wei: Nondual Action." *Philosophy East and West* 35, no. No. 1 (1985): 73–87. http://ccbs.ntu.edu.tw/FULLTEXT/JR-PHIL/loy3.htm., Accessed 2/7/2017.

Littejohn, Ronnie (Belmont University). "Daoist Philosophy ." Internet Encyclopedia of Philosophy, www.iep.utm.edu/daoism/. Accessed 31 Aug. 2014.

———— "Wuxing (Wu-Hsing) [Five Agents]." Internet Encyclopedia of Philosophy ISSN 2161–0002. www.iep.utm.edu/wuxing/. Accessed 12 Nov. 2014

Lynn, Richard John. "Truth and Imagination in China: Opposition and Conciliation in the Tradition," Symposion, Académie du Midi: "Imagination East and West," Alet-les-Bains, Languedoc-Roussillon, France, May 16, 2016 to May 20, 2016

Mathews Zenon, Cetnarski Ryszard, Verschure Paul F. M. J. "Visual anticipation biases conscious decision making but not bottom-up visual processing." Frontiers in Psychology, Vol. 5, 2015, 1443, DOI: 10.3389/fpsyg.01443.

Montagne, Gilles, Julian Bastin, and David M. Jacobes. "What is visual anticipation and how much does it rely on the dorsal stem?" UMR Mouvement et Perception, Marseille, France: Université de la Méditerranée & CNRS. http://www. uam.es/gruposinv/gipym/MontagneEA2008web.pdf

Næss, Arne. "The Shallow and the Deep, Long-Range Ecology Movement. A Summary." *Inguiry*, #16, 1973, DOI: 10.1080/00201747308601682, 95–100.

Nickerson, Raymond S. "Confirmation Bias: A Ubiquitous Phenomenon in Many Guises." *Review of General Psychology* 2, no. 2 (1998): 175–220. Accessed December 9, 2015. doi:10.1037//1089-2680.2.2.175.

NG, Wai-Ming. "The History of 'I Ching' in Medieval Japam." *Journal of Asian History*, vol. 31, no. 1, 1997, pp. 25–46. JSTOR, www.jstor.org/stable/41931054.

Ou, Xinyi. "The Successful Integration of Buddhism with Chinese Culture: A Summary." *Grand Valley Journal of History*, Article 3, 1, no. 2 (April 9, 2012). http:// scholarworks.gvsu.edu/gvjh/vol1/iss2/3.

Peterson, Willard J. (Princeton University). "Making Connections: 'Commentary on the Attached Verbalizations' of the Book of Changes." *Harvard Journal of Asiatic Studies* 42 (1982): 67–116. Accessed September 1, 2014. Http://www. biroco.com/yijing/Peterson_Making_Connections.pdf.

Raphals, Lisa. "Divination in the Han Shu Bibliographic Treatise." *Early China* 32 (2008): 42–102. Accessed March 15, 2015. http://faculty.ucr.edu/~raphals/ pubs/2009earlychina.pdf.

Rubin, Vitaly A. "The Concepts of Wu-Hsing and Yin-Yang." *Journal of Chinese Philosophy* 9 (1982): 131–37. Wiley Online Library.

Schallert, Diane, Glen Kieman, and Ann Rubin. "Analysis of Differences Between Reading and Oral Language (Technical Report No. 29)." 2007. MS, Large Scale Digitization Project, University of Illinois at Urbana Center for the Study of Reading, Urbana, IL. http://journals.sagepub.com/doi/ abs/10.1177/0022057409189001-204 , Access 12/2/2017.

Smith, Richard J. "Knowing the Self and Knowing "Other": The Epistemological and Heuristic Value of the Yiching." *Journal of Chinese Philosophy* 33, no. 4 (December 2006): 465–77.

———— "The Psychology of Divination in Cross-Cultural Perspective," Paper of ICRH Conference on "Ming and Fatum--Key Concepts of Fate and Prediction, July 204, 2010.

———— "The Book of Changes as a Mirror of the Mind: The Evolution of the *Zhouyi* in China and Beyond." *International Consortium for Research in the Humanities, Erlangen, Germany*, April 10, 2009, 1–40. Accessed August 9, 2014. http://www.ikgf.uni-erlangen.de/content/articles/RichardSmith_-_Book_of_Changes.pdf.

Wang, Robin R. "Zhou Dunyi's Diagram of the Supreme Ultimate Explained ("Taijitu Shuo"): A Construction of the Confucian Metaphysics." Journal of the History of Ideas 66, no. 3 (2005): 307–23. www.jstor.org/stable/3654184.

Wong, Eva. *Taoism, An Essential Guide* (Previous edition was titled Shambala Guide to Taoism, 1197). Boston: Shambala Publishing, 2011.

## ARTICLES, LECTURES, AND WEB SITES

"About Jung." The Jung Page: Published By: Jung Center of Houston, TX. Accessed September 23, 2014. http://www.cgjungpage.org/learn/about-jung.

"Chinese Text Project", https://ctext.org.

"Mandarin Chinese Pinyin English Dictionary." Yabla Chinese. Accessed August 28, 2014. https://chinese.yabla.com/chinese-english-Pinyin-dictionary.php?define=lao.

"YellowBridge Chinese Dictionary and Language Tools." YellowBridge.com Published by J. Lau. Accessed September 04, 2014. http://www.yellowbridge.com/.

Auge, Edward O., "Meditation," *Christian Science Sentinel,* 19 March 1921.

Biroco, Joel. "A Critical Survey of *I Ching* Books." Yijing Dao. Accessed March 17, 2015. http://www.biroco.com/yijing/survey.htm.

Robinson, Daniel N. *The Great Ideas of Psychology.* 2nd ed. Lecture Series, The Great Courses. New York, NY: Teaching Company, 2008.

Sturgeon, Donald, (Editor). "*I Ching.*" Chinese Text Project. Accessed August 24, 2014. http://ctext.org/book-of-changes.

Turk, Margaret McCauly , "Divine Mind's Control," *Christian Science Sentinel*, 12 July 1950.

## UNPUBLISHED

Olsen, Barbara Jean, and Kathryn Marie Olsen-Klattenhoff (Editor). *Collected Works of Barbara Jean Olsen.* Round Rock, TX: Kathryn Klattenhoff, 2013 (Unpublished).

## *I CHING* TRANSLATIONS & PARAPHRASES REVIEWED BUT NOT CITED

Bertschinger, Richard. *Yijing, Shamantic Oracle of China*, London: Singing Dragon, 2012.

Christensen, Lars B. Book of Changes, The Origanal *I Ching*. Self Published. 2015.

Crouch, Freeman. *I Ching: The Chameleon Book,*. Austin, TX: Brazos Media, 2005.

Danjun, Liu, Wang Dongliang, and Raymond Tartaix. *Les signes et les mutations,* Paris: L'Asiathèque, 1994 (French).

Dening, Sarah. *The Everyday I Ching.* New York: St. Martin's Griffin, 1997.

Fendos Jr., Paul G., *The Book of Changes: A Modern Adaptation and Interpretation,* 2018.

Liu, Da. *I Ching Coin Prediction*, NewYork: Routledge & Kegan Paul Books, 1975.

Karcher, Stephen. *I Ching Plain and Simple*, Hampton Roads Publishing, Charlottes-ville, VA, 2017. (Published in 2008 as *Simply I Ching*).

Karcher, *Steven. I Ching, The Symbolic Life,*

Kaser, R. T. *I Ching in Ten Minutes*, New York: Avon Books, 1994.

Liu, Da. *I Ching Coin Prediction*, 1975.

Jing-Nuan, Wu, *Yi Jing*. Taoist Center, 1991.

Johnson, Julia Tallard. *I Ching for Teens*, Rochester, VT: Bindu Books, 2002.

McElroy, Mark. *I Ching for Beginners: A Modern Interpretation of the Ancient Oracle*. Woodbury, MN: Llewellyn Publications, 2005.

Ming-Dao, Deng. *The Living I Ching*, Harper, San Francisco, 2006

Ming, Chan Chiu., and Xu (Calligraphy) Qinghua. *Book of Changes: An Interpretation for the Modern Age*. Singapore: Asiapac, 1997.

Moran, Elizabeth and Master Joseph Yu. *The Complete Idiot's Guide to the I Ching*, Alpha Books, Indianapolis, 2002.

Olsen, Stuart Olive. *Book of Sun and Moon (I Ching)*. Vol. Vo.1 1 & 2. Phoenix, AZ: Valley Spirit Arts, 2014.

Padma, Ma Deva, *Tao Oracle*, New York: St. Martin's Press, 2002.

Martin Palmer, Martic, Joanne O'Brien and Kwok Man Ho. *The Fortune-teller's I Ching*, Ware, UK: Wordsworth Editions, 1993.

Riseman, Tom. *Understanding the I Ching*. Aquarian, 1990.

Schorre, Jane and Carrin Dunne. *Yijing Wondering and Wandering*, 2003.

Sessions, *Wisdom's Way, The Christian I Ching,* Christian *I Ching* Society, 2015.

Stein, Diane. *A Woman's I Ching*. Berkeley, CA: Crossing Press, 1997.

Stephenson, Susan. *I Ching A Book of Changes Ancient Guidance for Contemporary Persons*. Self Published eBook — Available on iTunes.

Trainor, Robert. *I Ching 2015*. Self-Published, Kindle, 2015.

Walker, Brian Browne. *The I Ching, Or, Book of Changes: A Guide to Life's Turning Points*. New York: St. Martin's Press, 1992.

Wing, R. L. *The Illustrated I Ching*. Garden City, NY: Dolphin Books/Doubleday, 1982.

Wu Wei. *I Ching Wisdom*. Revised Edition. Los Angeles: Power Press, 2005.

*~ I continue to review I Ching books — See iChing.wiki/which-book. ~*

# INDEX

www.ingramcontent.com/pod-product-compliance
Lightning Source LLC
Chambersburg PA
CBHW041829090426
42811CB00038B/2367/J